Inga D. Schmidt, Thomas Döbler, Michael Schenk

E-Commerce:
A Platform for Integrated Marketing

Markt
Kommunikation
Innovation
(MKI)

herausgegeben von

Prof. Dr. Michael Schenk

Forschungsstelle für Medienwirtschaft
und Kommunikationsforschung
Universität Hohenheim

und

Prof. Dr. Bruno Neibecker

Institut für Entscheidungstheorie und Unternehmensforschung
Universität Karlsruhe

Band 4

LIT

Inga D. Schmidt, Thomas Döbler, Michael Schenk

E-Commerce:
A Platform for Integrated Marketing

Case Study on U.S. Retailing

LIT

Die Deutsche Bibliothek – CIP-Einheitsaufnahme

Inga D. Schmidt, Thomas Döbler, Michael Schenk,
E-Commerce: A Platform for Integrated Marketing : Case Study on U. S.
Retailing / Inga D. Schmidt, Thomas Döbler, Michael Schenk. – Münster :
LIT, 2000
   (Markt, Kommunikation, Innovation (MKI) ; 4.)
   ISBN 3-8258-4661-x

NE: GT

© LIT VERLAG Münster – Hamburg – London
  Grevener Str. 179 48159 Münster Tel. 0251–23 50 91 Fax 0251–23 19 72

Distributed in North America by:

Transaction Publishers
New Brunswick (U.S.A.) and London (U.K.)

Transaction Publishers
Rutgers University
35 Berrue Circle
Piscataway, NJ 08854

Tel.: (732) 445 – 2280
Fax: (732) 445 – 3138
for orders (U.S. only):
toll free 888-999-6778

Table of Contens

Table of Exhibits

Table of Appendices

Table of Abbreviations

AICPA:	American Institute of Certified Public Accountants
AMA:	American Marketing Association
AnyCo:	Anywhere Corporation
ARPA:	Advanced Research Projects Agency
CAGR:	Compounded Average Growth Rate
CEO:	Chief Executive Officer
CERN:	European Laboratory for Particle Physics
CICA:	Canadian Institute of Chartered Accountants
DMA:	Direct Marketing Association
E:	Estimate
E-com:	Electronic Commerce
EDI:	Electronic Data Interchange
EFT:	Electronic Fund Transfer
E.g.:	Et gratia (for example)
E-mail:	Electronic mail
Etc.:	Et cetera (and so forth)
E-tailing:	Electronic Retailing
EU:	European Union
FAQs:	Frequently Asked Questions
FTC:	Federal Trade Commission
FTP:	File Transfer
GVU:	Graphics, Visualization & Usability Center
HTML:	Hypertext Markup Language
IDC:	International Data Corporation
I.e.:	It est (that is to say)
Inc.:	Incorporated
IS:	Information Service

MIT:	Massachusetts Institute of Technology
MS:	Morgan Stanley
NSF:	National Science Foundation
PC:	Personal Computer
QFC:	Quality Food Center
RNPs:	Really-new Products
SKUs:	Stock-keeping Units
U.S.:	United States of America
VANs:	Value-added Networks
VP:	Vice President
V.s.:	Versus
WM:	Wal-Mart Inc.
WWW, Web:	World Wide Web

To be specific, the point of greatest peril in the development of a [new] market lies in making the transition from an early market dominated by a few visionary customers to a mainstream market dominated by a large block of customers who are predominately pragmatists in orientation.

Geoffrey A. Moore, author of
Crossing the Chasm

Section I: Overview

1 Introduction

Irresistibly the Internet spreads around the world. It has created an ever increasing communication infrastructure with global magnitude, influencing both consumers and businesses and even touching the structures of our society.

We live in a world of change; the way we work, the way we play, the way we shop, the way we organize our lives, the way we do things, the way we communicate with each other.[1]

Strategies proven to be successful in the market place might falter in the future and give way to new, not yet truly understood approaches - electronic commerce. Many traditional companies do not take the recent development in the virtual market place as a serious threat. However, Walter Forbes, founder of CUC International, forecasted that electronic commerce would not need to be huge to harm traditional business, since a five percent swing in revenues could bring a retail giant to its knees.[2] Today, the impact of electronic commerce on traditional retailing in the U.S. is below one percent. In Europe, this percentage is currently even lower. However, forecasts like for example made during the European IT-Forum in September 1999 in Paris, France estimate tremendous growth. In fact, estimates for European electronic commerce growth rates are even higher than the ones for the USA or Canada, which might turn Europe into the largest connected cyber market in only a few years. The IT-Forum further estimates that only in Germany electronic commerce will become a $62 billion business.[3] However, extensive investments of major competitors in technology, knowledge and marketing concerning the new tool might change the picture sooner than initially forecasted, leaving behind those who were not prepared. It does not seem advisable to

---

[1] Ghosh 1998, p. 126.
[2] Schwartz 1997, pp. 102-104.
[3] Spiegel Online 1999, www.spiegel.de/netzwelt/ebusiness/.

15

join the chicken and egg discussion of whether electronic commerce will make the Internet successful or whether, on the other hand, it is the existence of the Internet that will create a meaningful base for electronic commerce.[4] However, a company's strategic decision whether to wait or to engage in the virtual market place should neither be based on trivial assumptions nor on media hype but on a thorough analysis of the current circumstances. Such is the goal of this book.

This book will analyze electronic commerce from several aspects leading to an illustration of how AnyCo could take advantage of the current developments. Note that AnyCo, is a real-world company, operating in the West of the United States. Due to competitive circumstances, the company wants to stay anonymous and will therefore in the following be named with the artificial name Anywhere Corporation (AnyCo). All terms used in this introduction will in later Sections be thoroughly developed and discussed.

2 Approach

There are many different aspects of business-to-consumer electronic commerce, which need to be introduced and discussed. The book will therefore follow a flow of thoughts starting with the generics and than zooming more and more into the specifics.

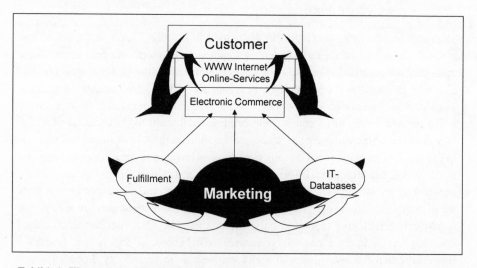

Exhibit 1: Illustration of the Book's Framework

Exhibit 1 illustrates the proceeding in a graphical way. The Exhibit also seeks to point out that the emphasis of this book will be on the consumer needs. Therefore, after a

---

[4]   Ryan 1997, p. 39.

brief introduction, the current developments of electronic commerce will be discussed – always having the customer in mind.

Section I: Overview. The book starts off with an introduction of the book's subject and the hypothesis on which it is based on. Then, an analysis of barriers to the adoption of innovations, the concept of the technology adoption life cycle, and the chasm between different segments of the cycle follow.

Section II: Age of Change. This Section is based on an in-depth desk research of secondary data and current literature that focuses on the present changes in terms of Internet, electronic commerce, and consumers. After the technological background and the development of electronic commerce have been introduced, its influences on consumers and on retailers will be discussed in detail. Additionally, several population dynamics that can be expected to influence the development of electronic commerce will be highlighted. Last, based on a specially developed Custom Tailored Mercantile Model a scenario will be illustrated, how all these identified changes might influence the relationship between consumers and retailers in the future. At this point it needs to be mentioned that up until now, there is not even a standard measurement of collecting and reporting Internet usage data in a consistent way, making it extremely difficult to compare different sources on the amount of actual usage.[5] In addition, on this new topic of electronic commerce, existing studies do not only fail to grasp the entire picture but furthermore are partially inconsistent both on methodological and outcome wise grounds. For this reason, combining existing research and modifying this material if necessary will develop a new angle to view electronic commerce.

Section III: Primary Market Research. This Section is based on a primary survey trying to tie in where the desk research from Section II left off. This primary survey, fielded in a metropolitan trade area[6] in the west of the United States, serves three purposes. First, to determine the readiness of the Analyzed Trade Area for business-to-consumer electronic commerce. Second, to identify products and strategies to approach the market best with a business-to-consumer electronic commerce concept. Last, the primary survey seeks to validate the veracity of analyzed secondary data regarding the subject of business-to-consumer electronic commerce.

The interpretation of the market research data not only describes the findings but also further analyzes the true relationship between different variables. This Section ends with a recap of the most important survey findings, leading the way into the last Section of this book.

---

[5] Maguire 1998, p. 19.
[6] Following, this region will be titled as Analyzed Trade Area.

Section IV: Entrance to the Electronic Commerce World. In this concluding Section, all information is combined to create a strategy of how AnyCo should deal with the new phenomenon of business-to-consumer electronic commerce. The Section starts by pointing out that a successful engagement in online retailing will require the company to change from the current industrial age business model to an information or communication business model. A discussion on reasons for hesitation, challenges and opportunities follows a proposed vision statement for AnyCo's e-tailing venture. Then, a new architecture, consisting of several pillars and suitable for AnyCo to enter the electronic commerce world is introduced. Here, the strongest focus is on "Customer Interaction", being the first pillar, which contents is also applied on a case study of a hypothetical AnyCo e-tailing venture for pet care. The second pillar "Asset Configuration", discusses the acquisition of critical assets and resources from external markets. The Section ends by drawing final conclusions.

3 Basic Considerations

3.1 Hypothesis

PC usage in the U.S. has crossed the chasm from the early adopters to the early majority, and the Internet usage recently crossed this chasm too. Now, the hypothesis raised here is that business-to-consumer electronic commerce will within the next three to five years have crossed the chasm too, which in turn will transition the channel into a profitable and mainstream tool for the U.S. retail industry.

The question arising from this hypothesis is how the U.S. retail industry should prepare for the advent of electronic commerce as a new tool to sell to customers. How should the community prepare to be ready to react to the new developments and how should retailers act to be able to model the evolution?

3.2 Barriers to the Adoption of Really-New-Products

For the purpose of the book it is important to note that electronic commerce is not really a product but the means to the end of purchasing products over the Web. However, for the following discussion of five different sources of barriers to adopt "really-new products" RNPs, electronic commerce can be treated as such. Additional sources name RNPs as "discontinuous innovations" or "technological discontinuities"[7], which contrast continuous innovations, referring to the normal upgrading of products

---

[7] According to Tushman and Anderson, so-called technological discontinuities can be classified as competence-enhancing or competence-destroying changes. The latter one, being fundamentally different from previously dominant technologies and representing a new way of doing certain transactions with customers, seems to be applicable to the underlying discussion of really-new-products. For a detailed discussion and literature review on technological discontinuities see Tushman & Anderson 1988.

or innovations that do not require a change in behavior.[8] It is out of question that electronic commerce fulfills the characteristics of discontinuous innovations, therefore also applying to the aspects of RNPs.

RNPs, whose concept is of fairly recent origin, are defined as "products which revolutionize product categories or define new categories" and which "shift market structures, represent new technologies, require consumer learning, and induce behavior changes."[9] According to Tushman and Anderson, "such discontinuities offer sharp price/performance improvements over existing technologies. Discontinuous innovations represent technical advancement so significant that no increase in scale, efficiency or design can make older technologies competitive with the new technology."[10]

RNPs Define New Product Categories. Several years ago, when IBM managers predicted personal computers never to be widely used, they made the mistake of viewing RNPs from the perspective of an existing product category.[11] This perceptual limitation led to the failure of recognition of the potential use of computers, as we know them today. Therefore, it is important to understand that RNPs revolutionize existing product categories or define new product categories, which cannot be measured with old scales. Consumers apply cross-category comparisons, driven by the absence of established standards, which are hard to grasp and to communicate. It can be concluded that electronic commerce is a new product category leading to the above-presented difficulties.[12]

RNPs Represent New Technologies. Electronic commerce utilizes new technologies and also offers new technologies to the consumers. For them, electronic commerce poses the problem of incompatibility with existing purchasing channels as well as performance, financial,[13] and product[14] risks.

RNPs Shift Market Structures. In fact, the introduction of RNPs might alter market structures in several ways. On the one side they may require new alliances and partnerships between different market players, resulting in a change of the competitive market structure. Here, the planned venture of Fortune 500 Companies joining forces

---

[8]   Moore 1991, p. 10 and Tushman & Anderson 1988, pp. 91-93.
[9]   Urban, Weinberg & Hauser 1996, p. 47.
[10]   Tushman & Anderson 1988, p. 91.
[11]   Chposky & Leonsis 1988, p. 107.
[12]   Aggarwal, Cha & Wilemon 1998, pp. 359-361.
[13]   Performance risk is the possibility that the product will malfunction or fail to work as supposed, while financial risk is the potential monetary outlay associated with the initial purchase price as well as the subsequent maintenance costs of the product. Grewal & Marmostein 1994, p. 146.
[14]   Product risk includes product-category risk, which is "inherent in purchasing any particular product in a specific product category as well as product-specific risk where the risk is associated with the particular product being considered in the product class." Dowling & Staelin 1994, p. 120.

to launch an electronic mall in Fall of 1999, providing customers with a one-stop-shopping experience that will offer unique benefits that no current brick-and-mortar retailers can offer to date,[15] suits as an example. Important on the consumer side is that the transition from the old market structure to a new one may take some time. The consumer may face difficulties in this transition, which might perform as a barrier to the adoption of RNPs.[16]

RNPs Require Consumer Learning. A potential adoption of electronic commerce will require a significant cognitive investment and active learning on the part of the consumers. In case the information referring to the RNPs is not available to consumers or difficult to understand, assimilation and internalization of information is difficult. To prevent this, businesses might provide consumers with as much information as possible, creating an information and innovation overload, which instead of stimulating learning, proves an impediment to learning. Both cases might create barriers to the adoption of electronic commerce.

RNPs Include Behavior Changes. Last, a potential adoption of electronic commerce will call for a significant modification in customer behavior. In short, it can be said that there are several obstacles which electronic commerce providers must overcome to induce behavioral change. According to Aggarwal, Cha and Wilemon, businesses must "first establish an information exchange relationship with potential adopters in order to inform and educate them about the new product." Second, "[a positive] attitude (intent) toward the offering must be created, [and finally,] intent must be converted to actual purchase behavior."[17]

It has been shown that several significant barriers need to be overcome by both consumers and businesses in order to adopt electronic commerce successfully. The following paragraph will illustrate that not every party exposed to electronic commerce is likely to overcome the above-presented barriers at the same time.

3.3 Technology Adoption Life Cycle

The mechanism, how new products and innovations diffuse in the market place, can be explained with the help of the technology adoption life cycle. The diffusion theory, defined by Rogers "as the process whereby an innovation is communicated via certain channels, through time, between the members of a social system",[18] has been studied extensively. In order to understand the acceptance and the diffusion process of an innovation, it is essential to learn which individuals obtain it, when they do so, and the

---

[15] For a preview of this venture visit http://www.countdown9199.com.
[16] Aggarwal, Cha & Wilemon 1998, pp. 361-362.
[17] Aggarwal, Cha & Wilemon 1998, p. 362.
[18] Rogers 1983, p. 5.

motives which led them to do so at one given time or another. Taking this into account, it can be said that if one succeeds to identify the "individuals according to the moment in time at which they adopt, [one] will be able to characterize their behavior [...] according to the degree of innovative behavior they present." [19]

Since Bass developed his initial innovation diffusion model thirty years ago, several other researchers have developed more sophisticated methods for obtaining adopter categories.[20] In 1983, Rogers introduced the classification of five different categories (innovators, early adopters, early majority, late majority and laggards)[21] among the adopters of new products. He further illustrated that the adoption follows a "bell" shaped curve or normal curve, which assumes an adoption distribution close to normality.[22] It is important to note that the divisions in the curve are roughly equivalent to where standard deviations would fall.[23]

3.3.1 Adopter Categories

In 1991, Moore adapted Roger's model in order to build the technology adoption life cycle, especially designed for high-tech enterprises, which are continually confronted with RNPs or discontinuous innovations (see Exhibit 2).

It has previously been shown that electronic commerce qualifies to be a RNP, therefore it appears suitable to apply the life cycle model in a slightly modified way for the adoption of electronic commerce.

Exhibit 2 illustrates the five different adopter categories including their percentage wise distribution among the population exposed to the innovation. The lower half of the Exhibit roughly sketches the current market penetration of computer and Internet usage as well as the adoption of business-to-consumer electronic commerce. The adoption life cycle curve needs to be read from left to right, meaning that the innovators are the first to approach the innovation, followed by the early adopters and so on. For computers, a penetration of 60% illustrates that innovators, early adopters, early majority and some of the late majority segments are already computer users. Following, the five different adopter categories will be described.

---

[19] Martinez, Polo & Flavián 1998, p. 325.
[20] Bass, Mahajan & Muller 1990, pp. 1-2.
[21] The categories must meet the following characteristics: They must be exhaustive, they must be mutually exclusive, and they must derive from one main classification.
[22] Martinez, Polo & Flavián 1998, pp. 324-327.
[23] Moore 1991, p. 12.

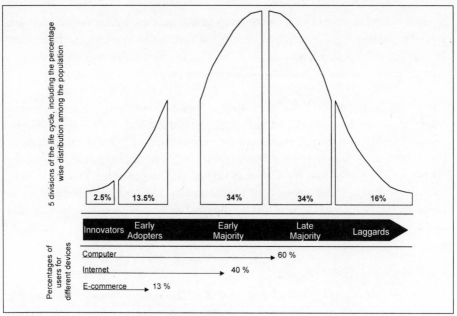

Exhibit 2: Technology Adoption Life Cycle[24]

Innovators (Technology Enthusiasts). The prerequisite for a diffusion process of innovation is that this innovation is adopted by a series of individuals who have what is known as "innovativeness".[25] They pursue new technology eagerly and often appreciate technology for its own sake. This segment of people may have technology as a central interest in their life, which motivates them to pick new products before a formal marketing campaign has been launched (often only for the pleasure of using the product before anybody else). As Exhibit 2 illustrates all three innovations (computer, Internet, and business-to-consumer electronic commerce) are beyond the first stage of the adoption life cycle.

Early Adopters (Visionaries). Being the second segment of adopting to innovations, these individuals also buy into new concepts very early in their life cycle. However, they are not as technology savvy as the preceding segment but they find it easy to imagine, understand, and appreciate the benefits of an innovation and they are the least price-sensitive segment of any segment in the cycle. They are not looking for a simple improvement; they are looking for a fundamental breakthrough. Early adopters do not base their adoption decisions on well-established references, but rely on their own intuition. While computer and Internet usage is already beyond this stage of adoption,

---

[24] Adopted from: Ernst & Young 1998, p. 4, Moore 1991, p. 12, Nielsen Media Research 1998, p. 1, Nieschlag, Dichtl & Hörschgen 1994, p. 906.
[25] Martinez, Polo & Flavián 1998, p. 327.

electronic commerce is assumed to be currently performed only by individuals belonging either to innovators or early adopters.

Early Majority (Pragmatists). One in three individuals exposed to the innovation fall in the category of the early majority, illustrating that an innovation planning on going mainstream must win their business. These individuals' adoption decisions are motivated by a strong sense of practicality and the feedback they gain from other people who use the innovation already. The early majority also relies on well-established references before any further investigation of the matter. While computer usage is already beyond this stage of adoption, Internet usage is currently in this stage, while electronic commerce seems not yet to have overcome the hurdle between early adoption and early majority.

Late Majority (Conservatives). Individuals included in the late majority share all characteristics of the early majority plus one more: They are not comfortable with their ability to handle a technology product and they are against discontinuous innovations. Therefore, they wait until the innovation has become an established standard or they may receive intensive buying or usage support. Again, this segment accounts for another one-third of the total population exposed to the innovation and so far, only the computer usage managed to reach into the late majority segment.

Laggards (Skeptics). These individuals, accounting for roughly 16% of the exposed population, will not adopt to the innovation until "hell freezes over" and can therefore be neglected in further considerations.[26]

It has been shown that technology assimilates to any given community in stages corresponding to the psychological and social profiles of various segments within that community. As mentioned before, business-to-consumer electronic commerce is assumed not yet to have overcome the hurdle between the stage of early adoption and early majority. Furthermore, as Exhibit 2 illustrates, the gap between theses two stages seems to be wider than the gaps between the other stages. It seems therefore appropriate to take a closer look at this so-called chasm.

3.3.2 Chasm

A gap stands for the dissociation between two groups that is "the difficulty any group will have in accepting a new [innovation] if it is presented in the same way as it was to the [preceding] group."[27] Even though there are four gaps, only the first three need to be considered further. The last one, between the late majority and the laggards, can be neglected due to a lack of interest of the laggards as already stated above.

---

[26] Moore 1991, pp. 9-15.
[27] Moore 1991, p. 17.

The first gap, being fairly small, is between the innovators and the early adopter stage. This gap occurs when an innovation cannot be readily translated into a major benefit for the individuals of the second segment.

However, since all three innovations including business-to-consumer electronic commerce have crossed this gap previously, it seems more important to take a look at the second fairly small gap, occurring between the stages of early majority and late majority. Until today, only computer usage managed to traverse this gap. Here, it is imperative to comprehend that while the early majority is willing and able to become technologically competent, this is not true for the segment of the late majority, who will only adopt if the innovation is increasingly easier to handle.

After having discussed the two cracks in the bell curve it is now time to take a look at the so-called "deep and dividing chasm", dividing the stages of early adoption and early majority. The reason for this chasm can be found in very different buying motivations: Early adopters adapt to an innovation in order to be ahead of the crowd and to profit from early-movers advantages. They are aware of the radical discontinuity between the old and the new ways and they are willing to master these challenges in order to gain the above mentioned advantages. The opposite is true for the individuals belonging to the early majority segment, who expect to utilize an innovation in order to achieve productivity enhancements for existing operations. In other words, they aim for technology to amplify, not overthrow, the established way of doing things and they expect it to function properly.[28]

It has been shown that missing one of these gaps (especially the chasm) results in missing an opportunity to reach the next segment, thereby never gaining the anticipated "profit-margin leadership in the middle of the bell curve."[29]

3.4 Outlook

Exhibit 2 presents it in a graphical form: Business-to-consumer electronic commerce is approaching the chasm between the early adoption segment and the early majority segment, yet segregating it from being a mainstream shopping tool for customers and a profit generating tool for the marketers.

The hypothesis raised in paragraph 3.1 "Hypothesis" of this Section, states that business-to-customer electronic commerce is going to cross the chasm within the next three to five years. However, this event will not take place automatically instead it needs to be thoroughly nursed and grown.

---

[28] Moore 1991, pp. 18-59.
[29] Moore 1991, p.17.

It has been illustrated that pragmatists, accounting for every third person in a given population, are different types of persons than the ones who were previously attracted by electronic commerce. To pragmatists, it seems most fruitful to sell where they want to be instead of selling them the bridge to get there. This may lead to the presumption that the electronic commerce market is about to experience a shift both on the demand side (types of customers attracted) as well as on the supply side (retailers providing the opportunity for Internet related purchases).

How American retailers can successfully pull the right triggers in order to attract the mainstream population to business-to-consumer electronic commerce - and to become profitable by doing so - will be the content of the remainder of this book.

Ultimately, the risk for established businesses is not from digital tornadoes but from digital termites.

Shikhar Ghosh, author of
Making Business Sense of the Internet

Section II: Age of Change

4 Internet and Electronic Commerce – the Basics

Today, virtually everyone talks about the Internet as a new and exciting medium challenging traditional ways of interacting, communication, and doing business.[30] To get a better understanding of what the reasons are that cause these changes, it seems advisable to take a closer look at how the Internet got started.

4.1 History of the Internet

4.1.1 Initial Invention

In September 1969, the words "Are you receiving this?" were sent from Boutler Hall at the University of California at Los Angeles across a four-node network. The Internet worked. The project was part of the Advanced Research Projects Agency (ARPA) of the U.S. Department of Defense. The project's initial goal was to create a system in which networked computers from the military, government agencies, and academic researchers and scientists could communicate with each other even if some of them went off-line (e.g. if they were to vanish in a nuclear attack). This network should be without a central point of control and each computer on the system was supposed to share the same amount of responsibility as the others. Soon, more and more researchers connected and everyone experienced the network as a great advantage.

In 1984, the National Science Foundation (NSF) realized the opportunity of the Internet to distribute expensive supercomputer power. In order to make the Internet more stable, the NSF created a national backbone of high-speed communication lines,[31]

---

[30] Pricewaterhouse 1998a, p. 231.
[31] Sterne 1995, pp. 13-14.

27

and in 1991, the NSF eased restrictions and allowed commercial parties to connect to the Internet. In the retro-perspective, this action was equivalent to "opening the floodgates of the Amazon River."[32] In the mid-1990s, commercial enterprises and individuals fully discovered the advantages of being part of the Internet, creating a mass-market phenomenon.[33]

4.1.2 World Wide Web

Tim Berners-Lee created the World Wide Web (WWW or Web) originally for internal use at the European Laboratory for Particle Physics (known by its French acronym CERN) in 1989. He figured that users would want to link multiple documents through hypertext, which would enable them through clicking on a highlighted phrase to access electronic references and additional information.[34] Such global information-sharing architecture turned the user-unfriendly, text-based Internet landscape into a colorful cyber-world full of social, artistic, and commercial opportunities. Often times the Web and the Internet are used synonymously, which is formally not correct. The Web, like file transfer (FTP), electronic mail, or news groups are applications using the transport functions of the Internet. The Web is an assortment of distributed documents referred to as "pages" located on computers or servers around the world. These servers store hypertext markup language (HTML) files and respond to the requests of users. Users, in order to connect to the Web, need a special piece of software called a Web browser, which acts as a graphical interface between the user and the Internet. [35] However, for the rest of the book, the terms Internet and Web will be used synonymously describing the World Wide Web.

4.2 Electronic Commerce

What is electronic commerce (e-com) exactly? Although literally hundreds of references to electronic commerce have appeared in both the popular press and the academic literature in the past couple of years, no agreed-upon definition currently exists. Pricewaterhouse defined it in 1998 as follows:

> *Electronic commerce is the use of electronic information technologies to conduct business transactions among buyers, sellers, and other trading partners. E-com combines business and electronic infrastructures, allowing traditional business transactions to be conducted electronically. [It] also enables the online buying and selling of goods and services via the communications capabilities of private and public computer networks, including the Internet.[36]*

---

[32] Kalakota & Whinston 1997, p. 32.
[33] Pricewaterhouse 1998a, p. 232.
[34] Sterne 1995, p. 15.
[35] Kalakota & Whinston 1997, pp. 63-66.
[36] Pricewaterhouse 1998a, p. 554.

While this definition occurs to be quite complete, it is helpful to consult an additional source to get a broader picture:

> *[Electronic commerce stands for using] technology to facilitate business-to–business and business-to-consumer transactions resulting in improving revenues and/or profits. [Another] important characteristic associated with the successful implementation of e-com is that all parties must be willing to rethink the way they do business.*[37]

Splitting these definitions reveals that the nature of electronic commerce consists of four different components:

- *Communication.* E-com is the delivery of information, products/services, or payments via telephone lines, computer networks, or any other means.
- *Business Process.* E-com is the application of technology toward the automation of business transactions and workflows.
- *Service.* E-com is a tool that addresses the desire of firms, consumers, and management to cut service costs while improving the quality of goods by increasing the speed of service delivery.
- *Online.* E-com provides the capability of buying and selling products and information on the Internet and other online services.

It almost seems as if electronic commerce is for individuals and organizations to define themselves. Some parties view electronic commerce simply as a tool to further penetrate the market. They seek doing so by improving execution of existing business due to more effective performance, greater economic efficiency, and more rapid exchange of goods or services. Other parties realize e-com as an opportunity to reach existing customers with new products or to reach new customers with existing products. Again, others see an entrepreneurial potential in electronic commerce, which motivates them to try new ways and to risk an investment in new opportunities to generate business value.[38] For an in-depth analysis please refer to the Chapter 6.2.1 "Classification of Online Retailers" in this Section.

After having defined the business aspect of electronic commerce it is worthwhile taking a look at its abilities. Due to its multi-dimensions, it is able to combine previously separated functions as well as old and new services and technologies (refer to Exhibit 3).

Electronic commerce represents the paperless exchange of business information using electronic data interchange (EDI), electronic mail, Web supported faxes, electronic bulletin boards, electronic fund transfer (EFT), and other similar technologies. It also stands for a new online approach to performing traditional functions such as payment

---

[37] Supermarket Business 1998a, p. 30.
[38] Kalakota & Whinston 1997, pp. 1-5.

and fund transfer, order entry and processing, invoicing, inventory management, cargo tracking, electronic catalogs, and point-of-sale data gathering. Last, organizations view e-com as a new medium enabling them to redefine the means of advertising, marketing, and customer support.[39]

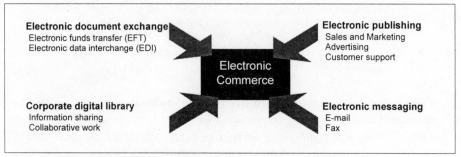

Exhibit 3: Electronic Commerce has the Ability to Combine Functions[40]

4.2.1 Different Types of Electronic Commerce

As mentioned earlier, electronic commerce is what one defines it to be. Therefore, there are very different forms of transactions, such as EDI, Internet commerce and Web commerce, all summarized under the same name – electronic commerce.

EDI, once the main form of electronic commerce, is a program-to-program communication that lets business applications in different organizations exchange information automatically to process a business transaction. These transactions involve predefined relationships between the involved parties and usually are carried over specialized networks known as value-added networks (VANs). The private networks of EDI provide users on the one hand with the main advantage of a high degree of security and reliability, however, on the other hand with the just as large disadvantage of not being suitable for ad-hoc business relations. New technologies and capabilities developed for Internet commerce are influencing the EDI technology, trying to remove the EDI hurdles. Web commerce, a child of Internet commerce, goes beyond using the Internet as a transport mechanism and assumes that participants have Web access. As stated in the second definition of e-com (refer to Chapter 4.2 "Electronic Commerce" in this Section), Internet-based electronic commerce is usually divided into business-to-business and into business-to consumer-commerce.[41] Following these two types of transactions will be discussed.

---

[39] Anderer 1998, pp. 10-11.
[40] Adapted from Sterne 1995, pp. 19-21.
[41] Pricewaterhouse 1998a, pp. 555-556.

4.2.2 Business-to-Business

The Web browser as a universal software client and the Internet as a provider of a ubiquitous infrastructure are the compelling advantages of the Web as an infrastructure for business-to-business commerce.[42]

Today, Web-based electronic commerce is the most widely used form of Internet commerce, it is more attractive than EDI, is growing faster, and will be much larger, both in terms of participants and in the value and volume of transaction. According to a study from Forrester Research, business-to-business commerce over the Internet will account for 78% of the dollar value of cyber-transactions in 1998. The report further estimates that by 2002, businesses will exchange goods and services over the Internet (here mainly the Web) with a worth of almost $330 billion.[43]

4.2.3 Business-to-Consumer

Although business-to-consumer Web-based electronic commerce has gained more and more attention, it currently only accounts for a relatively small fraction of the overall Web-based e-com. From a consumer standpoint, what exactly is business-to-consumer electronic commerce? First, it supports consumers' social interaction, by enabling them to communicate with each other (and businesses) through electronic mail, videoconferencing, and news groups. Second, it provides the means to manage investments and personal finances using online banking tools. Third, and most important for the business side, consumers can conveniently purchase products and information from their home. This might especially be important in times when convenience is of growing importance and time becomes more and more precious.[44]

Among the main reasons why consumers, compared to businesses, are much more reluctant to use the means of Web-based electronic commerce are security concerns and the relatively poor performance of the medium. While businesses can often build upon existing knowledge and the necessary technology infrastructure, consumers have only recently started to purchase equipment to make use of - and learn about - the Web on a large scale. Internet congestion and slow modems are other sources of complaints. However, concerns about secure payment alternatives seem to be the most important hurdle for consumer electronic commerce. Here, it is very interesting to note that business-to-business electronic commerce is not so much suffering from this hindrance. Electronic commerce merchants in a business-to-consumer transaction expect payments at the time an order is placed (and consumers want to be able to pay direct to avoid the delay and inconvenience associated with having to mail a check to the merchant). In the case of a business-to-business transaction, however, electronic

---

[42] Pricewaterhouse 1998a, pp. 556-557.
[43] Rainhardt 1998, p. 132.
[44] Kalakota & Whinston 1997, pp. 20-21.

commerce merchants are willing to invoice the buyer and collect the payment later. In the latter transaction, no sensitive data like credit card numbers are needed to be sent through the Web.[45] The issue of secure payments for consumers will be addressed again during the course of this book.

The remainder of this book will focus on the validation of the opportunity for Web-based e-com for the business-to-consumer side of retailers. Unless otherwise specified, the terms electronic commerce (Internet purchasing, or online purchasing) will refer to Web-based electronic commerce in a business-to-consumer relation.

5 Dimensions of Internet and Electronic Commerce from a Consumer Perspective

In virtually the blink of an eye, the Internet has given new meaning to the terms of growth. Ever since it opened up for public use, the number of participants increased astronomically. Following are some examples to give the reader an idea of the growth. In 1994, the traffic on the WWW grew by 350,000%[46] and from June 1993 until April 1995 the number of Web servers exploded from 130 to 15,700[47]. Earlier in 1998, the U.S. Department of Commerce illustrated that web traffic has been doubling every 100 days and more than 100 million people are now using it worldwide.[48] In August 1998, the number of Internet users over the age of 16 in the U.S. and Canada has reached 79 million; this is an increase of 36% compared to the previous study one year ago.[49] The following will explore the size of the Internet. The amount of secondary data available is immense, however, it is advisable to be careful analyzing the data, since most of the pieces of information are collected from different institutes, represent different populations, or are based on different assumptions.

5.1 Estimate of User Base

Speculations about the future role of the Web in everyday life are as manifold as the number of studies trying to predict the future size of the market. In order to get the most objective outlook, it is therefore advisable to take several different studies into consideration. The Morgan Stanley (MS) report on "Internet Retailing in the U.S." from 1997 suggests to first take a look at the adoption curves for various media. This assures to get a handle on the possibilities for the Internet as *the* new medium.

---

[45] Pricewaterhouse 1998a, pp. 557-558.
[46] Sterne 1995, p. 34.
[47] Kalakota & Whinston 1997, p. 64.
[48] U.S. Department of Commerce 1998, p. 8.
[49] Nielsen Media Research 1998, p. 1.

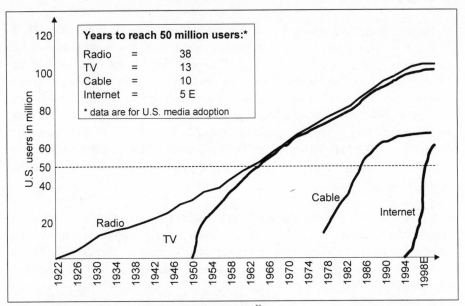

Exhibit 4: Adaptation Curves for Various Media[50]

By looking at these curves, illustrated in Exhibit 4, it becomes obvious that the adoption rates for new media have accelerated over time (numbers are not adjusted for population growth). For example, consumers adapted faster to TV than to radio[51] and Internet has certainly surpassed all of the other media in its rate of adoption. According to the study, it will take the Internet only five years (until 1999) to reach the critical mass of 50 million users, while it took cable television ten years to reach the same number of people. For the MS research team this is more proof that the Internet is the next mass medium in modern society. The team further believes in May 1997 there were 30-35 million Internet users in the U.S., which was an increase of 400% over the course of only two years. Compounded annual growth in Internet users until the year 2001 is predicted to be 54%, which would mean that more than 150 million people will utilize the Internet by the year 2000.[52]

Another study published in The Oregonian, estimates that 33% of the U.S. population[53] was online in July 1998. The CommerceNet/Nielsen Internet Demographic survey computed in June 1998 an Internet population of 79 million and a WWW population of 68 million over the age of 16 in North America. Even though these estimates might not be perfectly correct, they are precise enough to prove that by now about one third of the North American population is online.

[50] Morgan Stanley 1997, p. 2-2 – 2-3.
[51] For a detailed discussion about the technological developments of the radio earlier this century and parallels that can be drawn from there to the World Wide Web, see Hanson 1998, pp. 46-55.
[52] Morgan Stanley 1997, p. 2-2 – 2-3.
[53] Oregonian 1998, p. C02.

By the year 2000, the CommerceNet/Nielsen study forecasts for North America 132.75 million users on the Internet and 126 million on the Web, this is about half of the adults in the United States and Canada. This forecast suggests that more users of the Internet also make use of the Web.[54] The International Data Corporation (IDC) computed for the period from 1995 to 1997 a compounded average growth rate (CAGR) for Web users of 106%. The corporation estimated for the period from 1998 to 2000 a CAGR of 31%. This equals an estimate of 81 million U.S. Web users (and 163 million world wide Web users) in December 2000.[55] Note that this forecast was published in August 1997, from today's standpoint it seems to underestimate the development.

It becomes obvious that the estimates for the Internet usage in the year 2000 differ between the research conducted by Morgan Stanley versus Nielsen Media Research and CommerceNet, let alone the International Data Corporation. However, the results are suitable to give an estimate about future Internet usage and to illustrate the degree of uncertainty.

5.2 Online Consumer Profile

5.2.1 Internet Consumer

According the Ziff-Davis InternetTrak Research,[56] almost 60% (110 million) of the American population used a personal computer during the first quarter of 1998. Almost one-third visited the Web during the last three months prior to the survey (57 million individuals).[57] Who are these people?[58] Is the stereotype about the typical web user – young white male, above average income, and computer nerd – true or false?

Gender. The study concludes that men remain more active Internet users than women. While one-third of the overall male population used the Internet during the last three months prior to the survey, only 23% of the overall female population did so. However, a Nielsen Media Research study concludes that 43% of Internet users – 34

---

[54] CommerceNet 1998, pp. 1-2 and Nielsen Media Research 1998, pp. 1-3.
[55] Goldman Sachs 1997, pp. 28-30.
[56] This is an ongoing study of Web users in the U.S. and their online activities. Findings are based on monthly telephone surveys with a sampling group 18 years or older, conducted by ICR Research.
[57] Note the difference to the above-presented estimate of 68 million users from CommerceNet/Nielsen. This study estimated the usage for North America as a whole and did not specify the term "Web user". In the Ziff-Davis study, Web users are defined to be U.S. Americans, who used the Web during the three months previous to the survey.
[58] The following discussion of Internet users is based on Ziff-Davis 1998a Ziff-Davis 1998b unless otherwise indicated.

million persons – are women, which again is an example for the discrepancies among different study results.[59]

Age. Web usage is highly correlated with age. During the second quarter of 1998 more than half of the total population between 18-24 years and 40% of the total population of 25-34 years olds have been using the Internet. Here, the new medium has reached the critical mass, while one-third of the population between 35-44 accounts for Internet users, the same is only true for one-tenth of the ones over 55 years old. Refer to Exhibit 5 for detail.

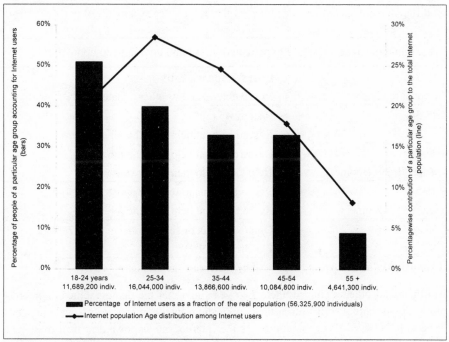

Exhibit 5: Age Distribution among Internet Users[60]

Income. The fraction of Internet users correlates positive with the household income, so it is not surprising that the average income of Web visitors is with $56,940 almost one-third above the national average income of $43,960. Almost one-fourth of the Internet population has a household income ranging between $50,000 and $74,999 (on a national base it is only 16%) and even more striking, Internet users are twice as likely as non-Web users to have an income higher than $75,000.

[59] Nielsen Media Research 1998, p. 2.
[60] GVU 1998, www.gvu.gatech.edu/user_surveys/survey-1998-04.

Education. It is not astonishing that the education of Web users is higher than the national average. One-in-three (31%) have some college (compared to 23% nationally), 28% are college graduates (17% nationally), and 13% are postgraduates (national average is 7%).

Performed Online Activities. Gender wise, men tend to participate in a wider variety of Internet activities, such as obtaining product information or researching about computers and computer peripherals, or personal finance. The only online activity performed more often by women than men are researching about topics like local community issues and clothes. The following Exhibit 6 presents some of the highlights of different online activities performed by the different age segments of users.

Age segment (in years)	Favorite activities (sum does not add up to 100%)
18-24 Generation X	• Chat with people (50%). • Receive news and weather updates (50%).
25-34	• Plan travel (56%). • Research about help with the job (55%).
35-44 Young Baby-Boomers	• Research about help with the job (58%). • Help kids to do their homework (45%).
45-54 Old Baby-Boomers	• Receive news and weather updates (67%). • Research about help with the job (58%).
55 and over	• Obtain product or service information (79%). • Plan travel (49%).

Exhibit 6: Online Activities Performed by Different Age Segments[61]

Hoffman and others believed about two years ago that the demographics of Internet users would rapidly shift to turn the new medium into a "mainstream" medium. They especially believed this to continue "as the Internet moves toward critical mass as a commercial medium."[62] While their prediction partly became true and the number of Internet participants continuously rose - and not only computer freaks participate anymore - it appears that Hoffman and other enthusiasts were wrong about the Internet going mainstream very soon. The discussion about Internet users states clearly, Internet is not for everyone – yet?

5.2.2 Electronic Commerce Customer

Do Web users equal online purchasers? Before examining this question, Gupta and Chatterjee suggest breaking down the Web users in two separate categories, namely

---

[61] Ziff-Davis 1998b, pp. 4-8.
[62] Hoffman 1996, www.microtimes.com.

36

the information seeking-stage and the buying stage.[63] After the addition of a third group, individuals not interested in online shopping at all, three groups of Web users can be identified as illustrated in the following Exhibit 7.

Purchasers	Individuals using the Web for ordering, paying for, and acquiring products or services
	• 32% of consumers with online access have purchased products or services over the Internet in early 1998.[64] • Estimates are that by the end of 1998, 40% of Web users have purchased goods or services over the Internet.[65]
Browsers	Individuals using the Web for visiting commercial sites, and searching and evaluating products or services
	• They don't account for online purchases, but the Web has influenced their shopping behavior.[66] • 50% of the Web community search online for detailed product and price information and then order the merchandise by fax or telephone. • 66% of the Web community research on the Web and then go to local brick-and-mortar stores to do the actual purchase. • 66% of the Web community indicate their research is beneficial to purchasing decisions. • Almost 50% of browsers are unlikely to give online purchasing a try during 1999.[67]
Non-shoppers	Individuals neither purchasing from nor browsing through commercial Web sites
	• 75% of non-shoppers indicated they would be unlikely to become online purchasers during the next twelve months.[68]

Exhibit 7: Three Groups of Web Users

As Exhibit 8 reveals, online purchasers are very likely avid moviegoers, gardeners and individuals doing some type of volunteer work. They also like to travel, to cook gourmet food and to play golf.

---

[63] Gupta and Chatterjee 1997, p. 124.

[64] Ernst & Young 1998, p. 4.

[65] Nielsen Media Research 1998, p. 1.

[66] The Vice Chairman of Industry Services at Ernst & Young formulates it this way: "The Internet is much more than a passive advertising vehicle, it's a shopping tool that fills the role of the knowledgeable salesperson consumers need, [...]. The Internet appears to be accelerating purchase decisions." Ernst & Young 1998, p. 6.

[67] Ernst & Young 1998, p. 6 and Jupiter Communications, 1998, www.jup.com.

[68] Jupiter Communications, 1998, www.jup.com.

Hobbies and Interests of Online Purchasers	
51%	... are avid moviegoers
48%	... are gardeners
38%	... travel for recreation
36%	... do some kind of charity or volunteer work
32%	... attend concerts/plays/performing arts events
25%	... enjoy gourmet cooking
21%	... play golf

Exhibit 8: Activities very Likely Performed by Online Purchasers[69]

Most of the above-presented characteristics are clearly pointing it out: Online purchasers are not average individuals. The Ernst & Young study concludes that online shopping is under the current circumstances mainly for well-educated, well-paid, middle-aged males. However, the study does not fail to mention the enormous future potential of the new commercial channel.[70]

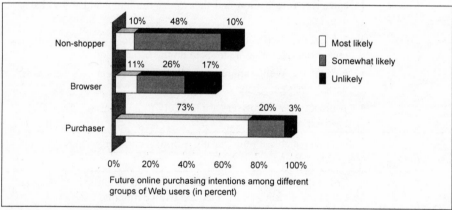

Exhibit 9: Online Purchasing Intentions[71]

Also interesting about online purchasers is that they are more likely than the average to make use of alternative shopping channels, such as mail-order (32% vs. an average of 25%) or telephone shopping (21% vs. 11%) and that those buyers shift purchases from these channels to the Internet.[72] Once in contact with the medium of online purchasing, customers were generally satisfied with their purchases and 95% indicated they would continue purchasing online in the future.[73] Exhibit 9 illustrates the future online purchasing intentions for the three types of Web users. It clearly points out people once

[69] Ernst & Young 1998, p. 5.
[70] Ernst & Young 1998, pp. 4-6.
[71] Jupiter Communications, 1998, www.jup.com.
[72] Ernst & Young 1998, p. 7.
[73] Jupiter Communications, 1998, www.jup.com.

convinced of online purchasing cling to the new purchasing channel, however, consumers not yet comfortable with this channel are difficult to convince.

6.3   Online Browsing and Purchasing Behavior

This part of the analysis (unless otherwise stated) is based on the 9th WWW User Survey,[74] conducted by the Graphic, Visualization & Usability Center's (GVU). Since the first survey was undertaken in 1994 a series of eight more followed. Today, it is the largest Internet based consumer survey.[75] The following discussion will first highlight some of the most important findings in regard to online browsing and purchasing in Exhibit 10 and will than address the implications of those findings for the future.

The influence of the Web on online purchasers and browsers cannot be neglected. While the influence is well visible in actual online purchases, it is not so easy to track when negative purchase decisions were made or when the actual purchase is made in a physical store. However, it is interesting to note that the habit of visiting the Web site of local stores, in which Web users normally shop in person, or other stores is quite common. It can be assumed that Web users' purchase behavior in brick-and-mortar stores is influenced by experiences they made on the retailers' Web pages. Interestingly, more mature people seem to base their purchase decision less frequently, exclusively on Web research, than younger people do.

Internet purchases are appreciated for their (assumed) ability to save time, to increase convenience and to deliver a clearer picture of the availability of different products. A recent study among people using the Internet on a regular basis, conducted by Zona Research revealed interesting information concerning this matter. According to Zona: One in three consumers have trouble finding products they are looking for. Most of them therefore abandoned online searches for merchandise at least once during the past two months prior to the survey. The chief economist at Zona concludes that if savvy Web users find it "extremely difficult or somewhat difficult, [...] the average population is having even more difficulty."[76]

---

[74]   GVU 1998, www.gvu.gatech.edu/user_surveys/survey-1998-04.
[75]   Methodology of the survey: It is conducted as a self-selecting, Web based survey. Announcements to participate are distributed through newsgroups, banners, www-surveying mailing lists and the popular media. The GVU offers incentive cash prizes of $250 awards. The survey consists of different sections, the ones used for the purpose of this paper are "Computer, Web and Internet Use" (9,150 respondents) and "Internet Shopping (Part 2)" (1,141 respondents). The GVU asks every user of the analysis to understand that the data has a bias toward the experienced and more frequent users than random digit dial surveys. The GVU conducts the surveys every sixth months as a public service to the WWW community.
[76]   Diederich 1998b, p. 1.

Visits on the Web Site of Local Stores
• 43% of Web users visit the Web site of local stores sometimes and 16% do so often.
• Women tend to visit Web sites of local stores less often than men.
• 20% of young customers (21-25 years) visit the Web sites often and almost 45% of people ages between 26-50 visit them sometimes.
Frequency of Online Browsing
• 20% use the Web several times per week or even daily to search for product information and more than 25% do so several times per month.
• Male Web users tend to use the medium more frequently to search for products than female users do.
• High frequency users tend to be mainly between 26-50 years old.
• 9% never use the Web to gather product information.
Purchase Decision Exclusively Depending on Online Browsing
• 33% of Web users (36% of all female Web users and 30% of all male Web users) make once or twice a month purchase decisions based solely on their Web research and more than 20% do so three to nine times a month.
• Web users 21-50 years of age use the medium most frequently (six and more times per month) as the basis of their purchase decision.
• People over 50 are the ones that base their purchase decisions less frequently or never solely on a Web research.
Reasons for using the Web for online purchases
• 80% name convenience as a main reason to use the Internet to make a purchase.
• 67% appreciate the Internet because of the feeling of no pressure while making a purchase.
• 65% appreciate the Internet because it saves time and 60% appreciate it because it encloses extensive vendor information.
• While men more often value vendor information, reviews, and recommendations from experts as most important, women consider personalized information based on customer profile (i.e. custom newspaper, book recommendations, etc.) more important.
Important Features When Doing Online Purchases
• 80% of online purchasers name security and variety of the offered goods as the most important features of online purchasing.
• Ease of ordering (76%), the quality of information (74%), and the Internet vendor's reliability (73%) are other highly important features of online purchasing.

Products Sought versus Bought Online
<ul><li>Computer and computer peripherals (75%), books and magazines (72%), travel arrangements (68%), and CDs (63%) are the most frequently online researched products.</li><li>Books/magazines (51%) and software with a value under $50 (50%) are the most frequently online bought items. CDs (38%) and software with a value over $50 rank second on the hit list of online purchases.</li></ul>
Amount Spent Over the Web
<ul><li>A little less than 33% have bought merchandise for up to $100, 33% have spent between $100-$500, and almost another 33% have spent more than $500 over the last six months prior to taking the survey.</li><li>Male Web users predominantly purchased the big ticket items (over $500), while more women than men purchased items for less than $50 over the last six months prior to taking the survey.</li><li>35% of Web users over 50 years of age spent between $100-$500 and another 34% spent over $500 over the last six months prior to taking the survey.</li></ul>

Exhibit 10: Online Browsing and Purchasing Behavior

In terms of Web merchandising, several requirements for successful utilization of a Web site can be concluded. It must be convenient and it must provide the customer with information, which may not be accessible through visiting a store, yet it ought not to be overwhelming, since the customer expects to save time by using the Web.

The question which product categories consumers search or purchase over the Internet is especially difficult to determine since different studies deliver somewhat opposing results. However, the 9th GVU study[77] as well as the Ernst & Young[78] study concluded that the product categories: Computers and peripherals, books, and travel arrangements are most frequently purchased online. A comparison of the results from the 8th and the 9th GVU survey reveals no big changes other than a 20% increase in both activities, seeking and purchasing. One reason for this wide increase might be a growing interest for online shopping, another reason might be that the GVU unfortunately changed the product categories[79] from the 8th to the 9th survey.

It is imperative not only to analyze which products are bought online but also how much money is spent there. Women seem to become curious about online shopping, while the heavy online purchasers are still mainly men. It becomes clear that the amount spent by Web users for online purchases is rising proportionally with his or her

---

[77] GVU 1998, www.gvu.gatech.edu/user_surveys/survey-1998-04.
[78] Ernst & Young 1998, p. 5.
[79] The 8th survey had a much wider product selection to chose from. It also had a category "other services", which accounted for two-thirds of seeking activities and one-third of purchasing activities. GVU 1997, www.gvu.gatech.edu/user_surveys/survey-1997-10.

age. While almost half of the smaller transactions (less than $50) are conducted by individuals younger than 20 years, one-third of the big ticket items (more than $500) are conducted by customers over 50 years of age. On average, the amount of consumer-spending dollars generated over the Internet is not tremendously high. Nevertheless, there is a strong tendency toward a rising importance of the Internet as a new purchase channel and there is the importance of the Internet as a location to spread product information and to create consumer appetite. Note that based on primary research, Section III "Primary Market Research" will elaborate further on characterizing current as well as future online purchasers.

6 Dimensions of Internet and Electronic Commerce from a Retail Perspective

First, the Internet has been introduced as one cause of recent changes in our society, its effects on the consumers were illustrated and now it seems worthwhile to determine these effects on the retailers.

In 1998, four out of five Fortune 500 companies[80] and every second U.S. retailer were present on the Internet. Another 40% of retailers were either seriously planing to be online or currently investigated the scene. During the same time period, one-sixth of these retailers actually sold products over the Internet and another quarter planed to do so in the near future. More than one-half had no plans to establish online sales. Exhibit 11 breaks down the details.

Retailers' Presence on the Web		Retailers' Intention to Sell Over the Web	
50%	Are present	12%	Sell online
20%	Plan presence within 12 months	22%	Plan to sell online within 12 months
20%	Currently investigate the scene	12%	Undecided in regard to future action
10%	No intention to establish Web presence any time soon	54%	No intention to establish online selling any time soon

Exhibit 11: Retailers' Current State of Mind in Regard to Being on the Web[81]

Despite these positive forecasts, it can be noticed that while traditional brick-and-mortar retailers have started to examine the Web as a marketing tool, they tend to use it to a lesser degree as a sales medium. However, the hesitation is partly understandable since online retailing is not successfully managed by creating a Web site with a "BUY"

---

[80] Puyear 1998, p. 3.
[81] Ernst & Young 1998, p. 10 and Wilson 1998, p. 13.

button, even though some proponents of online retailing sometimes map it to be that simple. The following discussion will therefore characterize online retailing by pointing out its advantages as well as its challenges.

6.1 Characteristics of Online Retailing

6.1.1 Five Advantages of Electronic Retailing

Robertson, Stephens & Company authors of "Webolution", a research study on the Internet, called it the ability to offer additional features and benefits to gain market share, Ghosh named it to be capable of becoming a customer magnet.[82] Both are referring to a unique set of advantages and opportunities of online retailing, which will now be introduced: Assortment, Information, Targeting, Direct Connections, and New Business Models.

Assortment. One enormous advantage of online retailing is the ability to offer a wider and deeper assortment then would be economically supportable in physical stores. This together with the Internet's ability to create an interactive and customizable communication with customers bares for online retailers the opportunity of creating a value proposition beyond traditional sales.[83] Etoys.com, an in 1997 founded Internet based toys and children's products company, offers a birthday reminder list, which might serve as an example. Here, Web page visitors are invited to insert the name and the date of birth of children. Then, two weeks ahead of the birthday, participants receive an e-mail, reminding them of the upcoming event and also directly linking them to a wide variety of gift suggestions for children of that particular age.[84]

Information. The Internet is filled with information and recommendations about goods and services. Online retailers can use this host of information to their advantage if they succeed linking content and commerce. The new medium also provides the opportunity to better understand customer's needs and wants.[85] It might be an especially helpful tool for selling products that require intense descriptions, reviews, or specifications. An example might be purchasing software. While stores are little help in transmitting detailed information about software, on the Internet, customers can download previews, read detailed descriptions or discuss it with an online discussion group. These opportunities of intense product research might eventually increase the customers' confidence and lead to an increase in purchases.[86]

---

[82] Ghosh 1998, p. 133.
[83] Robertson, Stephens & Company 1997, p. 16.
[84] Etoys 1998, www.etoys.com.
[85] Stewart 1998, www.deloittte.com/tidalwave.
[86] Robertson, Stephens & Company 1997, p. 17.

Targeting. The third advantage of the Internet is that any business on the Internet has the ability to reach and to be reached by many different types and communities of customers. On the sales side, this potentially opens up vast new markets. On the one hand, companies can reach out to customers they are particularly interested in, on the other hand, customers can search for the product that best fulfills their needs.[87] This phenomenon on the retailer side can be described as the technology and marketing leverage, which enables retailers to target those customer segments, most likely to purchase products. Take Tripod.com as an example. This company calling itself an electronic community, targets Generation X-ers, 18-35 years old, by providing information tailored to the needs and wants of this particular age group.[88] Retailers, focusing on a particular customer segment, enjoy exploiting such electronic communities since it provides them with already pre-bundled target groups. It becomes obvious that the Internet enables retailers to be both scalable and customer specific, by tracking consumer behavior and use this real-time data to make adjustments to their promotions, products and services.[89]

Direct Connection. The Microsoft slogan: "Where do you want to go today?" expresses the unique possibility for Web users to move to any desired location on a mouse click. In theory, online retailing represents the "ultimate in shopping convenience and maximum opportunity for impulse purchases."[90] However, it is anticipated that customers will prefer the convenience of shopping in one location. This will bring the opportunity for providers to host numerous suppliers under one virtual roof, outfitting customers with an easy, convenient way to compare and purchase products. On the other hand, this will force the individual suppliers to determine new ways to emphasize their unique values and to differentiate themselves from the competition.[91]

New Business Models. In the case of traditional retailers moving to the Web, Ghosh points out that" it will [...] be difficult to integrate electronic processes for commerce with existing physical processes that often involve numerous functions and many business units within an organization."[92] It also needs to be taken into consideration that start-up costs for an online retailing Web page and its maintenance are substantially high, and so are marketing and advertising expenses. However, online retailing is expected to lead to superior operating margins, since a centralized distribution versus a fragmented store distribution will guide to lower costs of goods sold. Also, marketing expenses as well as operating expenses are expected to decrease, while the return on investment is expected to increase. Experts justify these changes

---

[87] Stewart 1998, www.deloittte.com/tidalwave.
[88] Tripod 1998, www.tripod.com.
[89] Robertson, Stephens & Company 1997, p. 18.
[90] Robertson, Stephens & Company 1997, p. 20.
[91] Ghosh 1998, p. 134.
[92] Ghosh 1998, p. 135.

44

with a decrease in the size of the sales force, promotional expenses, as well as expenses for brick-and mortar stores.[93]

In the summer 1998, Activa Media Inc., a research company that has been surveying Web sites since 1994, published a survey revealing the profitability of online retailers: 46% of the surveyed sites revealed profits from current online sales. One-third believed to do so within the next one to two years and only seven percent of the interviewed online merchants indicated they do not expect profits within the next three years. One fifth of the interviewees did not generate revenue at their site.[94] However, it can be concluded that increasing online price wars among online retailers, leading to shrinking profit margins as well as difficulties in handling the back-end side of the operation, present the largest hurdles for retailers to sell online. Next, it seems advisable to take a look at additional drawbacks or challenges retailers are facing in regard to the new medium.

6.1.2 Customers' Risk Perception - a Challenge of Electronic Commerce

Electronic commerce holds a large degree of uncertainty for customers. Numerous research studies have been conducted to elaborate on the main reasons for consumers' reluctance to adopt the Internet on a large scale as a new purchasing channel. Again, different studies revealed different main causes, however *risk* has most of the time been identified as a major influential factor. What is risk and what can retailers do to minimize the perception of this risk? The following paragraph addresses these questions by first defining risk more precisely and then reflecting the current efforts of risk reduction. Jarvenpaa and Todd, differentiate risk in five dimensions (Exhibit 12).

Dimensions	Characteristics
Performance risk	Goods and services bought on the Web don't meet consumers' expectations.
Social risk	Purchasing on the Web is perceived as imprudent or socially unacceptable.
Economic risk	Using the Web to buy, leads to monetary losses through poor purchase decisions.
Personal risk	Online purchasing results in harmful personal consequences for consumers.
Privacy risk	The process of shopping on the Web puts the consumers' privacy in jeopardy.

Exhibit 12: Five Dimensions of Risk[95]

---

[93] Robertson, Stephens & Company 1997, pp. 17-22.
[94] Green & Browder 1998, p. 156.
[95] Jarvenpaa & Todd 1997, p. 146.

Retailers can generally counter performance risk by posting detailed product information on the Web page, by having a 24 hour phone service that can be contacted in case of concerns or questions and by offering a generous return policy. The issue of social risk will fade with the increasing popularity of online purchasing. Information on the bandwidth of products available over the Internet will also help to increase the social acceptability of online purchases.

More complicated to address are issues facing economic, personal and privacy risk. The conglomerate of these three risks is commonly described as the security and privacy issue. Jack Danahy, director of security services at GTE Internetworking Services, comments on these issues as follows: "Security and privacy are knottier problems. Today, Net security is practically a contradiction in terms. The Internet is a medium developed to provide wide access to information, but security means being able to restrict access selectively."[96] The current situation calls for improvement.

The Security Issue. As presented earlier, customers are still hesitant in regards to providing financial information. Three main causes explain the hesitation. First, merchants cannot determine whether the user of a credit card is in fact the owner or a defrauder. Second, if retailers keep the customer's card number electronically, it could also be accessed for subsequent fraudulent use. Third, customers have only restricted means to verify, whether a particular Web merchant was a legitimate company or in fact a trap to collect personal information for fraudulent use.[97] Today, the overwhelming majority of online merchants use credit cards as the medium of payment.[98] Experts assure a certain degree of security when encryption techniques are employed to transmit the sensitive data and other information about the transaction. Only a fraction of online retailers currently accept payments in a form other than credit cards, however, there are several other alternatives emerging. Among the most promising are: (1) the alternative to include a trusted intermediary service that provides credibility for both buyer and seller, (2) digital check payment, a network-based replacement for the paper check that uses secure encrypted data interchange, and (3) digital payment cash that uses serial-numbered digitally signed tokens.[99] The following discussion on the privacy issue will explain how merchants may succeed in building customer trust.

---

[96] Gross & Sager 1998, p. 166.
[97] Pricewaterhouse 1998a, p. 574.
[98] Visa plans to spend about $25 million on electronic commerce promotions, which is more than 10% of Visa's estimated annual advertising budge. According to estimates from the Wall Street Journal, electronic commerce transactions accounted in 1998 for less than 0.5% of all Visa payments in the U.S. The company estimates that EC transactions with its cards will hit $100 billion, or 10% of all U.S. Visa payments.
[99] Ritzer Ross 1998, p. 28.

The Privacy Issue. New sophisticated software increasingly enables retailers to collect, analyze, store, and transfer customer-specific behavioral data. Today, consumers leave "digital footprints" as they correspond, search, and purchase over the Internet. While retailers are eager to collect consumer demographic and psychographic profiles as complete as possible, these profiles assist them to forecast future demands as accurately as never before, most customers are reluctant to reveal private data. This dilemma in regard to customer information is considered one of the hottest online issues. Customers mainly raise concern over their lack of control over the possibility that their personal information is stolen or copied and sold to virtually anyone without their knowledge or consent.

On the first glance, one might consider to simply forbid companies to store personal data on individuals. On the second glance, this action would confront electronic commerce with an entirely different kind of threat. Why? Because precisely tracking consumers' preferences and tailoring products to those users evolved as one of the most promising online business approaches.[100] Here, the necessity to find alternatives in order to create a win-win solution becomes apparent.

Being up front with customers about the data being gathered and how it will be used, might be a conceivable compromise. The GVU survey revealed that a statement, addressing what kind of information is going to be collected and how it is going to be used, would convince the majority of the users to give out demographic information. More than one third would do so in exchange for some value-added services.[101] In this context it is also valuable to mention that almost two-thirds of current off-line computer users, indicated their likeliness to go online, if their privacy was protected. Almost two-thirds of online users indicated that a privacy policy would encourage them "a little" or even "a lot" to purchase products online.[102]

Different regions of the world are likely to install different alternatives to deal with the privacy issue. The European Union for example, by the end of October 1998, set its new Privacy Directive (Directive 95/46)[103] into effect. This Directive seems very extreme from a non-EU standpoint and in an era in which customer information is the lifeblood of economic success.

---

[100] Gross & Sager 1998, p. 168.
[101] GVU 1998, www.gvu.gatech.edu/user_surveys/survey-1998-04.
[102] Reda 1998, p. 41.
[103] Under this rule, companies are prohibited from transferring "personal information" – including names, addresses and personal profiles – across borders, if the country to which the material is being exported to does not have in place a national law on privacy and a regulatory agency monitoring the use of such information. Most countries, including the United States, do not fulfil these requirements. The EU justifies the new directive with the necessity to harmonize the diverse privacy protection regulations that where in place in the different member states of the EU in order to promote the freer flow of information within the EU. Savage & Warner 1998, AMA Presentation, November 3, 1998.

The U.S. currently experiments with market-based privacy-protection alternatives,[104] which were initiated by a warning served from federal officials in 1997 that the online industry had 18 months to put a self-regulation in place or else face government action.[105] The current state-of-the-art market-based initiatives addressing the consumer privacy issue are TRUSTe, Online Privacy Alliance, WebTrust, and the Direct Market Association efforts.

TRUSTe. Introduced in June 1997, is a global consumer privacy initiative, which is working in conjunction with existing standards such as SET[106] to increase the trust between buyers and sellers engaged in electronic commerce. TRUSTe issues so-called Trustmarks that certify compliance with three types of privacy standards[107]: No exchange, one-to-one exchange, or third-party exchange.[108]

Online privacy. This alliance is a coalition of more than 60 global companies that "leads and supports self-regulatory initiatives that create an environment of trust and that foster the protection of individuals' privacy online and in electronic commerce."[109]

WebTrust. This certification criterion developed by the American Institute of Certified Public Accountants (AICPA) and the Canadian Institute of Chartered Accountants (CICA) allows accounting firms to provide a certification service for business-to-consumer electronic commerce Web pages.

The criterion involves business practices disclosure, transaction integrity controls, and information protection controls. The aim of WebTrust is to provide a visible seal and corresponding attest report so that consumers may have confidence in the security of an electronic commerce Web page.[110]

Direct Marketing Association (DMA). The DMA has developed guidelines to provide marketers with answers to questions about implementing corporate fair information policies and complying with DMA's self-regulatory programs. In addition it has also defined so-called "Marketing Online Privacy Principles and Guidance", which uniquely address online and Internet marketing issues. The DMA guidelines, in

---

[104] Peppers & Rogers 1998a, www.1to1.com.

[105] Reda 1998, p. 46.

[106] Secure Electronic Transaction (SET) is an open standard that provides message integrity, authentication of all financial data and encryption of sensitive data. Davy 1998, p. 24.

[107] (1) No exchange – indicates that the site uses no personally identifiable information. (2) One-to-One Exchange – indicates that the site collects data, but only for use by the site owner. (3) Third-Party Exchange – indicates that the site may share, transfer, or sell personal information to other parties.

[108] TRUSTe 1998, www.truste.org and Pricewaterhouse 1998, pp. 408, 580.

[109] Online privacy Alliance 1998, www.privacyalliance.org.

[110] WebTrust 1998, www.verisign.com/webtrust/.

particular, address the issues of online notices, the means of opting out, unsolicited marketing e-mail, and online data collection from or about children.[111]

In June 1998, the FTC published its examination of the practices of commercial sites on the Web. The Commission's survey of over 1,400 Web sites revealed the industry's efforts to encourage voluntary adoption of the most basic fair information practice principle - notice - have fallen far short of what is needed to protect consumers. While more than four-fifth of all Web pages were collecting customer information, only 14% of those provided any notice in regard to information practices, and only 2% provided notice by means of a comprehensive privacy policy.[112] By March 1999, there were more than 80 bills related to privacy in Congress and the Internet was one of the primary drivers behind these bills. It can be said that electronic commerce freedoms hang in the balance. The Direct Market Association vividly informs retailers that they might be able to stop legislation by creating honest privacy policies.[113] Putting it all in a nutshell, in the matter of the privacy issue "a simple strategy, based on notice and consent: Do what you say and say what you do", would go a long way.[114]

The preceding discussion on the advantages and challenges of electronic retailing is meant as an anticipation of Section IV, which will highlight one alternative, how AnyCo - in case of an online venture - might cope with new requirements of this new and exciting way of doing business.

6.2 Participants of Online Retailing

6.2.1 Classification of Online Retailers

Who in the retail community is actually utilizing the Web as a sales medium? In general, these online retailers can be divided into four categories:[115]

- Retailers previously only operating brick-and-mortar stores,
- Catalogue and mail order retailers,
- Pure Internet retailers whose sales channel is exclusively the Internet, and
- Manufacturers exploring the potential to go "direct to consumers".

The reason, why these merchants, except the pure Internet retailers, moved to online sales is obvious. They experienced (or were anxious to experience) a gap, initiated by new online competitors, between originally anticipated and realized sales figures. They

---

[111] DMA 1997, pp. 3-11.
[112] FTC 1998, pp. 6-7.
[113] DMA 1999, www.the-dma.org.
[114] Davy 1998, p. 24.
[115] Kalakota & Whinston 1997, p. 224.

saw the solution in stepping in and participating in the modulation of the Internet as a new sales medium. On the other side, the pure Internet retailers were lead by the entrepreneurial spirit of a new business opportunity and the opportunity to challenge the existing business practice.

The product-market matrix from Ansoff, encapsulating how product and market opportunities are mapped against an existing or new status, is a suitable tool to categorize the different types of online retailers and their approaches to utilize the Web for sales purposes.[116] The matrix is base on four distinct strategies, which are in the following first defined and than applied to characterize online retailers (refer to Exhibit 13).

- Penetration: The increase of market share of existing products in existing markets at the expense of the competition.
- Product expansion: The identification of new product possibilities for existing markets.
- Market expansion: The identification of new potential markets for existing products.
- Diversification: The identification of new potential products for new potential markets, which means the exploitation of good opportunities outside the scope of the current business.[117]

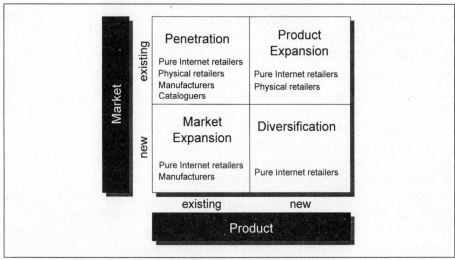

Exhibit 13: Modification of Ansoff's Product-Market Matrix[118]

---

[116] Nieschlag, Dichtl & Hörschgen 1994, p. 899.
[117] Ansoff 1957, pp. 113-115.
[118] Adapted from Nieschlag, Dichtl & Hörschgen 1994, p. 900.

The following discussion is based upon four assumptions: Online retailing is mainly a reaction to the Internet as a newly emerged tool (and not an action to become a high-tech innovator). The Internet in the following is understood as a new tool to reach the market. The product is goods that retailers offer for sale, and the market is the existing and potential customer base of a retailer, both in geographical respect as well as in respect to different customer segments.

Physical Retailers. The two prime reasons for retailers with an established physical store presence to go online seem to be a desired market penetration as well as a product expansion. As mentioned before, these retailers choose online retailing as a strategy to defend existing ground against emerging online competition (penetration). They seek to transfer their physical store expertise and name recognition into electronic retailing in order to differentiate themselves further from competitors as well as to increase their competitive advantage. Second, retailers move to the Web because it allows them to offer new products to existing customers. Online catalogues enable them to offer a much deeper and wider product selection than the constraints of a physical storefront would possibly allow them to do.

The Internet also opens up the possibility for online retailers to offer slow moving or very voluminous articles. This further supports retailers' effort to differentiate itself from physical and online competition.

Catalogue retailers. The prime reason for catalogue retailers to adapt to online selling is market penetration. Similar to the physical retailers, they aim to defend old ground against new competitors, which makes going online a pure reactionary strategy for them. For the most part they do not have the opportunity to offer new products or to access new markets - if such thing would be possible, they previously would have done so with their printed catalogues. Cataloguers, moving to the Web, are also aware that they cannibalize their own catalogue business, however they prefer this, than to standing the risk of being put out of business by the competition. One might ask, where is the advantage of online catalogues over mail catalogues. The Goldman Sachs report on cyber commerce from 1997 identifies speed as the potential edge. The report names as the big advantage the fact that browsing and selection processes are one in the same. On the Internet, customers load their shopping carts as they "surf" through the virtual aisles, with no need to transcribe item numbers and read them to an operator.[119]

Manufacturers. Manufacturers sense Internet selling as an opportunity to bypass some of the intermediaries to whom they used to sell their products and who then sold to the end customers. In the past, the alternative for manufacturers to sell the products directly to customers was mostly out of the question because it would have been too

---

[119] Goldman Sachs 1997, p. 93.

expensive for them to maintain physical stores. The Internet, however, allows manufacturers to sell in an economical way, directly to the customers. It also allows customers to approach manufacturers directly with a purchase request, which now seems in some cases more natural than taking the detour over to intermediaries. Manufacturers, moving to the Internet, exploit two strategies, market penetration and market expansion. In the first one, they sell the same products and the same people use it, however manufacturers bypass others in the value chain, which bares monetary advantages for them as well as for the end customers. Second, online retailing gives manufacturers the opportunity to employ the strategy of a market expansion, since it enables them to reach customers previously not being reached (e.g. because intermediaries didn't reach them or because of geographic distances). Besides the disadvantage of pirating in the value chain, there is the drawback of damaging long-standing relationships with other participants in this chain that should also not be forgotten.[120]

Pure Internet Retailers. For pure Internet retailers the picture is significantly different, since most of them are entrepreneurial start-ups who have no existing value chain to protect. Pure Internet retailers have the ability to utilize all four strategies of Ansoff's matrix. They utilize online retailing as a promising tool to penetrate the market and to challenge existing retailers by skimming up some of their profits. They also undergo a market expansion as they have the ability to develop new (geographical as well as customer segment wise) markets, which could not have been reached before. These new retailers also utilize the Internet for product expansion, since it allows the creation of things not possible before. Amazon.com, the virtual bookstore offers for example, the following service to customers, who look for a gift for someone else. Customers select the books or music they want to give, then they choose a gift-wrap and add a personal message, last they enter the gift recipient's address (while the customer gets the bill) and choose a shipping method.[121] This service allows customers to give something with a personal touch without ever having physically touched it. Last, Internet retailers are heading more and more towards a diversification strategy, since it allows them to sell new products to new markets (coming back to the previous example, Amazon.com is now able to offer the gift service to people in countries, which not even physical bookstores exist).

6.2.2 Movement Toward Market Concentration

One question arising from this discussion is, whether the boom towards online retailing will lead to a market share fragmentation or a market concentration. It has been shown that the perceived attractiveness of the Internet as a marketplace has recently drawn many new participants, which might serve as an indicator of low Internet market entry

---

[120] Ghosh 1998, p. 131.
[121] Amazon 1999, www.amazon.com.

barriers. However, experts forecasted a rising of the barriers in the near future. Their argument is, even though everyone can open a virtual store, only the ones with the biggest marketing budget and / or the best brick-and-mortar reputation will be able to accumulate the critical mass of customers.[122] Another reason for rising barriers is customer related. Once customers decide to do business with an online merchant they make an investment of their time and attention. They spend time to become comfortable with the procedures of a site, they might personalize the site according to their own needs and they offer sensitive information. Therefore, it can be assumed that the average customers, once they have established a relationship with one electronic retailer, are unlikely to go through the effort again with many suppliers as long as they are satisfied.[123] In such an environment, it shall become more difficult for new market entrants to find themselves a profitable position. It will therefore be concluded that the online market will gravitate to market concentration, much as we have seen in the traditional retail world.[124]

6.2.3 Identification of Beneficiaries

The Ernst & Young report on Internet shopping starts with the prediction that "the Internet has emerged as a shopping channel with undeniable power to facilitate and increase sales of a growing range of products."[125] So, how are the opportunities distributed?

In very broad terms it seems like commodities and durable goods, items with a trustworthy brand name and with consumer recognition will be successful in terms of Internet sales. Other attributes of successful items might be time-saving, convenience increasing, new, innovative, technically superior, hard-to-find or specialty.[126] Schwartz, author of the book Web-onomics, identifies two product categories to be likely to sell on the Web: Information-rich products that take time to find and to contemplate and information-poor products for which home delivery orders will be placed.[127]

Two forecasts, the Forrester Research and the Morgan Stanley report on Internet retailing, seem favorable to analyze opportunities for various retail categories. Forrester Research presents estimated revenues for different categories of the retail business until the year 2001. The overall revenue from online sales is expected to be between $5 and $9 billion in 1998, more than double as much from the previous year of 1997. Assumed that the total retail revenue in 1998 is similar to the figure from

[122] Morgan Stanley 1997, p. 3-8.
[123] Ghosh 1998, p. 129.
[124] Moschella 1998, p. 34.
[125] Ernst & Young 1998, p. 1.
[126] Morgan Stanley 1997, p. 3-4.
[127] Schwarz 1997, pp. 93-101.

1997, than Internet retailing takes about 0.2% of the total revenue in 1998.[128] For the year 2001, moderate estimates expect the total online retail revenues to rise to more than $17 billion, however, more enthusiastic estimates go up to $108 billion for the year of 2003. However, the revenues will not be distributed evenly among the different retail categories. Based on the Forrester estimates (Exhibit 14), the author suggests splitting the online retail community into three separate groups, currently holding different levels of performance potentials.

In Million U.S.$	1997	1998 E	1999 E	2000 E	2001 E
High market players					
PC hardware and software	863	1,616	2,234	2,901	3,766
Travel	654	1,523	2,810	4,741	7,443
Entertainment	298	591	1,143	1,921	2,678
Revenue	**1,815**	**3,730**	**6,187**	**9,563**	**13,887**
Revenue in % of total	74%	77%	78%	79%	80%
Medium market players					
Book and music	156	288	504	761	1,084
Gift, flowers, and greetings	149	264	413	591	802
Apparel and footwear	92	157	245	361	514
Food and beverages	90	168	250	354	463
Revenue	**487**	**877**	**1,412**	**2,067**	**2,863**
Revenue in % of total	20%	18%	18%	17%	16%
Small market players					
Jewelry	38	56	78	107	140
Consumer electronics	19	34	60	93	143
Sporting goods	20	29	43	63	84
Toys and hobbies	13	21	32	47	71
Health, beauty and drugs	11	16	25	36	50
Tools and gardening	10	22	31	44	59
Home furnishings	9	15	21	28	38
Other (pets, phones, etc.)	22	28	35	42	52
Revenue	**142**	**221**	**325**	**460**	**637**
Revenue in % of total	6%	5%	4%	4%	4%
Total	**2,444**	**4,828 ***	**7,924**	**12,090**	**17,387**

* Note that actual online retail revenues for the year of 1998 turned out to be over $8 billion.

Exhibit 14: Estimated Revenues from Different Sectors of Online Retailing[129]

First, the high volume players (PC hardware and software, travel, entertainment), which seem to be the immediate successors, second the medium volume players (Books, gifts, flowers and greetings, apparel and footwear, food and beverages), tend to be the medium-term successors. Third, the low volume players (jewelry, health, beauty and drugs, consumer electronics, tools and gardening, sporting goods, home furniture, toys and hobbies and other), being long-term successors. While the high volume players are estimated to hold more than three-quarters of the total online revenues, the medium volume players are expected to hold around 16-20% and the low

---

[128] The Seattle Times 1998, p. 15.
[129] Forrester Research 1998, www.forrester.com and Hof, McWilliams & Saveri 1998, pp. 122-125.

volume players only around 4-6% of total online revenues until the year 2001[130] (see Appendix 1).

On the other hand, the Morgan Stanley report, acknowledging that there is no proper estimate for future online sales figures, presents the online sales opportunities for different retail segments in a matrix form instead of real figures. This matrix compares fragmented markets, where selection, information, convenience and price are especially critical shopper variables with the Internet business opportunities (see Exhibit 15). A comparison of the two forecasts reveals no big differences, however, the Morgan Staley reports rates the chances for apparel lower and the chances for consumer electronics higher than the Forrester Research report. Note that in Section III, Chapter 11.4.2 "Online Sales Now and Then by Product Category" presents further information regarding online sales categories.

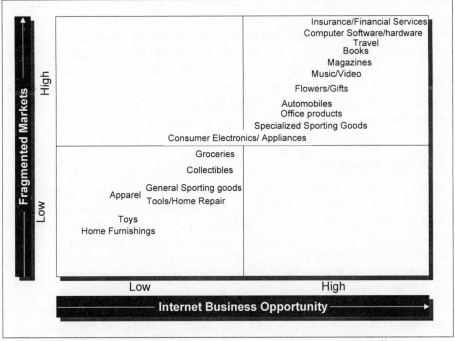

Exhibit 15: Matrix of Online Retailing Opportunities for Different Sectors[131]

[130] Forrester Research 1998, www.forrester.com and Hof, McWilliams & Saveri 1998, pp. 122-125.
[131] Morgan Stanley 1997, pp. 3-5.

7 Population Dynamics

In the U.S., there are currently broad demographic and lifestyle shifts underway, causing creeping but capital changes in society. Even though it can be assumed purely coincidentally that the current changes in society are parallel processes of the new technological advancements it is worthwhile looking at them since it can be assumed that changes in society will reinforce and influence developments in technology. Opportunities for online retailers seem to take on a tangible form.

7.1 Demographic Changes

7.1.1 Population Size and Population Growth

For the year 2000, the Bureau of Census projected the population will reach 275 million that relates to a 4.5% increase since 1995 or an annual average increase of 0.8%. This number may top 300 million around 2010 and by the middle of the next century, the population is expected to increase to 394 million, which is a 50% increase from today's population size.[132] Nevertheless with this large increase, the rate of population growth is projected to decrease during the next fifty years. In fact, since the introduction of "the pill" as contraception in 1965, the birth rate in the U.S. has fallen. Experts call this an historically unprecedented phenomenon,[133] which takes place among the American population a process of "deyouthing".[134]

7.1.2 Age Distribution

In 1995, children under the age of five have been at 19.6 million are as numerous, as they have been in the last 30 years. However, their numbers are expected to decline by 2000 and are then expected to rise again by 2010. In 1995, there have been 49 million children ages between 5 and 17 and this number is expected to increase by about 3 million until 2000 and by another 17 million until the year 2050. How about the age group 18 to 24 years? While during the early 1980's there were 30 million of them, the size of this group has declined to less than 25 million in 1995. Following the development of the younger age groups, this group of young adults will rise to 26 million in 2000 and 30 million in 2010. Accordingly, the total population under age 45 is projected to increase from 177 million today to 190 million in 2020.[135]

---

[132] Bureau of the Census 1998a, pp. 1, 5-6.
[133] While the population growth is declining in all industrialized countries, it is interesting to note that the growth rate of Americans is still the largest among these countries (e.g. the growth rate of the United Kingdom is 0.2%, Germany's natural growth rate is currently 0%). The role of immigrations in this context will be elaborated on later.
[134] Sheth & Sisodia 1996, p. 20 and Wolfe 1996, pp. 99-103.
[135] Bureau of the Census 1998a, pp. 1, 7-9.

About 30% of the population in 1995 was born during the Baby Boom after World War II (1946-1964). The early baby boomers have started to turn 50 recently. Subsequently, those in their 50's will increase by 12 million from 1996 to 2006, reflecting an increase of this age group by 50%. By 2005, almost forty percent of the U.S. population will be over 45 years old.[136] The age group 65 and over is projected to increase during the next 55 years, both in number and as a share of the population. The number of people ages 65 and over is forecasted to increase from 39 million in 2010 to 69 million in 2030 (this is when the Baby Boomers will enter this life stage). At this time, about 20% of the total population would be over 65, compared to about 13% today.

Not surprisingly, the future U.S. population will be older than it is now. The median age, of 34.3 years in 1995, will increase to 35.7 years in 2000, peak at 38.7 in 2035, and than decrease slightly to 38.1 by 2050.[137]

7.1.3 Ethnic Diversity

In 1997, almost one in ten individuals permanently living in the U.S. immigrated there from abroad, this number doubled from 1970. In 1995, three-quarters of the population was non-Hispanic White; nevertheless, this group will only contribute to about one-quarter of the total population growth during the next 10 years. From 2030 to 2050, the non-Hispanic White population is forecasted to add nothing to the U.S. population growth because it would be declining in size. In fact, the non-Hispanic White share of the U.S. population would steadily fall from 74% today to 72% in 2000 respectively to 64% in 2020 and 53% in 2050. This indicates that the percentage of non-Hispanic Whites decreases from three-quarters to one-half within the next half decade. By 2030, the non-Hispanic White population will account for less than half of the U.S. population under the age 18.

In comparison, the African-American population is expected to double its size to 61 million during the same time period. After 2016, more African-Americans than non-Hispanic Whites are expected to add to the population each year.

People with Hispanic-origin followed by the Asian and Pacific Islander populations have the highest rates of increase in terms of annual growth rates, which is expected to increase annually by 2% until 2030. Until 2050, the race/ethnic group that is forecasted to add the largest number of people to the population would be the Hispanic-origin population. The Bureau of Census further states that after 2020 the Hispanic population is projected to add more people to the U.S. every year than all other

---

[136] A.T. Kearney 1998, pp. 9-10.
[137] Bureau of the Census 1998a, pp. 1, 5-7.

race/ethnic groups combined.[138] These developments lead to the fact that the U.S. is becoming more racially and ethnically diverse.

Looking at these demographic changes from the perspective of today's retailers' point of view, it becomes apparent that in the future, retailers will be confronted with a different set of customer needs. On the one hand, the U.S. population will be "deyouthing" and the median age will rise. In other words, an increased number of older people will be faced with a decreased number of younger people to take care of them. Today's retailers might want to look at online retailing as a solution to satisfy the needs of tomorrow's (older) customers for features such as increased convenience, enhanced information or improved personal contact.

On the other hand, the U.S. in the future will be even more racially and ethnically diverse. Therefore, it can be expected that it will become even more difficult to identify and to address the target customer groups. Again, online retailing (easier than a brick-and-mortar store) would allow retailers to address different customer segments for example in different languages and with merchandise assortments from different ethnic backgrounds.

7.2 Lifestyle Changes

7.2.1 Women in the Workforce

In 1995 in the U.S., almost one half of all women were full-time employed and this percentage is going to increase to almost two-thirds by the year 2000. This leads to a change in the traditional family. Women will not stay home when they have decided to have children. Instead the opposite becomes more and more common, women must work if they want to have children. In 1980, the main reason for women to work was to make extra money (43%) and only one in five worked to support a family. In 1997, the picture has changed: 23% worked to earn some extra money and almost half of the women did so to support a family. Today, families loose the mother as a traditional anchor and move instead to a dual-career household. Not surprisingly, the different family members develop highly individualistic (some argue roommate types) lifestyles and behaviors. Another fact: From 1970 to 1995, the number of households led by married couples, declined by one-forth from 71% to 54%.[139]

Broadly spoken, households become relatively time poor and money rich. Time becomes a precious good, which will result in the fact that consumers will redesign tasks that consume too much time and embrace time-saving and time-shifting technologies. Experts therefore see over the next 10 to 15 years a massive shift to non-

---

[138] Bureau of the Census 1998a, pp. 1, 11-17.
[139] A.T. Kearney 1998, pp. 13-14.

store retailing emerging. They conclude that customers will demand hassle-free and convenient service on demand.[140]

7.2.2 Home Meal Replacement

As a result of the above-described movement, home cooking from scratch evolves to be a "dying art". Consumers, developing a negative attitude towards cooking, currently devote an average of 18 minutes to prepare a meal. While consumers do not relish cooking, they do enjoy dining at home. In 1997, 47% of U.S. food dollars were spent on restaurants, but more than half of these restaurant meals were takeouts.[141] Supermarket chains and food companies try to take advantage of this phenomenon by offering so-called Home Meal Replacement (HMR).[142] Recently, when consumers replaced a meal from the home, 23% bought a meal to go from a supermarket to consume at home.[143]

The above-discussed increasing diversity of the U.S. population also reflects on the food shopping patterns. For example, a comparison of similar income levels across different ethnic groups reveals that e.g. Hispanics tend to spend more money on food, while they dine out in restaurants less frequently than African-American or non-Hispanic Whites. Also important to note that second or third generations of immigrants have again different tastes than recent immigrants.[144]

In the context of cooking patterns, it seems worthwhile to take a brief look at the company Cybermeals, which discovered the link between HMR and the Web. Cybermeals, utilizing restaurant databases with large-scale geo-positioning software, provides customers free of charge with the ability to order meals online from neighborhood restaurants that are open and ready to deliver at the time of the order. Growing rapidly, Cybermeals' service is available nationwide with more than 25,000 restaurants under contract.[145]

7.2.3 Employment Issues, Income Disparities and Time Poverty

Today, the unemployment rate in the U.S. is the lowest in a generation and it is unlikely that unemployment will climb to high levels in the near future.[146] However, the drawback of the low unemployment rate is an increase in the wage inequality

---

[140] Schulz 1999, p. 48 and Sheth & Sisodia 1996, p. 21.
[141] Thompson 1997, p. 16.
[142] The HMR market reached $82.4 billion in 1996, estimates for 1997 are around $85.2 billion, with anticipated growth figures reaching $109.9 billion by the end of the year 2002. Barnack 1998, p. 31.
[143] Dwyer 1996, p. 13.
[144] A.T. Kearney 1998, p. 12.
[145] Cybermeals 1998, www.cybermeals.com.
[146] A.T. Kearney 1998, p. 16.

among the workforce. Therefore, it is not surprising that the forecasts predict the income gap between low-income and high-income segments to widen. In the future, while the U.S. will of course still have a sizable middle class, a massive percentage of the population will be affluent, and a sizable group will find themselves below the official poverty level. Experts more precisely forecast the middle class to shrink from two-thirds (in 1950) to one-third of the population in the year 2000. On the other side, the upper class is forecasted to grow from 10% to 30% during the same time period. In 1997, the real medium income of households mounted to $37,005, which has been the third consecutive year of increases.[147]

In this context also interesting to note is that Americans will be more educated in the future. By the year 2010, about 60% of the population will have attended at least one year of college, and beyond their general level of education, they will be much more technologically literate. However, just like income discrepancies split the population so will computers as the most ubiquitous electronic device and technology. The population will be divided into those individuals having access to computers and the Internet and therefore enjoying the benefits of technology and those who do not.[148]

Generally, Americans are working longer hours and thus believe they have less free time. In 1997, the average American adult spent almost 51 hours per week working (up from 41 hours in 1973) and perceived that he or she had only 19.5 hours of free time per week. Paradoxically, Americans' actual free time was more than twice that amount. This figure is actually up slightly from a generation ago, primarily because of the fact that people devote less time to housework, meal preparation and civic activities. However, the perception of having less free times stems from the fact that more workplace technologies (e.g. fax, e-mail, cellular telephones, and pagers) have overran people's home - creating visible interruptions of the home-based free time, and resulting in less perceived free time and higher stress.[149]

8   Scenario of a Relationship Change Between Customers and Retailers

8.1   Custom Tailored Mercantile Model

The following Chapter will draw a scenario of the Custom Tailored Mercantile Model on how changing consumer behavior trends, rooted in the increased availability of the Internet as a shopping and purchasing channel will effect the relationship between retailers and customers. In order to enhance the understanding of the scenario's thinking process, it seemed favorable to base it on a modified mercantile model.

---

[147] Bureau of the Census 1998b, pp. VII-XIII.
[148] Peterson 1997, p. 15.
[149] A.T. Kearney 1998, p. 14.

However, while many models are in place describing the relationship between customers and physical merchants, no models were found that described the mercantile model under both the influence of the Internet and the emerging consumer behavior trends in a fully satisfying manner. Therefore, the authors drew upon the existing models of purchase phases and consumer trends as well as ten anticipated consumer behavior trends, reengineered and complemented them and finally designed the Custom Tailored Mercantile Model. This model illustrated in Exhibit 16 below will be described on the following pages.

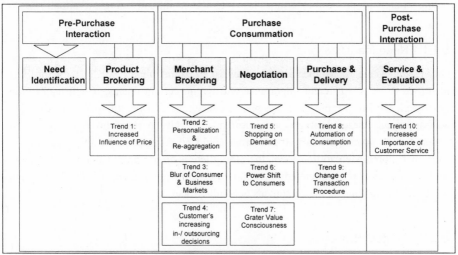

Exhibit 16: Custom Tailored Mercantile Model[150]

The reengineered online-based consumer mercantile model consists of six distinct Sections, which can be aggregated to three stages: Pre-purchase interaction, purchase consummation, and post-purchase interaction. The following discussion will analyze the sequence of necessary steps from both a consumer and a retailer standpoint, however, it will mainly emphasis on the purchase interactions, which seems to be the most important step for the purpose of this book.

Before discussing each of the three phases of the model it seems worthwhile looking briefly at the different types of consumers and shopping behaviors whose needs will be encountered in online sales. There are three types of consumers, first, impulsive buyers, who purchase goods promptly, second, patient buyers, who purchase goods after having made some comparisons. Third, analytical buyers, who engage in extensive research prior to purchase decisions. There are also two types of shopping behaviors. One is a so-called utilitarian behavior, carried out "to achieve a goal", which means that the result, not the purchase action itself is the key motivator. The opposite

[150] Adapted from Guttman, Moukas & Maes 1997, p. 2, Hawkins, Best & Coney 1998, pp. 26-29 and Kalakota & Whinston 1997, p. 235.

is true in the case of a hedonic shopping behavior, where shopping is regarded as entertainment or as a pastime. Here, the key motivator is the shopping procedure itself. Even though it seems that the hedonic shopping behavior makes up a large part of consumer online shopping behavior it has not been explored yet.[151]

8.1.1 Pre-Purchase Interaction

The nature of pre-purchase interactions will be discussed followed by an analysis how online retailers might be able to turn these interactions into advantageous situations.

8.1.1.1 Need Identification

During this stage, consumers become aware of some unmet need. If the need is identified to be of sufficient importance and within certain means, it will lead to the next level. During the pre-purchase phase, consumers can be stimulated to a certain action through targeted production information.[152] Up to now, no study has been undertaken to investigate how the Internet could be utilized during this stage of the Custom Tailored Mercantile Model, therefore there is no trend derivable yet. However, further research is recommended to zoom into possible alternatives on how the Internet might be able to support the customer's need identification.

8.1.1.2 Product Brokering

Merchants need to consider that the customer's inclination to purchase good is not simply created by setting up a Web page. In the real world, as well as on the Web, consumers go through a series of pre-purchase phases: Deliberation, comparison, and negotiation. During the deliberation phase, the consumer is retrieving information to determine what to purchase. It includes the evaluation of product alternatives based on criteria that are important to the consumer. This phase is much shorter for impulse or unplanned purchases, which account for one third of the total purchasing in physical markets. How this relates to the online world is not yet fully determined. Online retailers also need to find answers to several other questions in order to take advantage of the online deliberation process of their customers:[153]

- How much time are buyers allocating and spending on their purchasing decisions with respect to various products?
- What factors account for the differences in consumer decision time?
- What technology can be used or designed to reduce decision time?
- What shopping environment keeps customers happy and wanting to return?

---

[151] Kalakota & Whinston 1997, pp. 236-237.
[152] Hawkins, Best & Coney 1998, pp. 498-502.
[153] Kalakota & Whinston 1997, p. 238.

Trend 1: Increased Influence of Price. During the comparison and negotiation process, consumers are looking for information related to their purchase decision problem. Often times, consumers take the price of the goods as an indicator of quality. Here, the Internet confronts the retailer with a new challenge since it gives consumers the ability to do a much more extensive price comparison in less time. Therefore, the Internet might force many brick-and-mortar retailers, who are adding an online sales presence to rethink their pricing strategies.[154] This might result in a dilemma for them since on the one hand they want to be competitive on the Web but on the other hand do not want to undercut prices in their physical stores.[155]

The customers conclude this second stage (product brokering) of the pre-purchase interaction phase with a so-called "consideration set" of products.

8.1.2 Purchase Consummation

The purchase consummation comprises three different phases: Merchant brokering, negotiations, and purchase and delivery. It is important to note that some of the trends discussed might not exclusively occur in only one phase but might overlap several phases.

8.1.2.1 Merchant Brokering

During this phase, consumers combine the "consideration set" from the previous stage with merchant-specific information to help determine whom to purchase from, which also includes the evaluation of merchant alternatives based on consumer-selected criteria.[156] In the future, this phase is expected to change significantly.

Trend 2: Personalization and Re-Aggregation. In the past, a variety of mass marketing approaches have been put in place to serve a pretty homogenous mass market. Nowadays these once homogenous customers want to be treated differently, requiring marketers to launch so-called mass customization. Yet, customers are not always looking for customized products, and are sometimes happy with standard products. Still, to be able to personalize a service for specific customers, it seems helpful for marketers to keep in mind that mass customization not only applies to the products, but also to price, the advertising message, or the distribution mode. On the other hand re-aggregation of customer demand in the form of a pooling of interest is very likely to occur. These customer-driven actions will assure more bargaining power and better terms and conditions.

---

[154] Kalakota & Whinston 1997, p. 239.
[155] Browder 1998, pp. 160-162.
[156] Guttman, Moukas & Maes 1997, p. 2.

Trend 3: Blurring of Consumer and Business Markets. In the future, merchant brokering for the retail side will be more laborious since the lines between home and workplace will be increasingly blurred and customer decisions will become more like business decisions. For example, business applications such as e-mail are increasingly appreciated in the private sector. Customers, familiar with both sectors, expect product applicability in both of these environments.[157]

Trend 4: Customers' Increasing In- and Outsourcing Decisions. Customers - enabled through new technology - will increasingly take over part of the support and service functions previously performed by commercial companies. It is expected that self-service applications on the Web will be changing the rules in many industries. Customers will be increasingly comfortable doing things themselves because it provides them with control and convenience. They don't have to rely on someone else to handle the correct information. Currently main players in the sector of transportation and travel experience opportunities for an increased self-service. Transportation firms like Federal Express or UPS have enabled customers to track status information of cargo movements on a real-time basis and travel agencies allow customers on their Web site to book hotels, cruise ships, or rental cars. These types of services allow customers not only to bypass the customer service department but also to participate in increased service and convenience. A customer for example who disclosed to a Web travel site his preference to have window seating and a vegetarian meal while air-traveling can expect these features on succeeding flights without having to mention them again.[158] It is expected that these types of insourcing decisions will soon increasingly migrate to the retail industry. Also interesting for the retail industry is the perspective that customers will in the future be able to put their hands on the design and customization of products they purchase. Here, the customization of online books, where chapters are assembled according to the reader's preferences, serves as an example.

On the other hand, customers will outsource traditional household functions in order to free some time for new activities such as the ones described above. These trade-offs between make-versus-buy decisions will become increasingly necessary since time will be the bottleneck in customer decisions.[159]

8.1.2.2 Negotiation

The negotiation stage determines the terms of transactions. Depending on the market, negotiation varies in duration, importance and complexity. While previously traditional

---

[157] Sheth & Sisodia 1997, p. 30.
[158] Schwartz 1997, pp. 117-124.
[159] Sheth & Sisodia 1997, pp. 28-29.

retail markets left little room for negotiation, this picture is likely to change in the future.[160] Negotiation power on the customer side will not only be based on financial terms but also on the fundamental decision whether to give retailers the chance to contact potential customers.

Trend 5: Shopping on Demand. In the future, customers will no longer accept that their shopping patterns are constraint by time and place. The more mobile and technology savvy customers become the more they will look for shopping on demand, including anytime, anywhere procurement and anytime, anywhere consumption.

Trend 6: Power Shift to Consumers. The increase of competition and the availability of profound information will put the customer in the driver's seat of marketing activities. In fact, buyers might be viewed as marketers, while sellers then would be viewed as prospects in the market arena. In this case, "market activity will be driven almost entirely by buyer demand; marketing management will essentially become demand management: The task of influencing the level, timing, and composition of demand in a way that will help the organization achieve its objectives. [Spinning this idea even one step further leads to a scenario of information invitations.] Here, [...] companies would need to seek permission to present their case [e.g. advertising or product information] to consumers by inducing interest."[161]

Trend 7: Greater Value Consciousness. Customers will be more educated and informed about products. Given the efficiency, with which information will be shared between customers and companies as well as among customers themselves, companies will have to deliver top value to maintain a positive performance. Customers will expect innovation-based differentiation and value-based marketing in return for the three primary resources at their disposal: Money, time, and effort. Customers will only be willing to pay more for a product if additional value is offered, which exceeds the incremental price. Otherwise customers will expect cheaper prices for better products. Nevertheless, since time will be even more valuable in the future, customers might be inclined to trade higher prices for something that saves time, while it increases convenience and simplicity.[162]

8.1.2.3 Purchase and Delivery

After the termination of the previous stage, the actual purchase and delivery take place. Similar to the previous stages of the customer buying behavior model, this one will also be faced with new consumer trends.

---

[160] Guttman, Moukas & Maes 1997, p. 3.
[161] Sheth & Sisodia 1997, pp. 30-31.
[162] Sheth & Sisodia 1997, pp. 28-30.

Trend 8: Automation of Consumption and Nature of Relationships. Customers will have an increased tendency towards automated transactions with marketers. These transactions either may take place directly between (large) consumers and manufacturers or in the case of small customers via intermediaries. Since these developments will resemble today's business-to-business marketing arena, topics like supply chain management, electronic data interchange, or customized pricing are expected to step into the consumer-marketing arena. Over time, consumers will also ask marketers to share the benefits of cost cutting with them and marketers will focus more strongly on customer loyalty retention since this will be so much more economical than acquiring new customers.[163]

Trend 9: Change of Transaction Procedures. In every form of retailing, purchasers and sellers need to interact somehow to carry out the mercantile transaction of exchanging goods for payments. However, in the case of online retailing, these necessary transactions tend to be more difficult since they involve a yet unfamiliar procedure, for example the one outlined below. After a potential buyer has approached a vendor's Web site with purchase intent, the seller states the price of the desired product and the buyer and seller engage in negotiations. This action is mainly customer driven since his keystrokes determine the beginning of the transaction. If the buyer agrees to purchase the product, he authorizes (mostly) encrypted payment to the vendor. The vendor ships the product, after his billing service has verified the purchaser's payment. Both will receive standardized messages holding the details for their records. By analyzing these procedures it becomes obvious how many steps need to be mastered and how much trust must be established, before goods and payments can be exchanged successfully.[164]

8.1.3 Post-Purchase Interaction

The last component of the mercantile model involves elements like product service, customer service, as well as the evaluation of the satisfaction of the purchasing experience and decision from a retro-perspective.

Trend 10: Increased Importance of Customer Service. Why is this phase so important for retailers? In their Harvard Business Review article with the title "Why satisfied customers defect?" Jones and Sasser revealed the following. If satisfaction is ranked on a 1 to 5 scale, from completely dissatisfied to completely satisfied, the 4's – though satisfied – are six times more likely to defect than the 5's.[165] Many other studies on consumer complaints document that out of 100 dissatisfied customers, only a fraction

---

[163] Sheth & Sisodia 1997, pp. 31-32.
[164] Kalakota & Whinston 1997, pp. 240-242.
[165] Jones & Sasser 1995, pp. 88-91.

of four will complain to the company. Of the 96 dissatisfied and not-complaining customers, 91 will exit.[166]

Why is this phase even more important for online retailers? First, customers know about the retailer's ability to easily monitor his or her transactions and expect therefore in return more efficient and knowledgeable service. Second, no online merchants can claim to have a monopoly (neither geographical nor contents wise), therefore, dissatisfied customers are only one keystroke away from competitors. Third, the power of word of mouth is on the Web even more distinct than in the real world. Virtual newsgroups, bulletin boards, or chat groups have the power to spread the "bad news" instantly and over large distances.

8.2 Recapitulation

Not without reason is this Section titled "Age of Change", which has shown the "rippling effect of the Internet [on consumers and retailers] that reaches well beyond its own waters."[167] Then, a parallel – not less impressive - process of consumers changing both in terms of demographics and lifestyles has been illustrated. Last, a scenario has been shown how the emergence of the new technology of electronic commerce together with the current lifestyle changes might influence the relationship between customers and retailers in the future.

What are the consequences retailers have to be aware of? In summary, it can be concluded that the Internet as a new marketing and sales medium offers four distinct types of opportunities for online retailers. First, it allows retailers to establish direct links to customers to conduct business more efficiently. Second, new technology enables companies to bypass other participants in the value chain. Third, retailers use the Internet to form and deliver new products for new customers. Forth, the Internet has the ability to shift the market dominance from established participants to new participants.[168]

As in traditional retailing, so in online retailing, the competition is fierce. However, the rules have changed. Geography and the size of real estate do not matter anymore. Also, the Internet is a pull medium, which means that information is no longer pushed to customers. In reverse, the Internet requires consumers' consent and their eagerness to pull information. And finally, online retailing describes a "back-to-the-basics-approach" of increasing knowledge about customers' needs and leveraging information on products.[169]

---

[166] Anderer 1998, pp. 53-55.
[167] Schwartz 1997, p. 201.
[168] Ghosh 1998, p. 127.
[169] Schwartz 1997, pp. 56-58, 95.

However, every retailer is not equal and the question whether a particular retailer is ready to engage in business-to-customer electronic commerce, cannot be answered in a satisfactory manner with a "one size fits all" answer. The following Sections will therefore analyze the readiness for AnyCo to commit seriously to Internet shopping.

The Internet is not about demographics, mass marketing, and prospects. The Internet is about people, interest, and information. Treat people and their time with respect.
The Ward Group, http://www.netpost.com

Research is to see what everybody else sees, but to think what nobody else thinks.
Albert Szent-Györgyi

Section III: Primary Market Research

After having discussed the current developments regarding business-to-consumer electronic commerce one raises the question, whether AnyCo should head out to claim its piece of this new market too. At this point it is advisable to step back and collect some first hand data then come back to make a decision based on measurable, objective, and honest arguments. The way to obtain this kind of measurable information is through primary market research. Berkman therefore precisely defined market research as:

> *[...] the systematic collection and objective recording, classification, analysis, and presentation of data concerning the behavior, need, attitudes, opinion, motivation, etc. of individuals [...] within the context of their economic, social, and everyday activities.*[170]

The following discussion of the market research project concerning a hypothetical launch of the company's online retail Web site aims to follow this definition. Further, it is based upon a series of distinct research steps, which are commonly found in the market research literature.[171]

9 Definition of the Research Problem

Conducting primary research serves three purposes for AnyCo. First, to determine the readiness of its market for business-to-consumer electronic commerce for both the existing customer base as well as for new customers, who are not necessarily loyal to brick-and-mortar AnyCo stores.

---

[170] Berkman 1996, p. 9.
[171] Barabba 1990, pp. 105-115, Churchill 1995, pp. 81-86, Crimp & Wright 1995, pp. 2-5, Hawkins & Tull 1994, pp. 43-55, Nieschlag, Dichtl, Hörschgen 1994, pp. 683-686 and Stevens 1997, pp. 12-17.

Second, to identify products and strategies to ideally approach the market with a business-to-consumer electronic commerce concept. What is the attitude of consumers towards online purchasing? How likely are these individuals to adapt to a possible AnyCo online retailing Web site and what are the critical factors to do so? Which product groups seem favorable to sell online via this Web site?

Last, as shown in the previous Section, the literature is packed with favorable reports on electronic commerce. Companies may be attempting to spur demand by presenting over-enthusiastic[172] data. Chances are that some people, having financial stake in the new technology,[173] might be creating their own demand by presenting some almost too optimistic looking data. A survey, especially designed and conducted for the means of this book, will produce exclusive data about the market and a means to validate the veracity of the secondary data.

The Anywhere Company (AnyCo)[174], located in the Western states of the U.S., features a multitude of one-stop-shopping stores with an average store size of more than 10 thousand square meter and more than 200 thousand food and non-food products. These super-stores are supermarket, department store, drugstore, home store, home improvement center, garden center, home electronics store and fine jewelers - all under the same roof. In particular, AnyCo designed its concept to meet the needs of time-poor customers who work, are responsible for families, have less leisure time and appreciate making one stop for all their shopping needs.

During the time when the underlying study was conducted, AnyCo operated a Web site, which manly functioned as a distribution tool for information, not making use of many of the existing Web marketing dialog tools, which will be highlighted during the latter part of this book. Also, AnyCo was not engaged in electronic commerce, however, it was seriously studying the issue as well as various strategies that could be employed.

10 Determination of the Research Design

10.1 Collection Methods

After an extensive desk research on the available secondary data presented in the previous Section "Age of Change" of this book, it was then time to collect primary data specifically to help solve the problems specified above. In the course of the research, the first choice to be made was an option between a so-called descriptive and causal

---

[172] Berkman 1996, p. 38.
[173] Brody 1991, p. 40.
[174] This study has been conducted for a real-world company, which however wants to stay anonymous. Therefore, the artificial name Anywhere Company (AnyCo) has been introduced.

70

framework. The latter, based on experiments, would have enabled the researcher to make strong cause-and-effect inferences.[175] However, due to the lack of possibility to quantify this data as well as effort and cost constraints, the decision was made in favor of a descriptive framework, enabling the researcher to gather data, investigate possible relationships between variables, and to make predictions about future events. In particular, a cross-sectional analysis, which provides a snapshot of the variables of interest at a single point in time and which is based on a sample of elements of some known universe has been chosen.[176] How this sample was determined will be discussed in Chapter 10.2 "Selection of the Sample" of this Section.

There are several methods to collect systematic information directly from respondents. The traditional methods are telephone, mail, and personal interviews.[177] Even though oftentimes neglected in academic theory, Internet surveys are becoming a common form of data collection, however, each method has advantages and disadvantages. In the case of the underlying survey, the alternatives of distributing the interviews by mail and obtaining direct personal interviews seemed to be the least preferable alternative. They take a long time to conduct, they are very expensive and at least for the mail option, there is no control over who answers the questions. Therefore, the two alternatives closer observed were Internet based versus telephone survey methods. Appendix 2 discusses the advantages and disadvantages of Internet based surveys.

When planing a survey on electronic commerce, an Internet based method seemed, due to the relatedness of the subject, preferable at the first glance. However, there are currently several disadvantages of Internet based interviews compared to a telephone survey: There is no (not even a close) master database for the Internet population, which makes it almost impossible to draw a probability sample. Internet surveys also have a strong self-selection bias towards people either extremely pleased or displeased with the subject matter. Also, the anonymity and the peculiarity of the Internet that many users like to invent new personas for themselves, make it difficult to validate the identity of interviewees. Despite several advantages of Internet based surveys, such as the (assumed) increase of the rate of response due to the novelty of the tool, a quick turnaround rate, and the ability to target highly specific research groups without screening a large random sample, a telephone based survey seemed preferable. Here, the disadvantages, such as the fact that more Americans today refuse to participate in telephone surveys and the limited length of time (10-15 minutes) until the interviewee generates fatigue are offset by the advantages of telephone surveys.[178]

---

[175] Hawkins & Tull 1994, p. 49.
[176] Churchill 1995, pp. 177-180.
[177] Hawkins & Tull 1994, p. 49.
[178] Blankenship, Breen & Dutka 1998, p. 90, Berekhoven, Eckert & Ellenrieder 1996, p. 109, Dodd 1998, pp. 61-63, Edmondson 1997, pp. 10-13, Harris 1997, pp. 269-270 and Predow-James 1996, www2.worldopinion.com.

The largest advantages of telephone surveys, based on one-on-one questioning and answering between an interviewer and an interviewee, is the utilization of computer-assisted telephone interviewing (CATI), enhancing speed, quality, and control.[179] Applying this technique, the interviewer reads the questions from a computer screen and enters the responses directly into the computer. CATI is able to "individualize" the questionnaire for each interviewee based on answers to prior questions. It can also rotate the order in which the answer alternatives are presented in order to minimize the bias due to question ordering. Therefore, a market research company was asked to conduct the actual research as a telephone survey, utilizing CATI.

The actual questionnaire consisted of three main sections: Screening, content, and demographic questions. Appendix 3 illustrates the different components of the questionnaire. While the screening of questions made sure that the respondents qualified for the survey, the demographic questions helped to classify the respondents' answers. The main emphasis lay obviously on the content questions, which again can be subdivided into four parts. Questions about the respondents traditional shopping behavior and shopping habits for both food and non-food items were succeeded by questions about general Internet usage and experience. Then, questions about actual and intended online purchase behaviors and the identification of product categories most likely to be purchased (again) over the Internet followed. The complete questionnaire is indexed as Appendix 4.

10.2 Selection of the Sample

For the purpose of this survey, the population should include households in the Analyzed Trade Area, representing the market of AnyCo Stores. Knowing that the chosen region is not truly representative for the entire AnyCo market, one nevertheless settled for this one for three reasons. First, the Trade Area Profiles (TAP) 1998, undertaken by a local newspaper, seemed suitable to complement the underlying survey. Second, region certainly accounts for one of the metropolitan areas in the West of the U.S., and as such is representing a wide spectrum of people. Last, monetary constraints limited the research to one local market. After having made the decision to conduct the research in this particular region, one also determined that it was not advisable to draw a random sample from the entire population of this area. The AnyCo survey was certainly not the first survey dealing with the subject of business-to-customer electronic commerce and as the previous analysis of other survey results showed (see Section II "Age of Change"), Internet users and more important online purchasers are not "average persons". They tend to be more technically informed, tend to have a higher level of education and a higher income and they seem to be between 30-55 years old. The authors therefore defined households, "most likely" to have a

---

[179] Blankenship, Breen & Dutka 1998, pp. 122, 202.

computer or a laptop with a modem as the population for the survey. In total, there were 54,160 households qualifying. A result, based on this sample group would certainly not be representative for the whole population – it would be biased. However, online purchasing is currently "not for everyone" so it seemed feasible to draw the sample only among those people who are potential target customers for online purchasing. In fact, it was hoped that this would deliver a clearer picture, since more individuals of the preferred segments could be interviewed.

Since there was no list of telephone numbers of private households, "most likely" to have Internet access for the Analyzed Trade Area, the authors created such a list. Appendix 5 illustrates the different stages of this multi-stage sampling process in a graphical form. The Analyzed Trade Area, consisting of 91 Zip Codes with each having a population of at least one household (43 Zip Codes only belong to mailbox addresses) was mapped against seven different lifestyles. These seven lifestyles, representing households, most likely to be Internet users,[180] were extracted from a total of 50 unique lifestyles, which classify every U.S. household.[181] Appendix 6 characterizes the seven extracted lifestyles further. The intersection of the seven lifestyles and the 91 Zip codes revealed a total of 58 different Zip codes, representing the above mentioned population of 54,160 households.

Following, a wide set of demographics for people living in the area to the 91 Zip Codes was analyzed in order to identify the top 25% of Zip Codes (total of 14) for the most suitable means for the survey. Here it is important to note that the previously identified seven lifestyles of households most likely to be Internet users were represented in the 14 Zip Codes (top 25% of 91 Zip Codes).

In a last step, based on a desired number of 300 completed surveys, which will be addressed later, and assuming a ratio of 1:20 (completion to attempt), a sample of 6,000 households was drawn.[182] There are two reasons for this high ratio: First, a high refusal rate was assumed since the survey was scheduled to be fielded during the second and third week of December, which is generally the busiest time of the year. Second, even though most carefully selected, not everyone on the sample list would qualify for the prerequisites of the survey. While the number of households in the sample per Zip Code was determined with the help of quotas, the sample within each Zip Code was based on a random sampling.

---

[180] These segments ranked highest among the 50 lifestyles in at least one of the following list of attributes: Ownership of a computer with modem connection, an online service, a laptop or notebook, or a computer with mouse.

[181] The MicroVision system created by National Decision Systems is a database combining consumers and micro-geographic targeting. It provides the set of 50 different market segment lifestyles, which are based on current-year aggregated consumer demand information and 1990 Census demographics. MicroVision 1995, pp. 2-10.

[182] The company First Data Solutions, using the database of MicroVision, provided the requested list of 6,000 households, consisting of name, address, and phone number.

The above mentioned number of 300 completed surveys seems to perfectly balance the desired scope of the questionnaire with statistical reliability and project costs. Assuming a sampling size of 300, a standard deviation of 0.5, and a confidence level of 90%, one accepts a sampling error of +/- 4.7%, which suits the purpose of the survey.

10.3 Collection of the Data

After the completition of a pretest with 13 individuals, the survey was completed on eight evenings during the month of December 1998 (December 3-14). Even though each weekday has been covered, the bulk part of the calling (75%) was undertaken during a weekend, since one assumed to reach the most people. Altogether, 5,249 calling attempts were made, 105 callbacks were scheduled, and more than 528 phone numbers were dialed more than once to complete the survey. It is interesting to note that only 8% of the individuals reached, refused to participate in the survey. Only one in twelve recipients fell through the cracks of the screening process, indicating that the person either did not have Internet access or was not primarily (or equally) responsible for the household's food shopping.

11 Analysis and Interpretation of the Data

The following Section will present the analysis organized in a logical way, taking the reader in a step-by-step progression through all of the key findings of the study.[183]

11.1 Portrait of Participants

Demographic Profiles (Appendix 7). The analysis of the basic demographics of resondents reveals that they are younger and higher educated than the average population. They also tend to have a higher income, which comes from overwhelmingly white collar or other professional work. Speaking in broad terms it appears that AnyCo's position in the market place shows similar trends compared with the profile of current online purchasers, indicating that online purchasers might very well be AnyCo customers and vice versa.

11.1.1   Basic Demographics

Basic Demographics (Exhibit 17 and Appendix 8). The gender distribution of the AnyCo survey (52% female versus 48% male) equals exactly the one in the Trade Area Profiles (TAP) 1998, undertaken by The Oregonian.[184] The same is true for the age of

---

[183] Stevens 1997, p. 267.
[184] TAP 98 1998, p. 3.

74

participants, having a median age of 43, which indicates that the age bracket of 35 to 44 ranks first (30%), followed by the age bracket of 45 to 54 (28%) and the age bracket of 25 to 34 (18%). Nineteen percent of the participants are older than 55 while 4% are younger than 25.

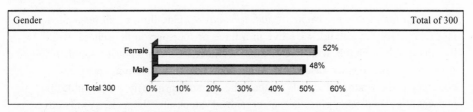

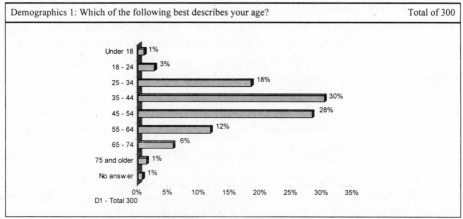

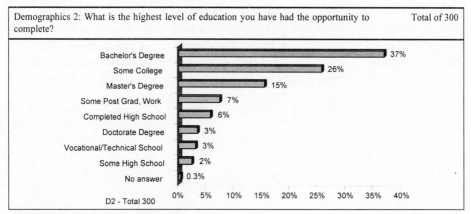

Exhibit 17: Basic Demographics

Thirty-seven percent of the participants have a bachelor's degree, which is slightly higher than the percentage for the overall population of the region published in the

TAP 98 (33%).[185] Astonishingly, 25% have at least a master's degree and 26% have completed at least some college.

11.1.2   Household Information

Household Information (Exhibit 18 and Appendix 9). One-third of all respondents live in a two person household, 43% live in a three or four person household, while 14% live in large households with five or more members. One in eight live by themselves. Anticipating the further discussion it can be seen that the more people live in a household, the more likely it is that the person primarily responsible for the household's food shopping is an organized stock-up shopper, compared to a convenience last-minute shopper. Corresponding with the number of household members is the number of children living at home with the respondents. Almost one-half (46%) of the respondents indicated they did not have any children under the age of 18 living with them. The majority of people living with children have either one (18%) or two (22%) children. Nine percent have three and only 4% have four or more children living at home. Compared with the results from the TAP 98, which indicated that 37% of the overall population of the Analyzed Trade Area have children under 18 at home,[186] it can be concluded that the survey population is more likely than the average to have children.

The majority of the respondents are married (76%) and only 16% are single. Here again, the population of the survey is above the average, since the TAP 98 indicated that only 59% of region's overall population is married. Singles, divorced or separated individuals are most likely to be convenience shoppers, interestingly however, they do not show any significant preference toward online purchasing, already indicating that this activity is not only carried out by those living alone. The vast majority (86%) of respondents owns the home in which they live, compared to an overall average of 68%. Age, annual household income and the likelihood to be a homeowner show a positive correlation, leading to the conclusion that more than 95% of those 55 or older and those with an annual household income over $100,000 own the home in which they live in.

---

[185] TAP 98 1998, p. 3.
[186] TAP 98 1998, p. 3.

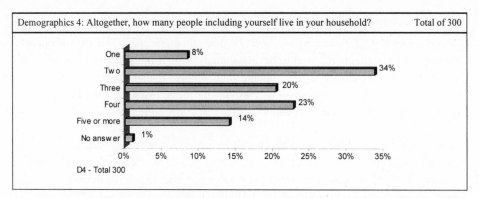

Demographics 4: Altogether, how many people including yourself live in your household?   Total of 300

One 8%
Two 34%
Three 20%
Four 23%
Five or more 14%
No answer 1%

D4 - Total 300

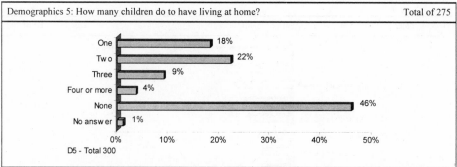

Demographics 5: How many children do to have living at home?   Total of 275

One 18%
Two 22%
Three 9%
Four or more 4%
None 46%
No answer 1%

D5 - Total 300

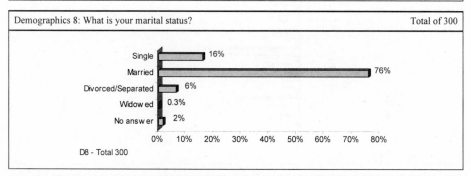

Demographics 8: What is your marital status?   Total of 300

Single 16%
Married 76%
Divorced/Separated 6%
Widowed 0.3%
No answer 2%

D8 - Total 300

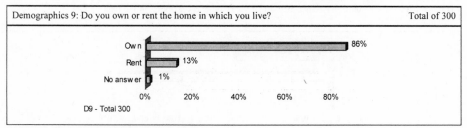

Demographics 9: Do you own or rent the home in which you live?   Total of 300

Own 86%
Rent 13%
No answer 1%

D9 - Total 300

Exhibit 18: Household Information

11.1.3 Occupational Information

Occupational Life Information (Exhibit 19 and Appendix 10). The overwhelming majority of respondents reported to having some type of white collar profession, such as professional/technical (27%), middle and upper management (12%), sales, marketing, and skilled tradesman (13%), or business owner (4%). Ten percent indicated they were homemakers and 9% of the respondents are retired.

Almost one-third of all interviewees reported to having at least one household member working in the high-tech industry. Overall, almost two-thirds indicated to having more than one working household member (51% have two and 13% have three and more), these numbers also correspond with the TAP 98 results.

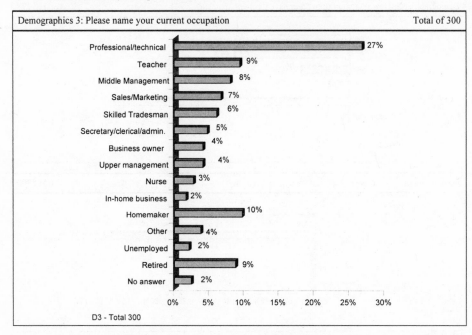

Demographics 3: Please name your current occupation — Total of 300

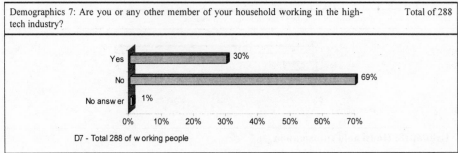

Demographics 7: Are you or any other member of your household working in the high-tech industry? — Total of 288

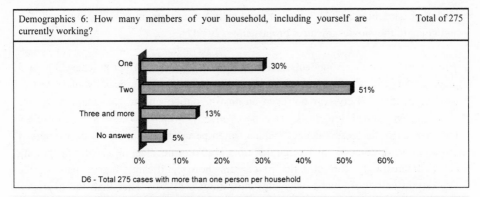

Demographics 6: How many members of your household, including yourself are currently working?   Total of 275

D6 - Total 275 cases with more than one person per household

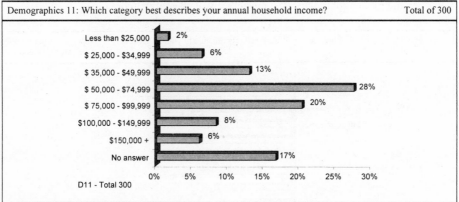

Demographics 11: Which category best describes your annual household income?   Total of 300

D11 - Total 300

Exhibit 19: Occupational Life Information

More than one-third (34%) described their annual household income to be over $75,000. Almost another one-third (28%) described their annual income to be between $50,000 and $74,999 and 19% indicated to having an annual income between $25,000 and $34,999. Seventeen percent would not reveal their income. The TAP 98 reported an annual median household income for the Analyzed Trade Area of $45,400,[187] which indicates that the income of survey respondents is higher than the average. Attractive is the fact that on average, individuals with household incomes between $35,000 and $100,000 seem to be more likely to shop at AnyCo than anywhere else.

11.1.4 Hobbies

Hobbies (Exhibit 20 and Appendix 11). Respondents seem to be very active individuals with manifold interests and hobbies. More than one-half pursue some type of outdoor sport (51%), others engage in outdoor recreation (38%), indoor sports and exercise

---

[187] TAP 98 1998, p. 3.

(20%), or gardening (17%). Other favored activities are reading (39%), music (20%), and going to the movies, theatres or museums (20%).

Thirty percent of all respondents and even 40% of current Internet purchasers named playing with animals as a hobby of their household. This is especially important to note, since this activity was not even an answer option on the questionnaire (it has always been named under the category "other"), which shows its extraordinary importance to the respondents.[188] Other often-perused pastimes are do-it-yourself projects (19%), domestic or foreign traveling (12%) or needlecraft, sewing or quilting (11%). Interestingly, current online purchasers show significantly higher than average interests in activities such as playing with animals (10% higher than the average), outdoor and indoor sport activities, music, as well as gourmet cooking.

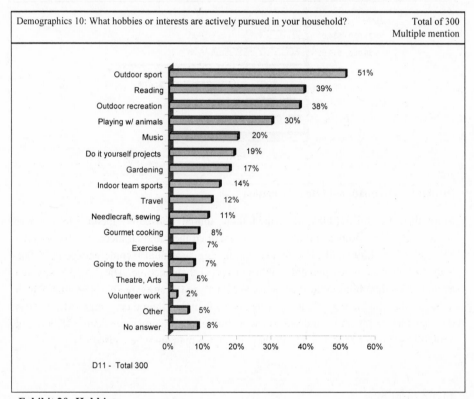

Exhibit 20: Hobbies

---

[188] Note the Section IV Chapter 14.2 "Customer Interaction - Creating a Critical Value Proposition" will draw a case study on how AnyCo could engage in e-com with pet care products.

11.2 Traditional Food Shopping - Opportunities

11.2.1 Characterization of Current Food Shoppers

Frequency of Shopping (Exhibit 21 and Appendix 12). Looking at grocery shopping behaviors several things become apparent. One in two respondents do their food shopping more than six times per month, a little less than that (39%) do so between three and five times per month and 14% do so only once or twice a month. It turns out that older people (55 and older) tend to visit a food store more frequently than younger people do, 59% visit a store six or more times per month, in comparison, only 35% of the 18 to 34 year olds do so. Also, individuals with a higher monthly food bill, probably having a larger family, do food shopping more frequently (40% of those with a monthly food bill higher than $500 go shopping more than eight times per month). Last, the annual household income and the number of monthly food shopping trips correlate positively with each other.

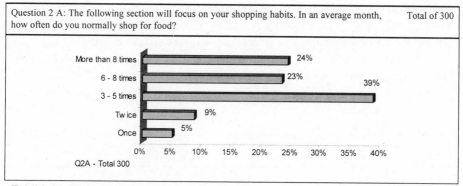

Question 2 A: The following section will focus on your shopping habits. In an average month, how often do you normally shop for food?   Total of 300

Exhibit 21: Frequency of Shopping

Type of Shopper (Exhibit 22 and Appendix 13).

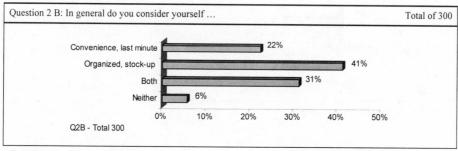

Question 2 B: In general do you consider yourself ...   Total of 300

Exhibit 22: Type of Shopper

While 41% characterized themselves as organized stock-up food shoppers, 22% indicated they were convenience last minute shoppers, and one third (31%) indicated they were both. The organized food shoppers represent all segments of annual household incomes more or less equally, however, compared to the lower income segments, the high-end income segment shows a tendency towards convenience last minute food shopping.

Food Expenditure (Exhibit 23 and Appendix 14). Almost one in two households (48%) have an average monthly food expenditure between $250 and $500, while having on average 3.3 household members and 1.9 children living at home. Another one in three households (35%) spend on average between $100 to $250 for food items and have an average of 2.5 household members, including 1.5 children. Twelve percent of the households spend even more than $500, they have an average number of household members of 4.4 including 2.4 children. Not surprisingly, higher income segments tend to have a higher food expenditure. However, in relative terms, the ratio of monthly food expenditure to total monthly household income tends to be higher for lower-income segments. So, three-quarters of low-end income households (less than $50,000) spend an average of 7 to 15% of their monthly income on food, while in comparison, three-quarters of households from the highest income segment (above $100,000) spend only an average of 2 to 5% of their monthly income on food. Another interesting finding is the slight tendency that respondents with lower food expenditure (less than $250 a month) are more likely AnyCo customers, both for food and non-food items, than those respondents with a higher average food expenditure (of $500 and up). A comparison of the comfort level of retailers tracking purchase actions and respondents monthly food expenditure revealed no significant correlation.

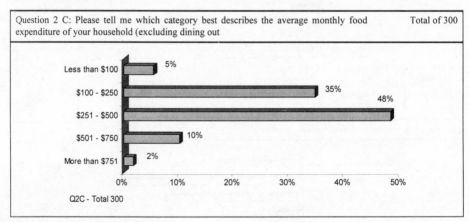

Question 2 C: Please tell me which category best describes the average monthly food expenditure of your household (excluding dining out   Total of 300

Exhibit 23: Food Expenditure

11.2.2 Shopping Locations

Food Shopping Locations (Exhibit 24 and Appendix 15). It turns out that for the respondents both AnyCo and Safeway (41% versus 42%) are close to equally popular locations to do the majority of food shopping. Albertson's ranks three (35%), followed by Thriftway (27%), and Cub Foods/Winco Foods (23%).

Question 4: In general, where do you do the majority of your food shopping?	Total of 300
	Multiple mention

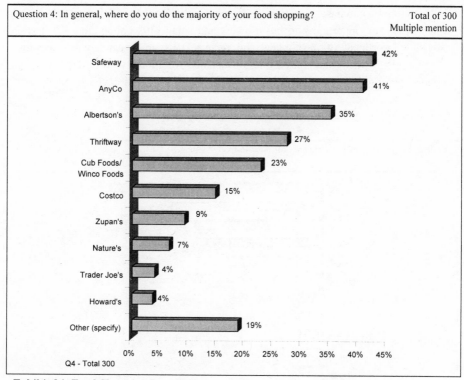

Q4 - Total 300

Exhibit 24: Food Shopping Locations

A comparison of the three most frequently visited food shopping locations discloses interesting findings. Convenience last minute food shoppers pick AnyCo more frequently over Albertson's or Safeway (43% versus 37% / 34%), while organized stock up shoppers tend to shop most often at Safeway followed by AnyCo and Albertson's (50% versus 40% / 33%). Respondents, marking themselves as belonging to both types of shoppers, prefer AnyCo a little over the other two competitors. Among people with a monthly food bill under $500, both Safeway and AnyCo rank top, followed by Albertson's. Not so for respondents with a monthly food bill of more than $500, who named Albertson's, Cub Foods/Winco Foods, and Costco (37% each) most frequently, closely followed by Safeway (34%), Thriftway (26%) and finally AnyCo (23%). Interestingly, food shoppers, being comfortable with both traditional and online retailers tracking their purchase activities are more likely to be AnyCo customers (45%), while customers feeling uncomfortable with the tracking activities are most likely to be Safeway customers (45%). Striking to the preceding statement is the finding that customers doing online purchasing are more likely to be Safeway than AnyCo customers (41% versus 35%), while customers exclusively purchasing in brick-

and-mortar stores are slightly more likely to be AnyCo than Safeway customers (46% versus 43%). This shows that online purchasers, who dislike the retailers' tracking activities, nevertheless prefer a supermarket that - through frequent shopper cards[189] - evidently tracks purchase activities. A reason for this might be Safeway's Web site, which offers the opportunity to buy flowers and small gifts online, and also has an extensive assortment of meal plans and recipes. Customers can create their own shopping list, which they may store or update. Additionally, registered frequent shopper cardholders receive advertisement and savings information via e-mail.[190]

Non Food-Shopping Locations (Exhibit 25 and Appendix 16).

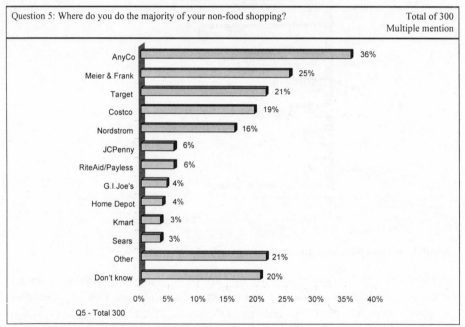

Exhibit 25: Non Food-Shopping Locations

Regarding non-food shopping, AnyCo clearly ranks number one (36%), followed by Meier & Frank (25%), Target (21%), Costco (19%), and Nordstrom (16%). This high preference for AnyCo continues across all ages, and - except one - across all segments of annual household incomes. The one exception are individuals with an annual household income over $100,000, who are more likely Meier & Frank than AnyCo customers. Also interesting is that 40% of those doing online purchasing are "offline"

---

[189] In return for several personal and demographic questions, Safeway customers receive a so-called Safeway Club card. The card needs to be presented at the check out in order to be eligible for price deduction. It is obvious that Safeway is tracking the customer's purchase activities, since - even in the case of a cash payment - the customer's name appears on the receipt. Safeway 1999, www.safeway.com.
[190] Safeway 1999, www.safeway.com.

most likely AnyCo customers, followed by Target and Meier & Frank (26% versus 25%).

11.2.3 Enjoyment and Comfort Regarding Food Shopping

Enjoyment of Food Shopping (Exhibit 26 and Appendix 17). Three-quarters of respondents expressed a rather negative attitude towards food shopping, while only one-quarter pointed out they enjoyed food shopping. Interestingly, convenience last minute food shoppers tend to enjoy shopping for food less often than the organized stock-up ones. The feeling towards food shopping reveals no significant differences between AnyCo customers and respondents who shop other retailers or between those who have made online purchases and those who have not done so.

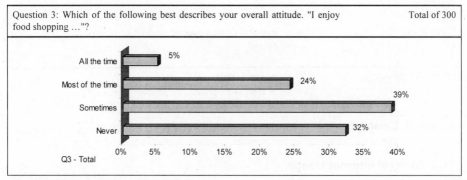

Exhibit 26: Enjoyment of Food Shopping

Comfort Level with Retailers Tracking Activities (Exhibit 27 and Appendix 18). How comfortable are shoppers with both traditional and online retailers tracking purchase activities to tailor offers to the customers' personal needs? It turned out that the customers' attitude towards tracking is rather negative, receiving an unmeaning average of 2.5. While one quarter of respondents felt somewhat or very comfortable, one half of respondents felt somewhat or very uncomfortable. About 20% felt more or less indifferent. Two regression analyses revealed first, a decreasing level of comfort with retailers tracking customers' purchase activities with an increasing age of the respondents. The second finding is a higher level of comfort for individuals who are either at the low-end (younger people) or at the high-end of the annual household income. Individuals with medium household incomes, who seem to be generally more conservative feel less comfortable about being tracked by retailers. Even though rather weak, a tendency can be seen that individuals enjoying food shopping are more likely to feel comfortable with retailers' tracking their purchase activities, than those who enjoy it less.

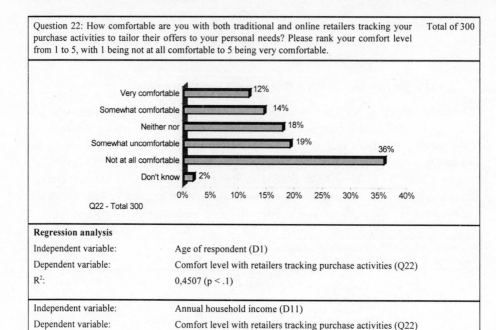

Question 22: How comfortable are you with both traditional and online retailers tracking your purchase activities to tailor their offers to your personal needs? Please rank your comfort level from 1 to 5, with 1 being not at all comfortable to 5 being very comfortable.   Total of 300

Regression analysis	
Independent variable:	Age of respondent (D1)
Dependent variable:	Comfort level with retailers tracking purchase activities (Q22)
R^2:	0,4507 (p < .1)
Independent variable:	Annual household income (D11)
Dependent variable:	Comfort level with retailers tracking purchase activities (Q22)
R^2:	0,5778 (p < .1)

Exhibit 27: Comfort Level with Retailers Tracking Activities

11.3 General Internet Usage

11.3.1 Internet as Part of Every Day Life

Internet Usage (Exhibit 28 and Appendix 19). The overwhelming majority of respondents (90%) have Internet access at their home and more than 40% access it from work. The time period since the respondents have had Internet access appears to be surprisingly long for such a young medium. Two-thirds have had access for more than two years (62%), one-fourth has been accessing the Internet for more than a year, and only 14% indicated to use the new medium less than a year. People with Internet access at work have been using the medium longer than people accessing it from home (73% versus 61% for an access period longer than two years). In return, people using the Internet from home account for twice as many short-term users as the ones accessing it from work (14% versus 7% for an access period shorter than a year). The frequency of using the Internet appears to be very high among the interviewees. Three-forths use the Internet more than four times a week (72%), another 20% use it between one and four times a week and only 8% use it less than weekly. Corresponding with the findings above, people accessing the Internet from work, seem to utilize it a little more frequently than the ones accessing it from home (83% versus 75% for a frequency of four or more times a week).

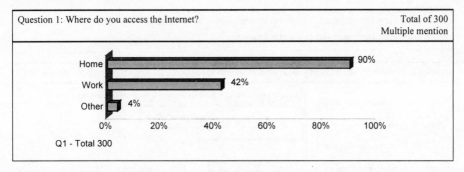

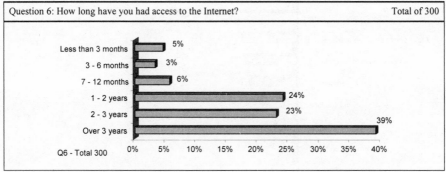

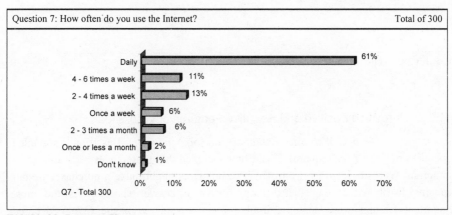

Exhibit 28: Internet Usage

Frequent Online Activities (Exhibit 29 and Appendix 20). It can be concluded that the Internet is generally used for a broad variety of activities. Communicating with others appears to be the activity most often performed over the Internet (66%), enjoyably followed by searching for product or service information (40%). Education related research, looking up news and daily information or business related contents are other frequently named reasons for Internet usage. One in five interviewees indicated to use the Internet for the purpose of entertainment and passing the time. Interestingly, 14%

of the interviewees named "making a purchase of a product or service" among the three things most often done with the Internet.

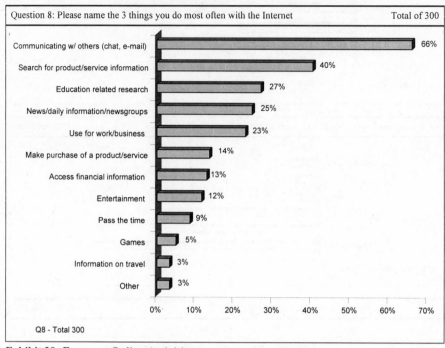

Exhibit 29: Frequent Online Activities

11.3.2 Perceived Positive and Negative Features of Web Sites

Positive Features of a Web Site (Exhibit 30 and Appendix 21). Based on a so-called goodness of fit test (chi-square), it can be concluded that preferences regarding most important Web site features, from which respondents might make a purchase, are not equally distributed among the different provided answer choices. As the most important features were named "simple to get around" Web site (37%), detailed product information (31%), and a secure site (22%), followed by prices, at least competitive to the ones in brick-and-mortar stores (21%) and a site that is colorful and interesting to look at (15%). Least often named and therefore least important for shaping a positive received Web page seem to be the delivery of suggestions, ideas and trend information, the number of payment alternatives offered, and a Web site reflecting the personality of the store.

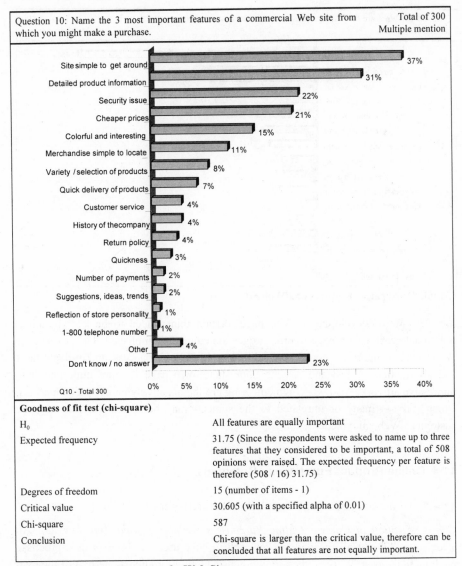

Question 10: Name the 3 most important features of a commercial Web site from which you might make a purchase.

Total of 300
Multiple mention

Q10 - Total 300

Goodness of fit test (chi-square)

H_0	All features are equally important
Expected frequency	31.75 (Since the respondents were asked to name up to three features that they considered to be important, a total of 508 opinions were raised. The expected frequency per feature is therefore (508 / 16) 31.75)
Degrees of freedom	15 (number of items - 1)
Critical value	30.605 (with a specified alpha of 0.01)
Chi-square	587
Conclusion	Chi-square is larger than the critical value, therefore can be concluded that all features are not equally important.

Exhibit 30: Positive Features of a Web Site

Negative Features of a Web Site (Exhibit 31 and Appendix 22). The issues most annoying about the Web or about a Web site seem foremost related to technical aspects of Web sites. Almost one-half of the respondents (45%) complained that it takes too long to open a Web page or to download material. Other major complaints were about too complex or chaotic Web sites (23%), making it hard or impossible to find the information looked for (22%). One in five respondents complained also about the multitude of ads and the so-called junk mail.

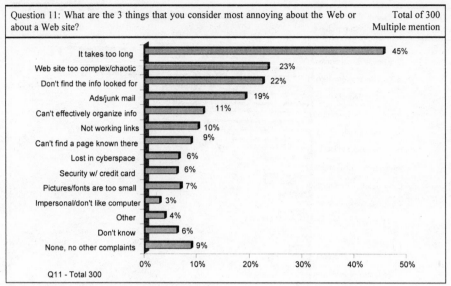

Question 11: What are the 3 things that you consider most annoying about the Web or about a Web site? Total of 300 Multiple mention

Q11 - Total 300

Exhibit 31: Negative Features of a Web Site

Remarks. When developing a Web page, certain things need to be kept in mind. Individuals visit a Web page in order to get something accomplished. They expect the Web page to support this goal by providing simple and quick access, and in-depth facts and information. A fast and easy to understand Web page is more important than impressive artwork. Also worth remembering are the negatively perceived banner ads, which - if too many or unrelated to the subject- may be disruptive, reducing the customer's Web enjoyment.

11.4 Online Product Purchases - Potentials

11.4.1 Characterization of Current Online Purchasers

Characterization of Current Online Purchasers (Exhibit 32 and Appendix 23). An astonishing 47% of all respondents reported to have used the Internet as a purchase medium in the past. Who are these individuals counting for almost one-half of the total sample? Characterizing the online purchasers, it can be said that they are more likely to be men then women (51% versus 42% of all male/female having participated in the survey). However, the gender distribution[191] is much more even than previously conducted research suggested, possibly indicating a closing of the gender gap among

---

[191] While studies of Ernst & Young as well as Nielsen Media Research stated by the end of 1998 that only 32% of all online purchasers are women, the underlying AnyCo survey concluded that women account with 42% for online purchasers. Ernst & Young 1998, p. 6, Nielsen Media Research 1998, p. 1.

Internet purchasers. In addition, they are more or less spread evenly among all ages. However, people falling into the age bracket of 45 to 54 are the largest and individuals older than 55 represent the smallest segment of Internet purchasers. Not surprisingly, online purchasers tend to be older than both the average AnyCo and the general Trade Area customer.

Almost two-thirds of current online purchasers have at least a college degree and therefore it is not surprising that the distribution of Internet purchasers among different income segments has a concave shape. While more than one-half of the individuals whose households have an annual income of either less than $35,000 or more than $100,000, are among the Internet purchasers, only 47% of individuals with a household income between $50,000 and $75,000 have purchased products online. Even more surprising is the finding that individuals from households with an annual income between $75,000 and $100,000 only contribute with 39% to the online purchasers.

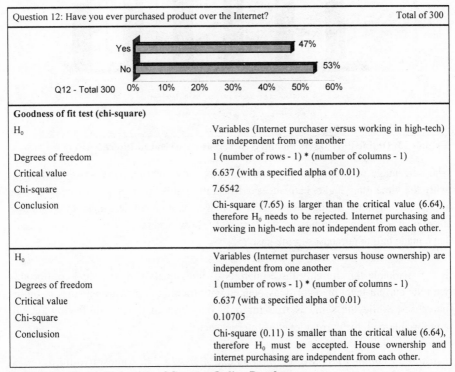

Question 12: Have you ever purchased product over the Internet?	Total of 300

Goodness of fit test (chi-square)

H_0	Variables (Internet purchaser versus working in high-tech) are independent from one another
Degrees of freedom	1 (number of rows - 1) * (number of columns - 1)
Critical value	6.637 (with a specified alpha of 0.01)
Chi-square	7.6542
Conclusion	Chi-square (7.65) is larger than the critical value (6.64), therefore H_0 needs to be rejected. Internet purchasing and working in high-tech are not independent from each other.
H_0	Variables (Internet purchaser versus house ownership) are independent from one another
Degrees of freedom	1 (number of rows - 1) * (number of columns - 1)
Critical value	6.637 (with a specified alpha of 0.01)
Chi-square	0.10705
Conclusion	Chi-square (0.11) is smaller than the critical value (6.64), therefore H_0 must be accepted. House ownership and internet purchasing are independent from each other.

Exhibit 32: Characterization of Current Online Purchasers

A chi-square test confirmed the relationship between having made Internet purchases in the past and having at least one household member working in the high-tech industry. Having zoomed further into this relationship, one discovered that sixty percent of households with at least one member working in the high-tech industry account for current online purchasers.

Also worth mentioning is the relation between the time frame since respondents have had access to the Internet and the percentage of respondents purchasing something online (Exhibit 33).

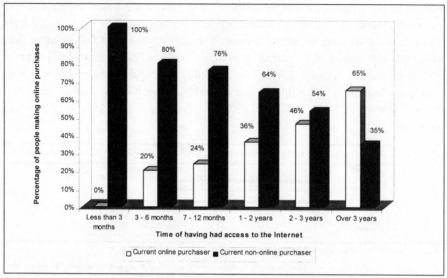

Exhibit 33: Online Purchasers among New versus Experienced Internet Users

The percentage of people buying something over the Internet increases almost linear with the time they have had access. Illustrating this incidence further it can be indicated that none of the respondents who were online for less than three months accounted for online purchasers, while 65% of those accessing it for over three years have made online purchases in the past.[192]

It is remarkable that roughly three-quarters of individuals feeling (very) comfortable with the current level of security associated with Internet purchases, engages in online purchases, while the same is true for only one-forth of those, not feeling (at all) comfortable with the current level of Internet security.

Reasons for Online Purchases (Exhibit 34 and Appendix 24). Almost two-thirds (59%) of people who have previously purchased something online, named convenience and the opportunity to shop at home as the issue most appreciated about Internet shopping over traditional shopping. More than one-third (39%) labeled the easy access to

---

[192] Chi square analysis analyzing a potential correlation between having made Internet purchases and house ownership revealed no relationship between these to variables.

products, followed by a 24 hour access to the shopping medium (19%), and the impression that it saves time (16%) as other advantages. Interestingly, two-thirds of organized shoppers and even three-quarters of those with a monthly food bill of over $500 named convenience and the ability to shop at home as their main driving factor towards online shopping. While younger people (less than 45 years) most often named convenience as the feature mostly appreciated about online purchasing, people over 45 years indicated easy access to products.

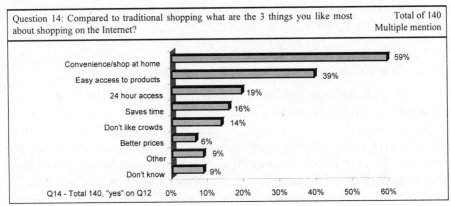

Exhibit 34: Reasons for Online Purchases

Reasons for Hesitating (Exhibit 35 and Appendix 25). People who previously had not undertaken Internet purchases were asked for their reasons for not having done so.

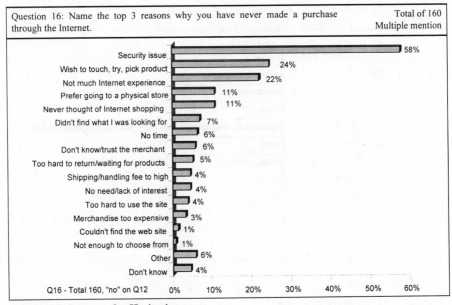

Exhibit 35: Reasons for Hesitating

93

Close to two-thirds (58%) responded that their hesitation is connected with the frequently discussed security issue. However, there are two more reasons, the first one is related to emotions, the second one is related to technical issues. People implied their wish to touch, try, and pick up the products they are actually going to purchase (24%) and they also expressed their preference for going to a physical store to shop (11%). The technical reasons for not having done online purchasing are interrelated. First, people felt that not having had enough experience with the Internet in order to engage in online purchasing (22%) and second, people also implied that they simply never thought of it (11%).

11.4.2 Online Sales Now and Then by Product Categories

Potentials for Different Product Categories (Exhibit 36 and Appendix 26). Respondents with online purchasing experience were asked to indicate, which types of products they have previously purchased online. In a next step, all individuals, those who previously made online purchases and those who have not done so in the past were asked to name the product categories, they might consider buying online (again) in the future. It will be shown that in the future, a much greater percentage of consumers are going to consider the online purchase of a much broader selection of products.

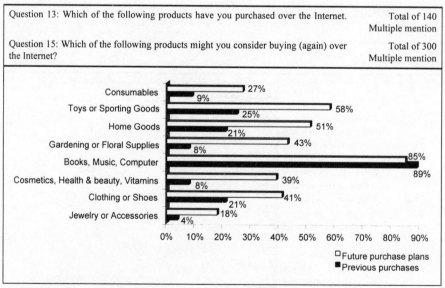

Exhibit 36: Potentials for Different Product Categories

Exhibit 36 illustrates the percentage of people who actually bought online (total of 140 respondents) versus the percentage of people who plan on buying (again) in the future (total of 240 respondents). Among those who previously bought online, it is worthwhile noting, that the longer respondents have used the Internet, the broader and more extensive is the mix of product categories they previously purchased online. There are several alternatives, how the above graph can be analyzed. Following, three of these alternatives will be discussed.

Looking at the Overall Percentage. The first alternative is looking at the overall percentage of products that people consider purchasing online in the future. It cannot be overstated that, with an overwhelming majority of 90%, favored product categories for online purchases now and in the future are books, music and computers items (including software, hardware and peripherals). Other high potential product categories seem to be toys or sporting goods (25% of actual purchases versus 58% considered purchases), home goods (21% versus 53%), gardening or floral supplies (8% versus 43%), and clothing or shoes (21% versus 41%). Nevertheless, the smaller percentage of interest, consumables like groceries, wine or perishables as well as jewelry also appear to be promising categories to be sold online.

Again, it is remarkable how much more likely individuals with a high comfort level in both, the current Internet security and retailers tracking activities, are among online purchasers. In fact, for categories not yet very popular among electronic commerce customers (such as clothing, home goods, or consumables), the likelihood that people with a high comfort level are among the purchasers is about two to four times higher compared to individuals with a low comfort level.

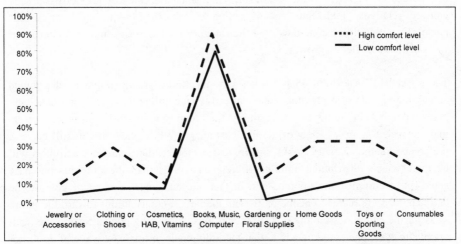

Exhibit 37: High and Low Levels Comfort with Current Level of Security Associated with the Internet among Online Purchasers of Differnet Product

With one exception it can be said that online purchasers with a low Internet-security-comfort-level account for only a few online purchases, while those with a higher comfort level account for much more online purchases. The one exception is the most established online sales category books, music, and computer items. While about 90% of online purchasers with a high comfort level have purchased something in this category, the same is true for almost 80% of those with a low comfort level (Exhibit 37). This indicates two things. First, online security is a very emotional issue. Second, retailers with mass-market presence can attract even those with low comfort levels through extensive awareness creation, advertising, and informal word of mouth. In short, convincing someone to purchase online does not necessarily increase the persons comfort level in doing so.

Distribution of Future Growth (Exhibit 38 and Appendix 27). Another alternative to analyze the potentials for online sales of different product categories is focusing on their distribution of future growth based on a comparison of previous purchase decisions of current online purchasers and future online purchase plans of current and going-to-be online purchasers.

Previously, one compared the number of current online purchasers with the number of future online purchasers. However, analyzing the increase in the number of future online customers in percent (see the top graph of Exhibit 38), one discovered quite different findings. Here, the categories gardening or floral supplies (1,080%), cosmetics, health and beauty, and vitamins (980%), and surprisingly jewelry or accessories (816%) seem to be the categories with the largest future growth potential. The category books, music, and computer items, displays only a moderate growth in new purchasers of 110%, which is not surprising since this category previously already enjoyed relatively high numbers of online customers. Looking at it from this perspective, it could be concluded that the category books, music, and computer items will only have moderate growth.

The lower half on Exhibit 38 illustrates how the future growth might be distributed among individuals who previously have already made online purchases and those who plan on doing so in the future. Interestingly, the group of going-to-be online purchasers may represent a new wave of online customers. While they might still have a preference for the category books, music, and computer, their purchase activities will be more widely distributed among different categories than the previous purchase activities of current online purchasers. In fact, the customer segment of going-to-be online purchasers seems to be the party with the largest contributions toward the future sales for the categories clothing or shoes and toys or sporting goods. Seeing this with optimistic eyes, one could conclude that the individuals of this new wave of going-to-be online purchasers are the forerunners of the mainstream customer segment.

Also, the segment of current online purchasers (those who have previously purchased over the Internet), too will discover the Internet's ability to sell more than books, music and computer items, since their future purchase plans will also much more resemble traditional shopping.

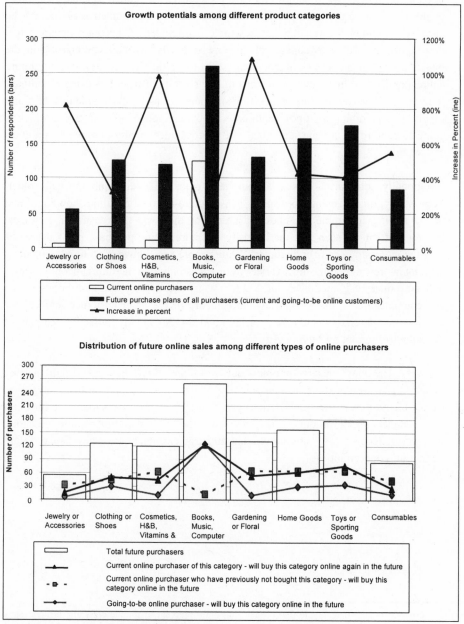

Exhibit 38: Distribution of Future Growth

Looking at Purchase Plans of Certain Customer Segments (Exhibit 39). A final alternative to analyze the different online potentials for different product categories is to focus on previous and future purchase preferences of AnyCo's primary customer segments.[193] Future purchase plans for the baby boomer and women segments can be discussed simultaneously since they resemble one another. It becomes apparent that these individuals plan to engage much more seriously in online purchasing in the future. Books, music and computer items seem to be the favored category for future online purchases (almost everyone plans to buy something from this category online), followed by toys or sporting goods (66%), home goods (55%), gardening or floral supplies, and clothing or shoes, (both around 50%). Another product group, which is going to capture significant attention, will be cosmetics, health and beauty products and vitamins.

Additionally, one also looked at purchase plans of individuals 55 and older. Surprisingly, this segment too displays heavy future interest in online shopping. Most of the findings resemble the ones illustrated for the two other customer segments. However, it can be seen that the intensity of future online purchase plans decreases with the increasing age of individuals. While people ages between 55 to 64, still show a strong interest in purchasing a variety of products online in the future, people over 65 indicate a more restrained behavior. Yet it is worth mentioning that, after books, music and computer items, the second favored category of the latter customer segment for future online purchases is toys or sporting goods (41%), clearly indicating the plan of utilizing the Internet for buying gifts.

Remarks. The above discussion points out two things. First, there are several starting points to analyze the future online potential of AnyCo's different product categories, from which different recommendations can be drawn. Second, it is extremely difficult to conclude, which product categories have the highest future online potential, however, it seems worthwhile noting that numerous product categories display future online sales opportunities.

---

[193] Respondents qualified for the first primary customer segment of middle class and affluent baby and boomers, if they were between 35 and 54 years old and had an annual household income of $50,000 or more. Respondents were considered to belong to the second primary customer segment of AnyCo namely working women, if they were between 18 and 54 years of age (unfortunately, no differentiation between working and non working women could be undertaken). Individuals, who did not know or refused to indicate their income, were left out.

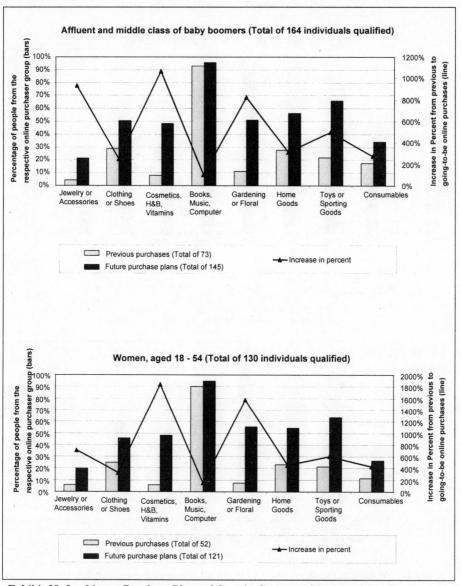

Exhibit 39: Looking at Purchase Plans of Certain Customer Segments (part 1)

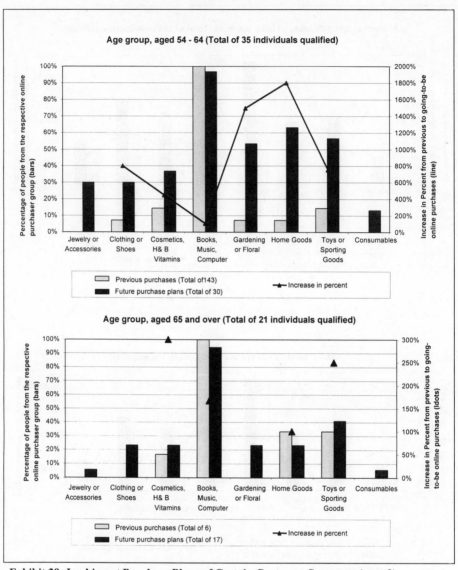

Exhibit 39: Looking at Purchase Plans of Certain Customer Segments (part 2)

11.4.3 Potential for Online Food Sales

The following paragraphs have been designed first, to learn more about online sales opportunities for food products, one of AnyCo's core competencies, and second to further demonstrate that in the future there are more categories than books, music and computer items suitable to sell over the Web.

Willingness to Pay for Service (Exhibits 40, 41 and Appendix 28). People were asked to indicate how much money (as a percentage of the total purchase amount), they were willing to pay for the convenience if their local food store offered online purchasing with two different delivery alternatives. The first alternative implies a full scale online purchase including the home delivery of the purchased items, the second one refers to a service, where the products are purchased online but then would need to be picked-up in front of the store. In general terms it can be said that people's opinions on both alternatives follow the same pattern, however they are willing to pay more for the home delivery and willing to pay less for the pick-up service.

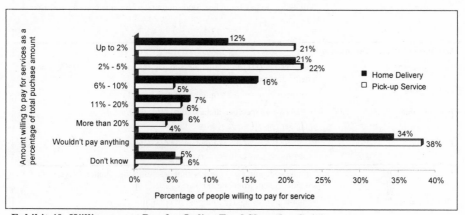

Exhibit 40: Willingness to Pay for Online Food Shopping Service

About one-third of respondents would be willing to pay up to 5% of the total purchase amount for a delivery service (43% would be willing to do so for a pick-up service). While 16% would still be willing to pay up to one-tenth of the purchase amount for a delivery, only 5% would pay this much for a pick-up service. Interestingly, Internet users accessing the Web from work appear to be willing to pay more than those accessing it from home are.

A look at the relationship between the respondents' willingness to pay for a home delivery and the type of shopper further supports the picture drawn previously about convenience shoppers. Last minute shoppers, over organized shoppers and over those belonging to neither of these two shopper types are willing to pay more for the service, further underlining their preference for convenience. Pleasant to note is that AnyCo customers are willing to pay slightly more for the two services than non-AnyCo customers (24% are willing to pay up to 5% for a pick-up services versus 19% of non-AnyCo customers).

Additionally, several so-called independence tests (chi-square) were undertaken in order to determine whether age or income was related to the willingness to pay for any of the two services.[194] Interestingly, the independence test revealed on the one hand a relationship between the variables age and willingness to pay for either of the delivery alternatives on the other hand, however, it revealed independence between the variables income and willingness to pay for the service. Unfortunately, the test cannot make any judgement on the level of dependency. Further analysis of the cross tables shows especially younger people and people with a lower annual household income to be willing to pay less money for any of the services than the average population.

Regression analysis	
Independent variable:	Type of shopper (Q2B)
Dependent variable:	Willingness to pay for online food shopping with home delivery (Q19A)
R^2:	0,9675 (p < .1)
Goodness of fit test (chi-square)	
H_0	Variables age (D1) and willingness to pay for home delivery (Q19A) are independent from one another
Degrees of freedom	6 (number of rows - 1) * (number of columns - 1)
Critical value	16.810 (with a specified alpha of 0.01) (for Q19A)
Chi-square	20.49991 (for Q19A)
Conclusion	H_0 rejected. Age of the respondents is not independents from the willingness to pay for a home delivery service.
H_0	Variables income (D11) and willingness to pay for home delivery (Q19A) are independent from one another
Degrees of freedom	9 (number of rows - 1) * (number of columns - 1)
Critical value	21.654 (with a specified alpha of 0.01)
Chi-square	10.13305
Conclusion	H_0 accepted. Income and the willingness to pay for a home delivery service are independent from each other.

Exhibit 41: Relationship of Age (Income) versus Willingness to Pay for Service

Last it seems worth taking a look at the roughly one-third of respondents who answered not to be willing to pay anything for the service. Highly interesting is the fact that individuals, who previously have done Internet shopping, are less willing to pay anything for any of the two services, suggesting that they may have encountered free of charge Internet purchase deliveries somewhere else on the Web. Individuals not

---

[194] It should be noted that people indicating either not to be willing to pay anything or not to have an opinion on the subject were left out of the analysis.

very likely to try online food shopping in the future and individuals who are not comfortable with the retailers tracking activities are least likely to pay anything for any of the services. Last, age and likeliness of not being willing to pay anything increase proportionally, meaning the older the respondents are, the less willing they are to pay anything.

Willingness to Try Service (Exhibit 42 and Appendix 29). Following, respondents were asked to state how likely they were to try online food purchasing with a delivery procedure most convenient to them. Interestingly, well beyond one-third (36%) of the respondents implied to be (very) likely to give it a try. Even though one-half of the respondents expressed their current unwillingness to give an online food purchasing service a try, the question nevertheless received an overall average of 2.7 (on a scale from one to five, with one being not at all likely).

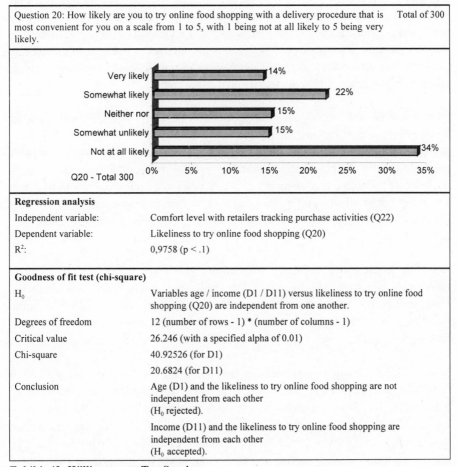

Question 20: How likely are you to try online food shopping with a delivery procedure that is most convenient for you on a scale from 1 to 5, with 1 being not at all likely to 5 being very likely.	Total of 300

Regression analysis	
Independent variable:	Comfort level with retailers tracking purchase activities (Q22)
Dependent variable:	Likeliness to try online food shopping (Q20)
R^2:	0,9758 (p < .1)

Goodness of fit test (chi-square)	
H_0	Variables age / income (D1 / D11) versus likeliness to try online food shopping (Q20) are independent from one another.
Degrees of freedom	12 (number of rows - 1) * (number of columns - 1)
Critical value	26.246 (with a specified alpha of 0.01)
Chi-square	40.92526 (for D1)
	20.6824 (for D11)
Conclusion	Age (D1) and the likeliness to try online food shopping are not independent from each other (H_0 rejected).
	Income (D11) and the likeliness to try online food shopping are independent from each other (H_0 accepted).

Exhibit 42: Willingness to Try Service

103

Further analysis, agreeing with previous discussions about the different shopper types, revealed that convenience shoppers over other types of shoppers express their likeliness to try online food shopping. Least likely to investigate further into online food purchasing appear to be those individuals neither subscribing to be a convenience nor an organized shopper. Another independence test (chi-square) claims that first, the variables age and the likeliness to try online food shopping are related with each other and second, the variables income and likeliness to try online food shopping are independent with each other. The significance of this finding is twofold. First, it further proves the results, stated earlier that age (not income) is related with the willingness to pay for a purchase delivery service. Second, it argues against common knowledge as well as against many findings in this analysis that online food shopping is more attractive to individuals with higher than average income. Further analysis illustrates that younger people, being more familiar with the new technology, are more likely than older people to give online food purchasing a try (42% of the 18 to 34 year olds are at least somewhat likely versus only 24% of the 55 and older). Nevertheless the above stated results it could clearly be shown that individuals with higher household incomes are more likely than ones with lower incomes to try online food purchasing. While 56% of respondents on the high-end of the income spectrum are likely to try it, the same is only true for 19% of the ones on the low-end.

Almost unbelievable seems the linear relationship between the respondents' comfort level with retailers' tracking their purchases and the likeliness to try online food shopping. Impressive is the result of another regression analysis, which attributes respondents who are not at all comfortable with the retailers' tracking activities, a likeliness to try online food shopping of barely two (on a scale from one to five with one being not at all likely). On the other side, it assigns respondents who are very comfortable with being tracked a likeliness to try online food shopping of more than 3.6.

Rounding up the above discussion, respondents were given the opportunity to name other ways in which the Internet might be helping them with food shopping. Unfortunately, one-half of the respondents did not contribute anything to this question, the others named the Internet as a tool to simplify comparison-shopping and to track hard to find (specialty) items, as well as a source of recipes and meal planning.

Remarks. It has clearly been pointed out that food is another category with a potential to be sold over the Internet. While people generally acknowledge that the service of delivering online bought merchandise requires an extra effort from the retailers, it appears, that the more mainstream the new sales medium becomes, the less willing people will be to pay extra for the service. From a medium-term perspective it can be argued that a free delivery service might be a tool to cut the competitive edge, in the long run, however, retailers should be prepared to provide this service free of charge on a standard basis. Having analyzed different influential factors on the likeliness of trying online food shopping, it becomes obvious that the educational aspect cannot be overestimated. Customers need to be able to fully understand the procedures of online purchasing and - almost more important - they must trust the retailers.

11.4.4   Online Security Issue

Comfort Level with Security (Exhibit 43 and Appendix 30). The question, asking interviewees to rank their level of comfort with the current level of security associated with Internet purchases (again on a scale from one to five with one being not at all comfortable) resulted in an average comfort level of 2.7.

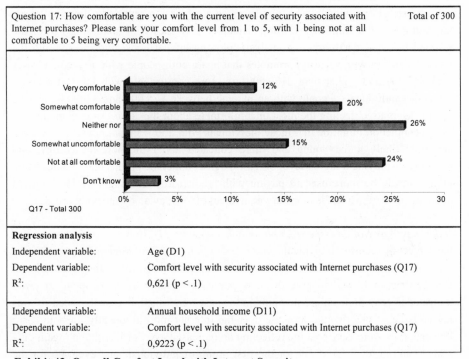

Question 17: How comfortable are you with the current level of security associated with Internet purchases? Please rank your comfort level from 1 to 5, with 1 being not at all comfortable to 5 being very comfortable.		Total of 300

Q17 - Total 300

Regression analysis

Independent variable:	Age (D1)
Dependent variable:	Comfort level with security associated with Internet purchases (Q17)
R^2:	0,621 (p < .1)

Independent variable:	Annual household income (D11)
Dependent variable:	Comfort level with security associated with Internet purchases (Q17)
R^2:	0,9223 (p < .1)

Exhibit 43: Overall Comfort Level with Internet Security

A look at the average comfort level with Internet security suggests that men tend to feel more comfortable than women do (average of 3.0 versus 2.6). In order to clarify whether this difference between the sample means occurred by chance or is based on statistical significance, one conducted an analysis of variance. This test has revealed that there really is a difference in the level of comfort between female and male.

Setting aside those who are undecided about the issue, it becomes obvious that people generally are more uncomfortable (39%) than comfortable (32%) with the current level of Internet security. It is therefore not surprising that more than three-quarters (77%) of people feeling uneasy about the issue named their distrust in the security as the main reason for not having given online purchasing a try in the past. Respondents, who have accessed the Internet earlier expressed a higher level of comfort than those who joined the online community only recently, resulting in an average of 2.8 for those having had access for less than three months versus 3.2 for those having had access for over three years. It obviously needs time until a high level of comfort with Internet security can be established. A higher level of confidence can be seen among the younger age brackets, for example people aged 18 to 34 exhibited a level of 3.0 while, people older than 55, only exhibited a level of 2.6. In fact, plotting age and comfort level with security associated with Internet purchases as a regression revealed a linear relation, indicating that the comfort level proportionally decreases with increasing age of the respondents. Another regression analysis, plotting annual household income and the level of comfort with security, promotes that again both people with an income lower than $25,000 and higher than $100,000 are more comfortable with Internet security than other individuals. People with an income between $75,000 and $100,000 are the most conservative, feeling the most uncomfortable about the issue. An explanation for this phenomenon might be that those individuals with a low annual household income are more likely to be young and more educated about the new technology, and therefore displaying a higher level of trust. High-end income groups on the other hand, might already be more used to paying with credit cards and might be less worried about the idea of losing the monetary equivalent of let's say an online book order.

If Security Was Not an Issue (Exhibit 44 and Appendix 31). In order to dig further into the subject of security, individuals who negated to have done online purchasing before were asked, in the case that security was not an issue how likely they would be to change their mind and to give the new purchase medium a try. Respondents who indicated to have done online shopping in the past were asked, in case that security was not an issue, if they would purchase over the Internet more frequently. In both cases the responses were very positive reflecting an increased average likelihood (again on a scale from one to five) of 3.4 for the first group of individuals and even 3.6 for the latter group.

In both groups one in two shoppers indicated to be (very) likely to do Internet purchases (more frequently).[195] No convincing significance between certain behaviors and age or household income could be found. However, the one finding worth

---

[195] Based on the previously mentioned different comfort levels with current security between men and women, two more analyses of variance were made in order to discover, whether likeliness to make Internet purchases (more frequently) and gender were dependent variables. However, the analyses produced no convincing indication for dependence between the two variables, suggesting that here, the differences between the sample means only occurred by chance.

mentioning is that especially individuals in the age segment between 35 and 44 years and the individuals with an annual household income between $75,000 and $100,000 are among the ones most likely to make use of Internet shopping more frequently.

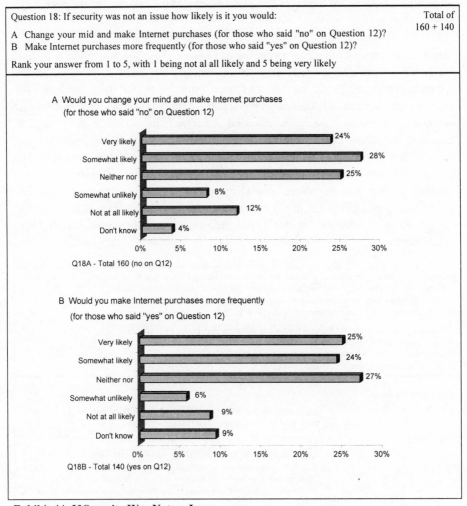

Question 18: If security was not an issue how likely is it you would:
Total of 160 + 140
A Change your mid and make Internet purchases (for those who said "no" on Question 12)?
B Make Internet purchases more frequently (for those who said "yes" on Question 12)?

Rank your answer from 1 to 5, with 1 being not al all likely and 5 being very likely

A Would you change your mind and make Internet purchases
   (for those who said "no" on Question 12)

Very likely — 24%
Somewhat likely — 28%
Neither nor — 25%
Somewhat unlikely — 8%
Not at all likely — 12%
Don't know — 4%

Q18A - Total 160 (no on Q12)

B Would you make Internet purchases more frequently
   (for those who said "yes" on Question 12)

Very likely — 25%
Somewhat likely — 24%
Neither nor — 27%
Somewhat unlikely — 6%
Not at all likely — 9%
Don't know — 9%

Q18B - Total 140 (yes on Q12)

Exhibit 44: If Security Was Not an Issue

11.4.5 Attitude Toward Online Purchasing

Attitude Towards Online Purchasing (Exhibit 45 and Appendix 32). AnyCo defined a set of four components, complementing one another to a "positive shopping experience": Delivery of quality, wide item selection, time saving, and the need to fit in ones lifestyle.

Therefore, a series of questions was designed to probe these four components against the perceived attitude towards Internet purchasing. To answer these questions, respondents were asked to rank their agreement from one to five (with one indicating their strongest agreement). The question whether "shopping over the Internet delivered the quality shopping experience expected", received an overall average of 2.8, indicating that about 20% agreed and 30% disagreed to the statement, however, the majority of interviewees is not very excited about the quality of Internet shopping. The question whether "shopping over the Internet gave better item selection" was rated similarly as the question above, and also received a 2.8. Setting aside the ones undecided, more individuals implied their disagreement (32%) than their agreement (20%), indicating that the Internet is not perceived as a provider of a better item selection.

Question 9: If you use the Internet, you are probably aware that today more and more retailers   Total of 300
offer their products over this new medium. Following are a few statements about Internet
purchasing. Please rank your agreement to each of the statements form 1 to 5, with 1 meaning
strongly disagree and 5 meaning strongly agree. How much do you agree or disagree that

A Shopping over the Internet delivers the quality shopping experience I expect.
B Shopping over the Internet gives me better item selection.
C Shopping over the Internet saves me time.
D Shopping over the Internet fits into my life style.

Analysis of Variance

Independent variable:	2 groups of shoppers, those who have made online purchases (group 1) and those who have not (group 2) (Q12)
Dependent variable:	Agreement to several statements about Internet purchasing (Q9)
H_0	Assumption that the two groups of shoppers have the same level of agreement to the statements about Internet purchasing and that the observed differences in the sample means are simply due to chance variations. Appropriately, the null hypothesis is that the population means are equal for both groups of shoppers.

	Q 19 A	Q 19 B	Q 19 C	Q 19 D
Significance level	$p < .01$	$p < .05$	$p < .01$	$p < .01$

Conclusion	The calculated F ratio exceeds the critical value, so one can reject the null hypothesis at the .01 level of significance (except for Q 19 B, which can be rejected at a level of .05). Thus, one concludes that there really is a difference from one group (online purchaser versus non-online purchaser), and that the differences between the sample means are too large to have occurred by chance.

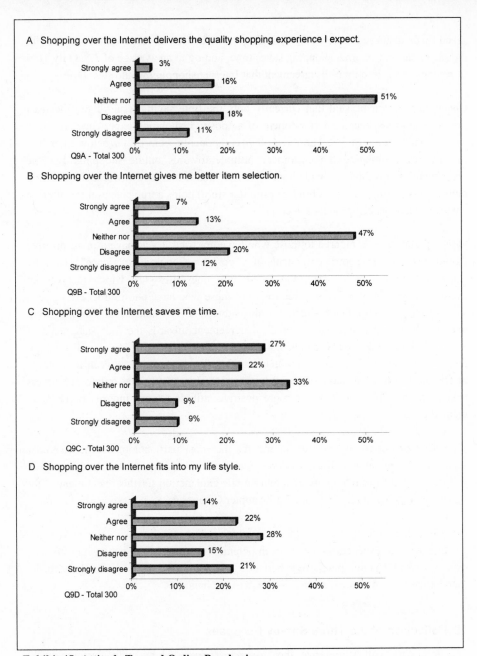

A Shopping over the Internet delivers the quality shopping experience I expect.

Q9A - Total 300

- Strongly agree: 3%
- Agree: 16%
- Neither nor: 51%
- Disagree: 18%
- Strongly disagree: 11%

B Shopping over the Internet gives me better item selection.

Q9B - Total 300

- Strongly agree: 7%
- Agree: 13%
- Neither nor: 47%
- Disagree: 20%
- Strongly disagree: 12%

C Shopping over the Internet saves me time.

Q9C - Total 300

- Strongly agree: 27%
- Agree: 22%
- Neither nor: 33%
- Disagree: 9%
- Strongly disagree: 9%

D Shopping over the Internet fits into my life style.

Q9D - Total 300

- Strongly agree: 14%
- Agree: 22%
- Neither nor: 28%
- Disagree: 15%
- Strongly disagree: 21%

Exhibit 45: Attitude Toward Online Purchasing

The statement, whether "Internet shopping fits into the persons lifestyle" received an average of 2.9, reflecting an equal percentage of people agreeing and disagreeing (36% for each) and 28% of people feeling indifferent about it. Asked if "Internet shopping saved time" disclosed more definite findings. One-half of all respondents agreed with the statement that Internet shopping saves time, adding to an average of 3.5. Only 18% of respondents raised their disagreement that Internet shopping would save time.

Concluding, it can be said that currently only the time saving issue, being the least personal and most technical component of a "positive shopping experience" receives an acceptable grade of 3.5. The three other components seem by far below their true potential of stimulating the customers' attitude towards online shopping. For the component of "displaying a wide item selection" this is insofar awkward, since selling online (over selling through a brick-and-mortar store) holds a true potential for offering a wide as well as deep product selection.

Online purchasers (compared to those who have not tried it yet) have a more positive attitude towards these four components of a "positive shopping experience". Here, the statement about "Internet shopping fitting into ones lifestyle", which receives an average agreement of 3.3 (compared to 2.6 of those who have not tried it) can be seen as an example. For further evaluation of this subject, several analyses of variance were undertaken, which compared the level of agreement towards the four statements of those who have and those who have not made Internet purchases. Interestingly enough, the analyses revealed for all four statements that the differences between the sample means are too large to have occurred by chance. This proves that online purchasers have - statistically significant - a more positive attitude toward Internet purchasing, than others do.

The fact that current online purchasers, for the most part, belong to the customer segments of innovators and early adopters, and therefore dispose of different motives to appreciate electronic commerce might be one explanation for this phenomenon (for details review Section I, Chapter 3.3.1 "Adopter Categories").

However, there are indications that the actual online purchase experience is more positive than the expectation it awakes in potential users. This gap between customers' expectations and online purchase experience will need to be narrowed to allow for its transformation into a true mainstream-purchasing channel.

12 Reflection of the Three Survey Purposes

The following will summarize the research analysis along with the previously introduced three purposes of the survey. Additionally, it will comment on the underlying hypothesis of this study, which states that business-to-consumer electronic commerce will within the next three to five years cross the chasm from the early adopters to the early majority. This will not only equip the reader with a recapitulation of the preceding contents but it will also lead the way into the concluding Section of this book, where a scenario of how AnyCo could dynamically enter the electronic commerce world will be drawn.

12.1 Readiness of the Analyzed Trade Area for Online Retailing

The Internet has become a part of the respondents' every day life. The compelling majority has Internet access at their homes and almost three-quarters use it more than four times a week. Enjoyably, searching for product or service information (40%) is among the favored online activities. One in seven interviewees named "making a purchase of a product or service" among the three things most often done with the Internet, and in fact, almost one in two respondents indicated to have purchased merchandise over the Internet. Also, the gender gap among customers making online purchases seems currently to dissolve. Interestingly, online purchasers are distributed almost evenly among all ages, showing only a slight tendency towards people younger than 55; also the income distribution among Internet purchasers has a concave shape.

Additionally, the survey highlighted the need for more education about online purchase logistics for consumables, like groceries, wine and perishables. Here, more than one-third of the respondents implied to be (very) likely to try either a home delivery or pick-up service. Last-minute shoppers over other types of shoppers are more likely to try online food shopping, further underlining their preference for convenience. Striking is the positive correlation between the respondents' level of comfort with retailers tracking their purchases and the likelihood to try online food shopping, indicating customers not comfortable with the retailers' tracking activities are not likely to try online food purchasing.

The current level of comfort with security associated with Internet purchases presents room for improvement. Almost 40% of respondents feel somewhat uncomfortable or not at all comfortable with the current level of security. Close to two-thirds of respondents who previously had not undertaken Internet purchases named distrust in the security as their main reason for not having done so. This is unfortunate, since from a technical point of view, the security of Internet based transactions is less an issue than from an emotional one. If security were not an issue, the likelihood to do online purchases (more frequently) would rise significantly. Among several components, currently only the time saving issue, being the least personal and most technical one, seems suited to create a positive shopping experience for customers' perceptions, while other components seem far below their true potential of stimulating a positive customer attitude towards online shopping.

However, while paying attention to the fact that there is room for improvement it can be concluded that the Analyzed Trade Area appears to be ready for business-to-consumer electronic commerce.

12.2 Identification of Products and Strategies for a Market Approach

Three different alternatives have been introduced to determine the product category with the largest online sales potential. Books, music and computer items (including software, hardware and peripherals) appear to be the favored categories for future online purchases, however, other categories with high potentials seem to be toys or sporting goods, home goods and clothing or shoes. Also reflecting future purchase interest are the categories gardening or floral supplies, cosmetics, health and beauty, and vitamin products. In a nutshell, a more serious engagement in the online purchase of a variety of product categories is apparent for the Analyzed Trade Area.

The above discussion named all of AnyCo's product categories at one point or another to be a high potential category, illustrating the extreme difficulty to identify *the* product category with the biggest online potential. Books, music, computer items appear to be the categories with the largest potential; however, there are several counter-arguments. These markets are heavily occupied by a handful of online merchants who previously have set up a hard-to-compete-with standard. Also, the respondents obviously expressed the wish to purchase online other product categories besides books, music and computer items. Many of these online category markets are not yet fully exploited and therefore still hold the opportunity for a niche marketer. Last, AnyCo holds an expertise in the arena of one-stop-shopping, emphasizing, on serving all of its customers' shopping needs at once. Keeping the above in mind, the question arises, why the company should limit itself in terms of different product categories. Why not apply this unique one-stop-shopping concept to the Web, since the knowledge and experience to deal with such a wide set of merchandise is already in place.

The best strategy to approach the current market of potential business-to-consumer electronic commerce customers is to build trust and to educate. Reasons for this strategy are manifold and have previously been highlighted. As mentioned earlier, only 12% indicated to be very comfortable with both traditional and online retailers tracking their purchase activities. The unease about being tracked appears to be the second reason for not (or not more frequently) making online purchases, after general security concerns. However, since detailed customer information is certainly the basis for successful online retailing, AnyCo will need to address this when building online commerce.

Also, AnyCo may focus on educating its customers about the different aspects and procedures of electronic commerce. This can be justified with the following. During the course of the questionnaire, respondents were asked to indicate their consideration to purchase several products over the Internet. Twenty-seven percent indicated they would consider online purchase of food. Several questions later, after the respondents had the opportunity to learn and reflect about possible distribution procedures of online purchased food products, they were asked again how likely they were to try online food shopping. Here, 36% indicated to be somewhat or very likely to do so in the future. Oftentimes, the reason for not having made Internet purchases does not seem to be based on dislike for the new medium but on uncertainty, something that also should be addressed in AnyCo's approach to the market.

12.3 Validation of the Veracity of Analyzed Secondary Data

The author of a previously discussed Ernst & Young report on electronic commerce summarizes her findings as follows:

> *Make no mistake about it: The Internet has arrived as a shopping channel. Like the telephone, the Web is reshaping the world, as we know it. The rapid pace of online adoption has given rise to a new breed of shoppers who are using the Net to research and purchase products.*[196]

Previously, this book has frequently expressed incredulity with statements such as the one just quoted. Many findings seemed unbelievable or just too good to be true. However, after having carefully analyzed the primary research on electronic commerce, one is willing to agree with the Ernst & Young statement and trust other secondary studies, which are coming to similar conclusions.

Interestingly, a comparison of the primary research findings with both types of secondary data material representing the entire United States and material focusing exclusively on the Analyzed Trade Area, revealed in many cases even more optimistic findings. There are two feasible explanations for this phenomenon. First, the region displayed a stronger predisposition towards technological advancements than average communities in the U.S. do. The Scarborough Report 1998,[197] which conducted the same market research study in the top 50 markets, ranked the analyzed region number five among major markets in home computer ownership. The same study also ranked the region number nine among major markets in Internet access (at home or at work).[198]

Second, the more optimistic findings of the primary research illustrate the enormous speed of change in this new and exciting market of business-to-consumer electronic commerce. One of the most significant proofs for this is the increased percentage of online purchasers among Internet users. Ernst & Young estimated in 1998 that 32% of online users utilize the medium to purchase merchandise, which is 15% lower than the findings from the primary research. Even more striking is the difference between this study and the TAP 98 (conducted during the first quarter of 1998). It concluded that

---

[196] Ernst & Young 1998, p. 1.
[197] The Scarborough Report is a syndicated, single-source, media/market study, which divides the United States, based on television broadcast markets, in 50 markets. TAP 98 1998.
[198] The Scarborough Report 1997, placed the Analyzed Trade Area on rank number 25 in the overall U.S. market.

only 26% of people with Internet access (or 11% of the overall population of the Analyzed Trade Area) made purchases over the Internet (compare these findings with the content of the following paragraphs and Exhibit 46).

Also worth mentioning is the proof that there is a broader spectrum of products with online potential than initially assumed, such as toys or sporting goods, gardening or floral, apparel, or food products.

12.4 Observations Regarding the Hypothesis

Are there indications that the community of online purchasers is going to cross the chasm between "early adoption" and "early majority" sometime in the near future? Looking at Exhibit 46 reveals that this certainly is the case. First, complementing primary research data with data from The Oregonian TAP 98 survey, revealed that currently 20% of all adults in the Analyzed Trade Area account for online purchasers (47% from 43% of the total Analyzed Trade Area population over 18 years). If one further takes into account the information gathered on the number of respondents with future online purchase plans, the implications are striking.

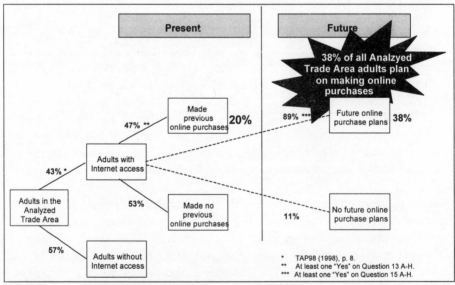

Exhibit 46: Present and Estimated Future Size of Analyzed Online Market[199]

This approach led to the discovery that 38% of all adults in the analyzed region (89% from 43% of the total region's population) plan on making online purchases (again) in the future. Note that the technology adoption life cycle (see Section I, Chapter 3.3.1,

---

[199] Based on TAP 98 1998, p. 8 and the underlying AnyCo survey (Q13 and Q15).

Exhibit 2) assumes that the customer segment of the early majority enters the scene after the new technology has approximately spread among 16% of the potential user market. If the above-presented percentage of current and going-to-be online purchases is true than electronic commerce has entered the stage of crossing the chasm. Note further that the percentages for future users presented in Exhibit 46 are rather modest estimates, since one assumes that the percentage of adults with Internet access would not increase further, which is very unlikely.

Second, the survey identified the advent of a new wave of going-to-be online purchasers, who appear to be the forerunners of the mainstream customer segment, and who no longer restrict their online purchases to the "traditional" online categories (books, music and computer items). The discussion on individuals belonging to the early majority customer segment[200] characterized them to be motivated by a strong sense of practicality. It is therefore important to note that the new customer segment, which is currently emerging on the online customer horizon explicitly pointed toward an increased importance of issues like time saving and convenience regarding Web transactions. This new customer segment is looking for productivity enhancements for existing operations, which corresponds with the characterization of individuals belonging to the segment of the early majority. Both of the presented indications are suitable to further support the hypothesis: The stage of crossing the chasm from the early adopter to the early majority electronic commerce customer segment is currently taking place. Based on the previous discussion, the concluding Section will therefore develop an architecture, suitable for AnyCo to benefit from the business-to-consumer electronic commerce world.

---

[200] See Section I, Chapter 3.3.1 "Adopter Categories".

The Internet is quickly emerging as one of the most powerful and dynamic forces in the retail industry today. It is transforming retailing, affecting everything from marketing to distribution, and creating entirely new relationships between retailer and customer.

Donna Iucolano, shop.org and
David Pecaut, The Boston Consulting Group

Section IV: Entrance to the Electronic Commerce World

13 New Strategic Focus

The bad news, the dynamics of the Internet are changing daily, therefore today's perfect solution might be outdated tomorrow.[201] The good news, there seem to be several orientation marks suitable to safeguard a company through the venture of discovering the Internet as a new sales channel.

The following Section will conclude the discussion of the preceding three Sections by emphasizing the most important things AnyCo will need to keep in mind when engaging in electronic commerce. Here, the authors will mainly concentrate on the business-to-consumer aspect of the topic and only highlight the so-called backend issues, such as technology and fulfillment.

The first part will suggest a "New Strategic Focus" for AnyCo to apply to the online retail venture. The latter will introduce a "New Architecture" suitable to handle the new requirements of a firm that wants to stay competitive in the twenty-first century. What exactly lies ahead? Some experts predict the emergence of a technology revolution, after which business will be conducted in the electronic world, and communities of people and businesses will be connected through networks of fiber-optic and satellite-based superhighways that transcend traditional boundaries. Distances will be measured in mouse clicks, not miles or minutes. However, other experts claim that, as the economics of distance will change, so will the economics of information, which in turn will give rise to the real revolution – the information revolution. They argue that while traditionally, information has been governed by a

---

[201] Carter 1996, p. 157.

trade-off between richness and reach,[202] the Internet will make it possible to have information-rich, customized interactions with large communities of individuals. This will eventually lead to the explosion in connectivity making it possible to unbundle information from its physical carrier, which eventually will revise the asymmetry of information between business and consumer. Again others conclude that the term information revolution is a misnomer and instead argue that the world is in the midst of a relationship revolution. Schrage, author of "The Relationship Revolution" argues, "to say that the Internet is about information is like saying that cooking is about oven temperatures; it's technically accurate but fundamentally untrue."[203] In his mind, information itself offers value only when presented in the context of a particular relationship. It therefore appears that an organization should not spend too much time figuring out what information it wants its networks to carry but instead to spend time on supporting the relationships that those networks create.[204]

Note that Appendix 33 holds an external benchmark on how Wal-Mart, a $104 billion revenue creating retailer, entered the business-to-consumer electronic marketplace. The study first covers Wal-mart.com's challenges and its strategic goals. Next, it reflects on the company's online merchandise mix and it concludes with online pricing practices and logistics.

13.1 Reasons for Hesitation

AnyCo and many other retailers share several similarities regarding a serious engagement to business-to-consumer electronic commerce: They are on the verge of implementing it, yet they are hesitant to take the first step. To find reasons for hesitating it seems useful to flip the coin - why are AnyCo and other retailers even bother considering a possible investment in the new medium? There seems to be two kinds of reasoning. On the one side a defensive strategy (defending against newcomers and old competitors who are attacking core markets), and on the other side profit reasons (when Internet retailing takes off, it will be too profitable to ignore). It appears that both are strong motivators to avoid unpleasantness (loss of customers and of course profit), while positive motivators such as the eagerness to explore new territory seem to be missing.[205]

---

[202] Richness is a function of bandwidth (the amount of information that can be communicated in a given amount of time), customization, and interactivity. Reach is a measure of connectivity – the size of the audience.

[203] Schrage 1997, p. 3.

[204] Evans & Wurster 1997, pp. 71-76, Matthews 1997, pp. 39-43, Schrage 1997, pp. 1-11 and Stewart 1998, www.deloitte.com.

[205] For a detailed discussion on motivation to work review for example Herzberg 1972, pp. 71-129 and Herzberg 1986, pp. 109-120.

Day, contributor to the Harvard Business Review, identified four reasons why established companies might have a more difficult time succeeding in electronic commerce than newcomers do. First, since there is currently not one single alternative (the definite business model), decision-makers in established companies may be nervous to "waste" money on alternatives that do not work in the end (but eventually lead the way to the winning strategy). A second reason might be that decision-makers decide to develop the complete venture in-house to save money. This might lead to picking the less optimal technology, either due to overlooking the possibilities for improvement or lacking capabilities to appraise technologies, or when a proprietary mind-set gets in the way. Third, decision-makers - rightfully concerned about the possibility of cannibalizing existing revenues or sacrificing long-term profits for an immediate revenue increase - may hold back from making follow-up commitments after their initial investment in a new technology. However, a company's follow-up investments may make or break its success. Last, established companies may have little patience for continued adverse results or surprises sometimes experienced during the gestation of a new technology. Also, in case the core business might not be doing too well, or other corporate challenges come up (e.g. mergers and acquisitions), the new venture might not receive the resources necessary.[206]

13.2 Opportunities

In spite of the above obstacles stated, many retailers seem to be quietly studying and researching the opportunities of electronic commerce,[207] while experts endlessly praise the opportunities of electronic commerce for retailers. For example, one can read that "there is reason to expect a glorious rate of return for those who catch and hold and ride the waves of light as the all optical network becomes reality"[208], which "[eventually] may prove to be the largest transition in the history of Western retailing [...]."[209] Others realize that "[electronic commerce] presents huge opportunities [as well as] formidable challenges."[210]

Even though such statements might be a little exaggerated at the moment it seems worthwhile to assess AnyCo's opportunities in the world of electronic commerce. To do so, it seems helpful to recap the most important input factors for this decision.

- Primary research has shown that there is a market for an Internet retailing venture. In the Analyzed Trade Area as an example, 20% of all adults have made online purchases in the past and almost 40% plan on doing so in the future. Review Chapter 12.4 "Observations regarding the Hypothesis" in Section III for details.

---

[206] Day 1996, pp. 158-159, Heller 1998, p. 23.
[207] Hennessy 1998, pp. 107-109.
[208] Audette 1998, www.adventive.com.
[209] Mathews 1998a, p. 22.
[210] Orler & Friedman 1998c, p. 52.

- Demographics of today's and tomorrow's online purchasers match AnyCo's primary customer profile, leading to the assumption that online customers could very well be AnyCo customers.
- Adopting decisions of individuals, belonging to the segment of the early majority (mainstream segment) are motivated by a strong sense of practicality (for details, see Chapter 3.3.1 "Adopter Categories" in Section I). Almost two-thirds of current online purchasers (the majority of them not yet belonging to the mainstream segment) named convenience as the single most appreciated thing about buying over the Internet. It can therefore be assumed that offering online retailing with a strong emphasis on increasing customers' convenience is a guarantor to attracting the early majority segment of customers.
- Studying other brick-and-mortar retailers, who have previously gone online, displayed the enormous momentum for merchants to shift their merchandise and/or customer focus. Here, the Wal-Mart Case study (Appendix 33) serves as an example.[211] The Internet enables retailers to target specific customer segments (e.g. more affluent customers) much more easily, while also providing different and more unique merchandise (e.g. slow moving or bulky items, taking up too much floor space in a traditional retail environment).[212]
- Research has further shown that customers in the future will be interested in purchasing a wider variety of retail merchandise than previously assumed (see Chapter 11.4.2 "Online Sales Now and Then by Product Categories" in Section III for details). Studying the online browsing behavior of Web users also indicates the ability of electronic commerce Web sites to drive customers to brick-and-mortar AnyCo stores for purchases (see Section II, Chapter 6.3 "Online Browsing and Purchasing Behavior" for details).[213]
- A most recent study on the state of online retailing, released by The Boston Consulting Group in November 1998, has shown that online sales were growing in excess of 200% over the last twelve months prior to the release of the study. Total online retailer revenues for 1998 in the U.S. turned out to be over $8 billion and modest forecasts estimate this number to reach $18 billion by the end of 1999.[214] Another study, published by Spiegel Online estimates that U.S. overall online retail revenues for the year 1999 will have been increased by more than two-third compared to the previous year.[215]

Pulling these factors together leads to the conclusion that AnyCo should definitely consider an engagement in Internet retailing. This would provide the company with the

---

[211] Wal-mart.com obviously tries to target a more affluent customer segment than reached through brick-and-mortar stores by selling online more upscale merchandise than available through stores.

[212] Heller 1998, p. 23.

[213] With AnyCo's e-tailing Web site on terminals in all brick-and-mortar stores, special could be serviced electronically.

[214] The Boston Consulting Group 1998, pp. 7-8.

[215] Spielgel Online 1999, www.spiegel.de/wirtschaft/konjunktur/.

opportunity to leverage its expertise regarding one-stop-shopping merchandise as well as its customers on the Web. However, succeeding in this new medium as a one-stop-e-tailer will require decision-makers at AnyCo to carve out a unique strategic model, which needs to be both, scalable and defensible. Whether this is seen as an opportunity or a burden is really up to the company.

13.3 Challenges

AnyCo's long-term objective can be defined as differentiating itself from the competition by establishing a customer-oriented, flawless, and profitable one-stop-e-tailing presence on the Web. However, to reach this goal, several external and internal hurdles need to be accomplished.

External. AnyCo will need to establish a brand name, providing certainty and familiarity. Since online customers, if faced with a broad choice and limited time, are most likely to reach for a comfortable and trusted brand name, it seems favorable to introduce the already well-know AnyCo name.[216] However, Schwartz, author of "The Nine Essential Principles for Growing a Business on the Web", points out that "it's better for a well-known brand not to go on the Web at all, rather than be there with a halfhearted, inferior, or useless Web site."[217] AnyCo could support and complement its online brand building efforts by establishing a targeted and value-adding dialog between the company and the online community. These relationships will serve several purposes. First, a customized online contact will help to establish or enhance the customers' trust and confidence in the new medium. It could also be used to involve customers in the development process of the online store, to anticipate future preferences, as well as to promote AnyCo's transparency in terms of dealing with private customer information. Last, truly value-adding contact will also help to attract new customers. This is especially important since online service - exclusively to currently loyal brick-and-mortar customers - will only result in trading pockets between traditional and online store and will therefore not complement the two channels.

Internal. To integrate the above activities, AnyCo will need to determine the most effective leverage between e-tailing and current brick-and-mortar marketing and sales promotions. How can existing offline advertising vehicles be used to create awareness and excitement for online activities? Additionally, since the Web is such a new medium, it will need to be consciously observed to recognize new developments or trend shifts as quickly as possibly.

---

[216] Mathews 1998a, p. 26 and Merril Lynch Forum 1997, pp. 3-6.
[217] Schwartz 1997, pp. 156-176, 161.

However, figuring out a home-run solution to promote its online activities is only one step in a series of tasks. First, AnyCo will need to specifically determine to whom (market), what (merchandise), and how (distribution) it wants to sell. Finding specific solutions to all of these questions will require the serious engagement of a cross-functional team of individuals as well as the top management.[218] Day even suggests established organizations to set up separate organizations specifically designed to pursue the new endeavor, which would create a boundary that enables the new group to do things differently while still permitting the transfer of resources and ideas from the parent company.

For AnyCo, the decision to adjunct the e-tailing Web site to its physical stores or to handle it as an independent operation seems highly situational. Most traditional retailers currently lean towards an integrated solution.[219]

They see the advantage for them in marrying traditional consumer marketing, product expertise, an extensive database, and back-end efficiencies with new Internet technologies. Nevertheless, separating and running the e-commerce venture as a stand-alone company might generate a more favorable response from financial markets. The near-term goal of electronic commerce is not necessarily generating cash flow (as in traditional retailing) but to capture market share. While the financial world accepts this in the case of "pure-play" online retailers, it might be less forgiving in the case of traditional retailers. Also, a separate company could profit from truly entrepreneurship and the opportunity to thing out of the box. One example for a retailer that decided to set up a separate unit is the office equipment supplier Staples.com. One of the company's Senior VP explains this step, "Running the Internet business separate from the core achieves the focus of mission. [...]. When we as a business unit are focused on the metric and measure, with specific revenue, profit and loss objectives, we are better able to measure success." There are advantages and disadvantages to both, and no one has cracked the code yet.[220]

13.4 Online Vision Statement

A vision statement may be used to address some basic questions about a business and it can be seen as a condensation of what the company expects to look like in the future.[221] It is important to note that a potential electronic commerce venture of AnyCo

---

[218] Hartnett 1999, p. 77 and Machlis 1998a, p. 43.

[219] Toys "R" Us, stared in 1997 to build its online sales toys store and launched the site one year later in 1998. To pursue this, the company set up Toys "R" Direct (even though not as a separate division) as a highly visible department that directly reports to the chief operating officer and president of the overall company. To keep the team on the track in terms of customized software, interface design, and logistics, the company also hired outside consultants and partnered with United Parcel Service (UPS). Chin Leong 1998, www.internetwk.com.

[220] Day 1996, p. 159, Ernst & Young 1999, p. 15 and Reda 1999, p. 26-30.

[221] Aaker 1995, pp. 30-11 and Stone 1996, p. 170.

requires the same goal-setting as well as result-determination clarity as using any other marketing technique.[222]

> - Exploit richness of the Internet to provide our customers with an opportunity to increase the convenience in their lives.
>
> - Exploit richness of the Internet to provide our current and future customers with a rewarding and distinct shopping experience.
>
> - Exploit richness of the Internet to create a dynamic and unique retail experience for our customers.
>
> - Exploit richness of the Internet to build a sense of affinity and community around our merchandise and our Customers.

Exhibit 47: Vision Statement for a Potential Electronic Retailing Venture

Thus, the customer related share of the new vision statement for a potential electronic retailing venture might read as illustrated above in Exhibit 47.

Why is this statement equipped to suit such a generic customer need? The answer lies in something that Levitt stated in 1960 in his classic article, "Marketing Myopia", and which still seems to hold true. He suggested that firms that myopically define their business in product terms can stagnate even though the basic customer need that they are serving is enjoying healthy growth.[223] Thus, firms for example regard themselves to be in the transportation rather than the railroad business and Visa, the credit card company, has defined itself as being in the business of enabling a customer to exchange value. Applying this to AnyCo's potential electronic retailing venture, one might suggest defining the company as being in the business of increasing the convenience of its customers rather then selling merchandise online. Aaker understands the definition of a business in terms of generic needs as extremely useful for fostering creativity in generating strategic options, something that is unquestionably necessary to master the realities of the Internet as a new medium.[224] Also interesting about the new medium, it enables existing companies by applying a different set of vision, to take on different shapes in the virtual reality of the Internet. However, it should be mentioned that redefining the business expands both the set of competitors and the range of opportunities.[225]

The above vision statement for the potential electronic retailing venture clearly articulates the goal of meeting the customers' generic need of increasing their

---

[222] Carter 1996, p. 157, Pricewaterhouse 1998b, p. 20, Reynoldson 1999, AMA Presentation, February 2, 1999.

[223] Levitt 1960, pp. 45-46.

[224] Aaker 1995, pp. 31-32.

[225] After redefining its business, Visa estimated that it had reached only 5% of its potential given the new definition.

convenience. The online vision statement also states the company's purpose of creating and keeping new customers with the means of the new technologies. Then, the statement focuses on utilizing the Internet's abilities to create a distinct shopping experience in ways that currently cannot be accomplished through traditional brick-and-mortar stores. The next statement of AnyCo's online vision invites the company to establish a unique retail environment by creating dynamic and customized products, which again could not be offered though AnyCo's traditional way of doing business. The last statement of the vision challenges the online retail venture to transform the existing (mostly) top-down communication between the company and its customers into an extensive dialog, which by definition always involves both parties.

14 New Architecture

As previously pointed out, if AnyCo will engage in business-to-consumer electronic commerce, it might discover that the current technology - information – or relationship revolution would challenge its traditional business logic on the Web. Venkatraman and Henderson, authors of a groundbreaking article on this matter summarize that "business models rooted in the industrial economy maybe in future [electronic commerce age] questionable,"[226] which led to their suggestion of a new architecture for a twenty-first century business model. Most probably motivated by the high level of uncertainty regarding the new medium, they did not suggest a distinct structure and instead concluded that a new architecture would need to be extremely flexible to adapt to changes along the maturation of the new medium. They therefore define architecture as

> [...] providing a framework for the conduct of life, not specification of what life should be. Architecture should facilitate, guide, and provide a context. It should not provide a rigid blueprint for conduct. [Moreover, the] building should preferably be ahead of its time when planned so that it will be in keeping with the times a long as it stands.[227]

14.1 Three Pillars

Venkatraman and Henderson conclude that the new architecture of an electronic commerce conducting firm should consist of three pillars: Customer interaction, asset configuration, and knowledge leverage.

Customer interaction. The first pillar deals with the new challenges and opportunities for business-to-consumer interactions.

---

[226] Venkatraman & Henderson 1998, p. 33.
[227] Venkatraman & Henderson 1998, p. 33.

Asset configuration. The next pillar focuses on the firms' requirements to be integrated in a business network, in sharp contrast to the vertically integrated model of the industrial economy. Firms using the Internet for business-to-consumer transactions can structure and manage a dynamic portfolio of relationships to assemble and coordinate the required assets for delivering value to customers.

Knowledge leverage. Finally the last pillar is concerned with the opportunities for leveraging diverse sources of expertise within and across organizational boundaries.

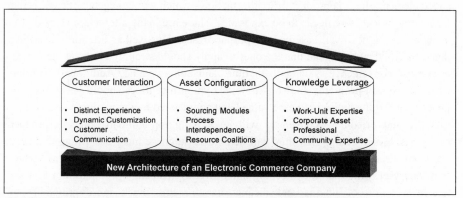

Exhibit 48: Architecture for a Twenty-first Century Business Model

All three pillars in one form or another exist in current business models, however they have previously been mostly independent from one another, since there was no common unifying platform to gather these different activities. This is, through the means of the Internet, possible today. In fact, only the interdependence of the three pillars creates the new architecture. Although each pillar is of equal importance, the following discussion will mainly focus on the aspects of "Customer Interaction", only highlight major aspects concerning the "Asset Configuration" and not further discuss the "Knowledge Leverage" since this would go beyond the scope of this book.

14.2 Customer Interaction – Creating a Critical Value Proposition

The new architecture will allow for establishing and leveraging a two-way information link between the company and its customers, which will not only enable the latter to interact with companies in new, innovative ways, but also make it possible to interact with fellow customers by constructing consumer communities. In order to have the above working to its advantage, AnyCo will need to determine how to leverage the functionality of customer interaction in crafting a successful marketing strategy. Following, three stages of customer interaction will be depicted.[228]

---

[228] Venkatraman & Henderson 1998, pp. 33-34.

14.2.1 Distinct Experience of Products

Looking back at the history of retailing, the first time customers experienced products separated by time and distance (distinct) was the advent of merchant catalogs. Customers made purchases without actually seeing or touching products. Certainly, the capabilities of the Internet have accelerated and redefined the possibilities of the distinct product experience, therefore, companies selling over the Internet will need to assess how its products can be experienced "virtually" in the new marketing infrastructure by creating superior linkages with customers. It appears that a value-added element - be it in product or in information - which would negate to be delivered from a traditional store needs to be exposed.[229] There are many alternatives for AnyCo to choose from, however, based on the primary research as well as literature regarding this subject, it can be argued that the ones to apply should strongly focus on increasing customers' convenience, saving them time, and adding value. Additionally, online customer reward-programs and (real-time) shopping incentives should be in place to give customers the feeling of being valued and appreciated by the retailer.[230] According to Orler and Friedman, consumers will be looking for a broad range of product categories, broad enough that they will be able to purchase most everything that they can from a traditional store. [231] In fact, retailers seem to be making a big mistake when they cherry pick the top stock keeping units (SKUs). Instead, a product mix of basics and a selection of unique and distinct items seems much more preferable to customers.[232] Customers will also appreciate everything that shortens the time required to do the shopping, such as automatic replenishment to help them control and manage the shopping experience. Additionally, customers will like information that allows and empowers them to make more informed choices (providing the same amount of information available in a store is the minimum requirement). For example, value adding might be a system telling customers that certain products do not meet dietary requirements,[233] or a Web site providing customers with recipes[234] and the opportunity to immediately order the required ingredients online. Besides groceries, there seem to be other categories in a AnyCo store that customers are seeking expert information about and that therefore could be utilized to attract customers to the Web. Categories such as baby care, health products, music[235] and entertainment planning as well as

---

[229] Schwartz 1997, p. 104 and Venkatraman & Henderson 1998, pp. 34-35.

[230] Radice 1998, p. 50 and Reda 1999, p. 27.

[231] Orler & Friedman 1998c, pp. 51-52.

[232] Progressive Grocer 1998, p. 96 and Schwartz 1997, p. 95.

[233] Orler & Friedman 1998c, pp. 51-52.

[234] Kraft Interactive Kitchen (www.kraft.com) is an example of a consumers products company keeping in touch with its consumers by providing information-based services like meal planners, recipes, tips, and cooking techniques. The company's intent is to have remote connections and interactions with consumers in new ways.

[235] CDNow (www.cdnow.com), an online music store offers its customers to test selections by playing CDs through audio clips. The site also makes recommendations to alert customers to other selections of possible interest, notifies customers on new releases via e-mail, and suggests customers to create their own personalized stores to meet their individual tastes.

apparel[236], gardening and pet care come to mind, however, this list could certainly be extended.[237]

Even though different categories certainly require different approaches to create a distinct online experience of products, all approaches should commonly share that the information provided would never be an impediment to making a purchase, but rather an area consumers can go to if they choose.[238] The following paragraph will draw an example of how AnyCo could leverage the Internet by providing customers with a value-adding and distinct experience for the category pet care. Based on the primary research note the following: Of all households that have made Internet purchases in the past, "playing with animals" (42%) is the second most favorite hobby or interest only surpassed by outdoor sports (52%) (see Appendix 11 for details).

AnyCo could become the one-stop, personalized pet care resource on the Internet.

The company could use the constraints of brick-and-mortar stores regarding pet care products as a leverage for Internet merchandising. Customers owning a multitude of different kinds of pets have obviously diverse needs that might - through brick-and-mortar stores - not all be fulfilled in a fully satisfactory manner. Consequently, the fact that the store does not carry the desired product or that the sales force is unable to address a particular issue will result in an unsatisfactory shopping experience for the pet owner. In comparison, a AnyCo online pet care store, not constrained by floor space, could promote items that are less popular and / or that logistically do not lend themselves to in-store displays (e.g. huge aquariums). One could engage in online relationships with a fragmented base of pet care suppliers, both exclusive suppliers to serve the upscale market as well as mainstream suppliers to fulfill the needs of a broad customer base. On the one hand, an online venture would therefore put AnyCo in the position to offer breadth and depth of selection. On the other hand, equally important, it would also provide the company with the opportunity to display not only its own but also its suppliers' and vendors' information about pets on the Web (care, nutrition, vitamins, toys, accessories, and FAQs). Such would offer customers the in-depth knowledge that previously was unavailable

---

[236] Land's End (www.landsend.com) selling apparel online, invites women customers to punch in their personal dimensions to view a "model" just their size. The "Your Personal Model" technology gives the customer a three-dimensional look at several style collections, all on her own body type. Additionally, the site offers different colors and complements to go with the selected piece of clothing.

[237] The Boston Consulting Group 1998, pp. 23, 29.

[238] Progressive Grocer 1998, p. 96.

in a physical store.

It becomes obvious, the company's e-tailing venture for pet care would only extract the full potential of the Internet if it were designed to provide much more than just merchandise online. Key to a distinct shopping experience (and therefore fully satisfied customers) is a successful integration of rich and relevant content, tailored to educate customers and to increase their confidence, add convenience, and finally to stimulate impulse buying.

Exhibit 49: AnyCo's e-tailing Venture for Pet Care (Part 1)[239]

The following Chapters will elaborate further on company's opportunities as an online merchant for pet care. Note that the presented suggestions for pet care shall only serve as an example. The concept can certainly be applied to other retail categories, such as for example music and video or gardening.[240] So far, the first part of this case study pointed out that AnyCo should focus on offering a unique product, providing a level and richness of content around the purchasing experience not normally offered by traditional retailers. The value-adding experience on the side of customers will also ensure defensibility against other online retailers.

14.2.2 Dynamic Customization of Products and Services

The second stage of the customer interaction pillar focuses on the opportunities and challenges in dynamically customizing products. Because competitive markets are rapidly eroding margins due to price-based competition, companies are seeking to enhance margins through customized offerings.[241] This, however, does not take place without hesitation on the side of the customers, as the following discussion will portray.

14.2.2.1 One-to-One Selling

While the concept of one-to-one selling can be expressed fairly simply, it is not so simple to implement it successfully as the current struggle of many companies efforts proves. For AnyCo, the way to create a dynamic and unique retail experience for its customers seems to be through establishing one-to-one communications with highly targeted markets or even individual customers through the vehicle of online retailing.[242] In fact, "one-to-one" seems currently to be the buzzword in regard to customization and personalization (as a mean of differentiation) and is apparently even called the

---

[239] Adapted from an example for garden products, found in The Boston Consulting Group 1998, pp. 24-26.

[240] Note that 21% of current online purchasers named "music" and 17% named "gardening" as interests actively pursued in their households, for further details refer to Appendix 11.

[241] Venkatraman & Henderson 1998, p. 36.

[242] Allen, Kania, Yaeckel 1998, p. 8.

customer-driven competition.[243] To determine what one-to-one means exactly for a corporation, it is worthwhile looking at Peppers and Rogers, authors of the book "Enterprise One to One", who defined four steps for establishing a so-called learning one-to-one relationship with customers:

- Find out what your customer needs through interaction and feedback.
- Meet these needs by customizing your products and remember the specifications.
- Continue interaction and feedback to learn more about the customer's individual needs.
- Keep your customers satisfied so you do not lose them to your competition.[244]

One might raise the question, what is it that is so new and exciting about doing business one-to-one over the Internet? It appears that what really distinguishes this one-to-one selling from the previously utilized selling methods is its database capabilities, which extends well beyond data mining and target-marketing, allowing for the creation of truly customized shopping experiences that customers – ideally - perceive as valuable and productive.[245] Take a retailer's apparel department as an example. The possibility of notifying its best customers about an upcoming event or the arrival of a spring collection could take on a whole different meaning.

If the company is able to integrate the customer data they have compiled (age, size, and preferences of style) on one side of their business with information coming through other doors, the retailer's apparel department could initiate a targeted communication with customers according to their needs.[246]

Pearce defines the new art of doing business as micromarketing. It is his understanding that so-called micromarketers "think about a market in terms of customer-specific characteristics, [since] without the ability to distinguish among customers and to remember their individual preferences and behaviors, a retailer cannot develop customized approaches to each customer."[247]

The literature is filled with positive exclamations about the new opportunities, such as the following:

> *We are about to see a return of one-to-one marketing, where retailers know their customers to the point where they can even anticipate their needs. With mass media came mass marketing. With the ability to use*

[243] Smith 1999, p. 37.
[244] Peppers and Rogers 1997, pp. 14-16.
[245] Arlen 1998, www.4interactivemarketing.com.
[246] Reda 1999, p. 28.
[247] Pearce 1997, p. 70.

data to customize our consumer portraits, we will come back to one-to-one selling.[248]

Getting the customer's name, address and purchasing history is only the beginning, however. AnyCo, as a one-stop-e-tailer, could record the customers' digital footprints (cookies) as they click through the retail site, taking note not only of purchases but also of so-called window-shopping. The promised end result is "a dossier that would allow the retailer to almost telepathically determine what that customer is most likely to purchase next – and then offer inducements to seal the deal."[249] Cookies will give the Web merchant a leg up on its brick-and-mortar stores, since they enable the company to follow a visitor and then use the information to target promotions at them on the fly or on return visits. For example, the company could rearrange the entire layout of a store in real-time, sticking an advertisement for parkas on the page when a "ski bum comes calling."[250] Such dynamic customization is possible since intelligent Web sites leverage in real time and can guide each user's experience to relevant contexts and products.

However, in reality one-to-one selling is not always that simple, since there are two hurdles to overcome. First, the online retailer will need to determine how to harness the huge amounts of raw data in a fashion that is meaningful and which eventually could be used as in the previous example above. Second, gained knowledge about customers should only be applied with great caution. In fact, the company should always verify whether the information it is about to share with its customers would be perceived as an invasion of privacy or a service.

14.2.2.2   Word of Warning

The Fingerhut Corporation, a \$20 billion database-marketing giant, collects up to 3,500 data elements per customer and will soon have a database exceeding 7 terabytes[251] in size,[252] thus making the company the leader in the cutting edge of life time value measurement.[253] Persecution mania – or a justified reason for customers to worry.

As illustrated above, the new, increasingly efficient ways that companies have of understanding and responding to customers' needs and preferences seemingly allow them to build more meaningful connections with consumers than ever before. Unfortunately, a close look indicates that the relationships between companies and

---

[248] Orler & Friedman 1998b, pp. 40.

[249] Wingfield 1998, R20.

[250] Wingfield 1998, R20.

[251] One terrabyte is more than 714 trillion floppy discs of space.

[252] Rogers & Peppers 1998b, www.1to1.com and Schulz 1999, p. 50.

[253] Customer lifetime vale: The stream of expected future profits, net of costs, on a customers' transactions, discounted at some appropriate rate back to its current net present value. For further information on the issue, see Berger & Nasr 1998 and Peppers & Rogers 1997, pp. 30-54.

customers are troubled ones, at best. Companies may enjoy learning more about their customers and being able to provide features and services to please every possible taste. But customers generally enjoy neither. In fact, customer satisfaction rates in the U.S. are at an all-time low, while complaints, boycotts, and other expressions of consumer discontent are on the rise. However, experts warn that this mounting wave of unhappiness has yet to reach the bottom line.[254] Note that the primary research, illustrated in Section III, Chapter 11.2.3 "Enjoyment and Comfort regarding Food Shopping" of this book revealed that more than 50% of respondents felt uncomfortable with both traditional and online retailers tracking their purchase activities (also review Exhibit 27 and Appendix 18 for details). Experts name fear and distrust regarding the loss of personal privacy[255] and lack of confidence in the newly developed one-to-one marketing machinery as two major impediments to full-scale integration of the electronic marketplace.[256] Borrowing the dramatic words of Fournier, Dobscha and Mick, the only solution to prevent a "premature death" is one-to-one marketing and selling to negate the "us versus them" mentality and become what it is meant to be – truly customer oriented.[257]

14.2.2.3   Understanding the Paradigm Shift

Traditional brick-and-mortar retailers, to become successful one-to-one Web marketers, will need to subscribe to becoming truly customer oriented. Marketers, who misinterpret the true meaning of customer orientation, engage in a kind of espionage of customers to squeeze out results, which they then translate into supposed customized products. Such behavior is not according to the above definition of one-to-one selling. It will not result in a positive outcome and will only cultivate negative customer responses. The sucessful online retailer will need to understand that the distinguishing factor between a one-way communication and a two-way dialog[258] is the simple matter of control. In true one-to-one selling, the relationship between marketers and consumers gets flipped on its head. Here, customers obtain control and they are able to direct the dialogue based on their own needs, while marketers will be the ones to listen and react.[259]

---

[254] Fournier, Dobscha & Mick 1998, pp. 43-48.

[255] The term privacy is usually described as "the right to be let alone," and is related to solitude, secrecy, and autonomy. Wang, H., Lee & Wang, C. 1998, p. 64.

[256] Campbell 1997, pp. 45-46 and Wang, H., Lee & Wang, C. 1998, p. 64.

[257] Fournier, Dobscha & Mick 1998, p. 48 and Hagel III & Singer 1999, pp. 4, 16.

[258] Wolfe identifies three requisites for true dialogues:
- Conversational reciprocity: each party allows the other to condition its responses: "I influence you; you influence me."
- Reciprocal empathy: each party reaches out to identify with and understand the other party's circumstances, feelings and motives.
- Reciprocal vulnerability: both sides in a relationship let down their guards to some level that remains safe and conformable yet allows information to flow and trust to build. Wolfe 1998, p. 450.

[259] Schwartz 1997, pp. 56-56, Smith 1999, p. 37, Wolfe 1998, pp. 449-450.

At first glance, this sounds scary. However, many experts, while further underlining the paradigm shift, also point toward a solution in the fight about customer information. While the experts point out that today's consumers know that they have more power than they had yesterday and are going to take ownership of their information, they acknowledge that customers will be interested in exchanging their information for something tangible and valuable in return.[260] Maes, professor at the MIT Media Laboratory puts it this way, "people like to contribute, especially if it will change things."[261] Retailers have many opportunities to offer their customers something valuable in return for information. Besides a monetary incentive, another alternative might be to promote the benefits for customers to engage in a one-to-one dialog. A benefit might include the reduction of information overload, which would help make customers' lives simpler and to make decisions to buy the right products easier.[262] Whatever the tools, they should always be designed to enhance a loyalty-increasing dialog with customers and to make purchasing more convenient.

It seems worthwhile to end these paragraphs on one-to-one selling with Wolfe's proposed new definition of one-to-one relationship marketing, which will summarize all of the above.

Old definition of Marketing:

Exchange relationship involving goods and services in exchange for payment

– this definition is object-oriented: Consumers being the object (of attention), in other words, the marketer "pushes" products.

New definition of one-to-one Relationship Marketing:

Product-related information processing

– this definition is subject-oriented: The consumer being the subject (of attention) to be served, in other words the consumer "pulls" the product.

Exhibit 50: Old and New Definition of Marketing[263]

Coming back to the previous example on a potential online pet care venture: How could the concepts of a dynamic customization of products and services be applied to AnyCo's opportunities as an online merchant for pet care?

---

[260] Hagel III and Rayport 1997, pp. 53-54, Schwartz 1997, pp. 55-57 and Smith 1999, p. 38.
[261] Schwartz 1997, p. 77.
[262] Smith 1999, p. 38.
[263] Wolfe 1998, p. 452.

The company could ask customers to introduce their pets to the Web site (name, birthday, kind of pet, special characteristics, concerns, etc.). This information could then be used to initiate a personalized contact with customers, and AnyCo could ideally take a regular part in the pet's life. Here, ideas are manifold. For example, one could provide special health or nutrition tips or one could send pet birthday notes to promote special custom-made gift items for the particular pet, or one could offer customers coupons targeted to the special needs of their particular pet. These coupons could be sent by e-mail (here it is important to make sure that customers have opt-in, in other words, agreed to receive promotional material over e-mail). Besides customized information, one could also provide customers with personalized space, where they could note down personal information. It might also be beneficial if one could save previous purchase data, so next time they come to replenish, they just click on previous orders.

Exhibit 51: AnyCo's e-tailing Venture for Pet Care (Part 2)

14.2.2.4   Customer Communication

The most profound aspect of interaction in the new architecture is the emergence of electronic customer communities. These communities are another signal of the power shift from business to consumer: The communities are information-gathering and information-disseminating conduits (note that previously, consumers could not be effectively linked together across time and space).[264]

Hagel III and Armstrong offer five defining characteristics of virtual communities: Distinctive focus, capacity to post their content for access to the wider community, appreciation of member-generated content, access to competing offerings, and commercial orientations.[265] Even though as of today no community could be found that incorporates all five components, they acknowledge that communities can also exist with only the first three. Critics argue that customer loyalty on the Web is frequently non existent, resulting in very high customer attrition rates. In order to prevent this, online retailers should make use of innovative techniques creating so-called sticky relationships with its customers. AnyCo should use the opportunity of online communities to build customer loyalty and to enhance the breadth and depth of customer relationships. This will also help the company's understanding of customer preferences and behavior, and enable it to become even more effective at personalization and cross-selling.[266]

---

[264] Venkatraman & Henderson 1998, p. 37.
[265] Hagel III & Armstrong 1997, p. 37.
[266] Ernst & Young 1999, pp. 15, 22-23 and The Boston Consulting Group 1998, pp. 26-29.

Online communities are basically homogenous affinity groups formed around a common interest. People join online communities for the same reasons as they do real world communities: They are bored or anxious or lack fulfillment, or just want human contact and all it brings. Myra Stark concluded her extensive research on online communities with the conviction that the groups emotional involvement holds powerful opportunities for marketers to build brands and loyalty. However, marketers should be careful not to invade the privacy of such communities. For an online retailer one alternative to honor privacy would be to create, sponsor or underwrite a community and then get out of the way.[267] Instead of treating the community as a place to sell products, the company could regard it as a marketing effort - a long-term alliance to build relationships. In fact, this kind of advertising is all the more powerful since it is not advertising.[268] How could the above be applied to AnyCo's online pet care venture?

> The company would have several opportunities to orchestrate a tight-knit community around its pet care customers. The company could provide twenty-four hour chat rooms, e-mailing services and a forum where customers could display photos and stories about their pets creating a sense of affinity among pet owners while stimulating their urge to purchase pet related merchandise. AnyCo could also set up a billboard where people could post questions or requests, (e.g. if somebody, living in the suburbs was looking for company when walking the dog) and they could sponsor a raffle to find the funniest pet name to build a database of pet owners. The site could motivate customers to participate and to submit information by e.g. setting out a price of one year of free pet food. The submitted e-mail addresses, in return, could then be used to keep contact between the company and the customers. The site could also put visitors directly in touch with veterinarians or breeders who could share valuable information and insights. It has been shown that there are many choices to create a lively online community among pet owners, however, it is important to update the site frequently (and to share this information with visitors) to give customers incentives to return on a regular basis.

Exhibit 52: AnyCo's e-tailing Venture for Pet Care (Part 3)

When AnyCo decides to join the emerging electronic commerce age, customer interaction will change dramatically. Customers will demand the retailer's attention.

---

[267] Amazon.com, the virtual bookstore, has found a very effective way of leveraging the power of customer communities. One example for this community is the fact that Amazon gives readers the opportunity to create and distribute their own content (by posting their own book reviews for everyone to read on the Web). This creates for Amazon a strong and loyal community of readers.
[268] Stark 1998, www.4interactivemarketing.com.

The generic mass customer will disappear. The new customer for the online retailer to address will possess unique needs and desires.

14.3 Asset Configuration

This pillar of the new architecture focuses on acquiring critical assets and resources from external markets. Venkatraman and Henderson suggest that many businesses in the electronic commerce age will refocus on their core competencies and concentrate on creating and deploying intellectual and intangible assets while sourcing tangible, physical assets from external sources.[269] The following discussion will briefly highlight what "asset configuration" means and how it could be applied in the case of AnyCo's online venture.

14.3.1 Sourcing Modules

This stage deals with the benefits of efficiently sourcing standard modules or components. In the New Age, the value-adding for all stakeholders of a company[270] lies in the creation and the controlling of an interactive architecture that combines the different modules. The question is: What assets can we outsource without losing our competitive advantage?

Why will the New Age require a stronger engagement into outsourcing anyway? In the specific literature on outsourcing frequently named reasons are first, an increasingly dynamic environment of the firm, second, accelerating paradigm shifts in technology, and third, an increased discontinuity of frameworks within which a company operates.[271]

Looking at it from the opposite side, another question should be is there enough time for the company to build certain modules from scratch or might this result in the sacrifice of valuable opportunities? Certainly, there are many different alternatives how electronic commerce could be handled within AnyCo. After all, this decision also depends on which categories the retailer decides to sell online since it is out of question that one-stop-e-tailing would require more extensive back-end settings than an exclusive engagement into e.g. music, books and videos. However, since online retailing is such a new and immature phenomenon it seems advisable for the company to obtain as much as possible from experts outside the company. This would guarantee the opportunity to be able to switch gears in case new and more favorable

---

[269] Venkatraman & Henderson 1998, p. 38.
[270] The general idea of the Stakeholder Theory: Individuals and groups who have a legitimate interest (stake) in the activities of a corporation include at a minimum suppliers, customers, employees, stockholders, and the local community, and the management.
[271] Perlitz 1997, p. 433 and Venkatraman & Henderson 1998, p. 38.

technological developments come into being. However, AnyCo should base its decision to obtain certain modules from outside the company on two criterions. The first criterion should be the costs involved (transaction cost theory). On the one hand, there are costs to find and to engage with a third party (so-called ex-ante costs) and on the other hand, there are the costs to integrate the outsourced module in existing operations of the company (so-called ex-post costs). Here, as another possible disadvantage of outsourcing should be mentioned the increased dependence of the company on sourcing partners.[272]

For AnyCo, assuring state of the art of e-tailing, one definite outsourcing target seems to be the Web site development, since this is the ultimate tool to attract and serve customers. With literally thousands of Web site developers flooding the market it can be a tedious task to pick the one most suitable.[273] While the attributes of the perfect Web site developer depend on the specific needs and wishes of the retailer entering the Web, it seems worthwhile to pick a developer who also offers Web marketing and advertising services. This will allow the company to benefit from the knowledge that the developer has gained with other clients.

Another classic candidate for AnyCo to be sourced from outside seems to be the complex payment processing and order fulfilling networks. However, any further specifications on this matter certainly depend first on what categories of merchandise will be sold over the Web and second which alternative the company will choose to fulfil the orders. Here, the retailer faces two fundamental alternatives. The company can either engage in strong alliances with suppliers making them responsible for a direct filling of the orders to the customers or filling the orders themselves out of its own warehouses or stores. In the first case, the online retailer could partner with a back-end expert such as e.g. the Lowell, Massachusetts based OrderTrust, which covers all aspects of the supply chain for online storefronts, including order fulfillment, routing and processing, payment, and fraud prevention.[274] Partners of OrderTrust

---

[272] Perlitz 1997, pp. 433-439, 527-532.

[273] The magazine "Business Marketing" conducted a national survey of Web developers, which resulted in the following Web site price index for 1998.

	Small Site	Medium Site	Large Site
National Lows	$5,645	$18,000	$80,400
National Medians	$44,500	$99,750	$302,975
National Highs	$653,000	$1,486,000	$2,641,000

Carmichael 1998, pp. 1-2.

[274] The following will illustrate the transaction process between SkyMall and OrderTrust as an example for what the company is doing exactly: Transactions from SkyMall are transmitted in batch or real time using EDI, FTP or encrypted e-mail and are fed into 55 Sun Microsystems Inc. Solaris servers. From there, the orders are parsed and translated into an internal format called LSF, a master data structure that contains all aspects of an order and its status, including credit card information, stock-keeping units, country code and specifics on an order. Based on rules established by the particular merchant, the LSF data is conveyed to the payment processor for credit confirmation and eventually routed to the merchant's suppliers. The orders are transmitted to the respective suppliers in whatever format they specify, including SMTP mail, FTP, fax and EDI.

simply drop the incoming customer order to them, and they rout it to the fitting merchant using the appropriate file format. Coming back to the previously mentioned criterions to base sourcing decisions on, it can be said that an engagement with a back-end expert would bare two main advantages. On the one hand, AnyCo would have its hands free to concentrate on core sales and marketing competencies without getting bogged down in the technical minutiae of creating interfaces to various merchants' systems. On the other hand, it would be completely scalable and would clear the way for growth without forcing the company in additional technology gear to handle an increased number of customers.[275] In the case that AnyCo would decide to fill orders out of its own warehouses, it would also need to consider partnerships with transportation companies such as the U.S. postal service, UPS, or FedEx.

14.3.2 Process Interdependence

This stage focuses on the interdependence of business processes across organizational boundaries. Venkatraman and Henderson argue that external specialists can carry out information-intensive business processes without the risk that companies may lose control. In fact, this trend of delegating business processes to an external provider who then owns and manages the process will even grow stronger in the electronic commerce age. The authors even elude that as "processes become more standardized and as the market matures with more stable participants, many companies will recognize the criticality of business process outsourcing."[276]

Based on the above discussion of processes qualifying to be handed over to external specialists, there appear to be several candidates within a potential AnyCo e-tailing venture such as inventory control, Web site advertising, and database analysis. While all of these processes are certainly important, none of them appear to be one of the company's future online retailing core competencies. The company should therefore not be ashamed to hand over some of these processes to external specialists who might be able to provide the same or better quality for less costs and hassles. For example, it might be beneficial for the e-tailing candidate to outsource everything belonging to Web site advertising to an expert company such as for example the San Francisco, California based Flycast. This company has specialized in providing most effective advertising solutions. Their services include identifying and focusing all Web advertising activities on areas that are yielding the best results for the particular client. Flycast also monitors all campaigns in real-time (tracking) to assure the quality of their client's advertising efforts at all times. Finally, Flycast bundles their efforts to easy-to-work with reports for ist customers, which would allow the the retailer to keep control without the hassle of actually bothering with all the technical details.[277]

---

[275] Shein 1998, p. 55.
[276] Venkatraman & Henderson 1998, pp. 39-40.
[277] Flycast 1999, www.flycast.com.

14.3.3 Resource Coalitions

This stage focuses on establishing a resource network, in which the company would be part of a vibrant, dynamic network of complementary capabilities. In other words, the company becomes - ideally - a portfolio of capabilities and relationships. Venkatraman and Henderson conclude their discussion of the second pillar of the new architecture for electronic commerce businesses with the forecast that positioning a company within a broader network of resources in the marketplace will be a driver of competitive advantage. Consequently, the strategic leadership challenge is to orchestrate an organization's position in a dynamic, fast-changing resource network.[278]

How could this be done in the case of AnyCo? To answer this question it might be helpful to look again at the approach of Amazon.com. Amazon, as part of its attempts to create a powerful business model, has been orchestrating affiliated sites as associates to serve as extended bookstores. It can be seen that the company's success will be significantly affected by its ability to centrally position itself in the constantly reconfiguring resource network. Therefore, one can conclude that AnyCo will also need to engage in relationships with potential affiliates. There are several choices for coalitions and as previously illustrated, the genius of the Internet is just that - networking and the seamlessly connecting of people.

Several coalitions, resulting in an additional stream of income as well as greater exposure for e-tailing candidate might be beneficial to look at. On the one hand, there are programs with affiliates or associates who could refer potential customers to the AnyCo site and vice versa, and on the other hand there are also many different possible programs with banner advertisers. However, Wilson, editor of "Web Marketing Today", points out that a serious downside of developing multiple coalitions is the potential of losing focus. He further illustrates that "a Web site needs a very clear focus. If it tries to do everything, it does nothing well."[279] Last, AnyCo might want to look into the opportunity to participate in one of the currently evolving - new - virtual malls. While coalitions hold many opportunities for the participants to establish themselves further in the electronic marketplace, good judgment to align the different coalitions into the complex net of Web activities will be essential.

15 Conclusions

The preceding paragraphs of this book suggested a new architecture, suitable to support AnyCo in meeting the challenges of a commitment to electronic commerce. However, the word architecture should not be misinterpreted as a ready to plug in tool for the company. In other words, the proposed architecture should be understood as a

---

[278] Venkatraman & Henderson 1998, pp. 40-41.
[279] Wilson 1999, www.wilsonweb.com.

guideline to point the direction for the company's further actions. Such will require a serious engagement of the retailer's top management, illustrating on the one hand the company's orientation toward the future and acknowledging on the other hand the existence of a new tool to reach its customers. Also, a thorough goal setting will be necessary, in order to define whether electronic commerce will be a tool for the company to further penetrate the existing market with current AnyCo merchandise. The downside of this approach is the risk that all the effort of implementing electronic commerce might only result in trading pockets between physical and online stores. Therefore, an alternative would be the goal to reach existing as well as currently not loyal brick-and-mortar customers with current as well as new merchandise that will not be available through the physical stores. While many questions still need to be solved, one thing became crystal clear during the analysis: Retailers in future will need even more than in the past to define customers as their center of gravity in order to succeed in the new environment. Therefore, one suggestion in defining AnyCo's motivation for engaging in e-tailing is not to sell merchandise online but instead as to increase the convenience of its customers.

The suggested new way of doing business is, on the front-end, synonymous with a power shift from retailers to customers. For a brick-and-mortar retailer to stay successful on the Internet- while acknowledging the power shift - it should consider several key points. The company's online venture should aim to provide customers with value-added features that could not be provided through traditional brick-and-mortar stores. By doing so, however, it will be important to respect the customers' privacy by inviting them to an honest dialog. This dialog should be used to learn more about each other and to fine-tune offers to the wants and needs of customers. Last, AnyCo, as a successful e-tailer, will need to provide customers with real incentives to stay loyal. On the back-end side, the new way of doing business will challenge the retailer to increase its engagement in partnerships with external sources. Such will require the company to trust outsiders, however, it will also open the opportunity to concentrate on its core sales and marketing competencies.

When planning the engagement into business-to-consumer electronic commerce, AnyCo will also need to be aware of changing business models. In fact, the online e-tailing future will require a change from the current industrial age business model to an information or communication age business model. Bill Gates, founder of Microsoft commented on this change that "competition today is not between products, it's between business models" and further that on the Internet irrelevancy would be a bigger risk than inefficiency.[280] But, for the moment at least, these drastic words only apply to business on the Web, which means that AnyCo's engagement as an e-tailer would not instantly require the company to change its current brick-and-mortar

---

[280] Hamel & Sampler 1998, www.pathfinder.com/fortune/.

operations. For the time being, it seems more fruitful to view electronic commerce as an add-on to current operations, as something that should be experimented with and that eventually will add to the bottom line.

It is extremely difficult to draw conclusions on a topic so new and unexplored as business-to-consumer electronic commerce. Everyday, popular press and academic literature publish new and exciting findings. Everyone seems convinced that his or her discovery is the key to master the current challenges of an electronic commerce application. However, even though this would be certainly desirable, it nevertheless appears that every so-called solution only raises new and unsolved questions. Now is not the time to accept seemingly agreed upon approaches to deal with electronic commerce. Instead, everyone dealing with the subject needs to keep an open mind in order to be optimistic for whatever the future will bring. And one more thing, one ought not to be impatient while seeking to get a handle on electronic commerce. The medium is not even a decade old and has merely been a mainstream tool for a few years, yet it has already had a fundamental influence on our life and the way we conduct business. There is only one fact one should consider: Electronic commerce is here to stay.

If that is the case, what conclusions can be drawn for AnyCo? While it may be too early to predict the ultimate impact of electronic commerce for the company, it should certainly be viewed as a source of business opportunity today. Pushing the envelope even further one could raise the assumption that the greatest threat of electronic commerce may be the risk of not acting on this unique opportunity.[281] Negative mid- and long-term consequences for not doing so may be numerous. On the one hand, the technological developments in the field of electronic commerce might be so profound and fast paced that simply catching-up might be impossible. On the other hand, the increasing importance of electronic commerce will eventually result in a massive shift of retail spending dollars from physical stores to the Web. In the long run, the bottom line for AnyCo will be that if the company is not planning on generating a part of its revenues from the electronic commerce world, it will be left with a much smaller market to compete in and to induce profits.

---

[281] Hartnett 1999, 76.

Appendices to Section II: Age of Change

Appendix 1: Estimated Share of the 3 Different Market Players on Total Revenues[1]

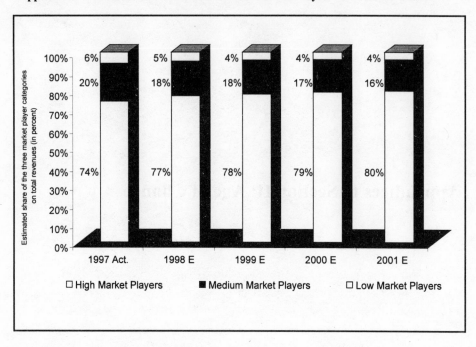

[1]   Forrester Research 1998, www.forrester.com and Hof, McWilliams & Saveri 1998, pp. 122-125.

Appendices to Section III: Primary Market Research

Appendix 2: Advantages and Disadvantage of Internet based Surveys[2]

Internet Based Interviewing	
Advantages	**Disadvantages**
	Universe The Internet lacks of a master database for its Internet population. There is no reasonably accurate sampling frame, nor is there likely to be one anytime soon.
Sample represenativiness Lack of representativeness is less an issue, if sample only requires certain groups, which have high levels of Internet usage. It makes it possible to find highly specific research targets without screening a large random sample. Applying quota and weighing the sample also increase the representativeness.	**Sample represenativiness** It is mostly not possible to draw a probability sample, which might make the survey research look suspect. People with Internet access are not representative. Although demographics of Internet population become more mainstream, the issue remains significant. While it is easy to track behaviors in virtual environments, it is much more difficult to thoughtfully understand people's motivations.
Honesty The absence of interviewer interaction reduces the socially desirable answers. Anonymity effect of the Internet can be helpful for some topics.	**Dishonesty and identity validation problem** It's a peculiarity of the Internet that some users like to invent new personas for themselves or just lie for the pleasure of it. While this is also true for any other type of survey, the likeliness is larger in Internet based surveys. The anonymity of the Internet increases the likeliness of dishonesty. It is difficult to keep people from answering an online survey more than once. The anonymity of the Internet makes it difficult (impossible) to validate the identity of an interviewee.
Response rate Errors caused by not-at-homes or refusals could be reduced, since online research allows for participation at the individual's convenience.	**Low response rate** Response rates may be dramatically lower than for any method other than mail. Online surveys are hampered by constraints on length and complexity. Response rates for un-incentivized questionnaires drop off precipitously after about 10-15 questions. In fact, response rate seems to be directly and negatively correlated with questionnaire length.

[2]   Dodd 1998, pp. 61-64, Edmondson 1997, pp. 10-14, Harris 1997, pp. 267-270, Nadilo 1998, pp. 12-13 and Predow-James 1996, www2.worldopinion.com.

The novelty of computer-assisted research might result temporarily in higher respondent interest.

Simple animation might increase response rate by 25%.

Very quick turnaround rate. In the past, most completed online surveys were returned in just 48-72 hours.

Invite fresh and invigorating new trends.

Technology

The data may be analyzed continuously, which might help to improve the quality of the survey. Also, the data can port directly into statistical tools and databases.

Less labor intensive and expensive

Even though the initial start-up costs of Internet based survey are high, the technique should pay off over time.

No need to hire and train interviewers, (and no chance that an interviewer's mistake will trait the results).

Break-ups after the interviewee is half way through. On an Internet survey, there is no interviewer to motivate the interviewee to continue.

Invitations to participate in a survey via e-mail are often considered "spamming", which might have negative consequences for the institution conducting the survey.

Technology and accuracy problems

Not everybody uses the same software. Difficulties may occur, while the interviewee copies the questionnaire into a text editor. Quick and easy clicks with the mouse can increase the chance of tabulation errors. Using standard e-mail systems might be too limiting and difficult.

Elaborate information-condensing grids of CATI phone and mail surveys do not translate well to either an e-mail or Web based delivery environments.

More labor intensive and expensive

It might be expensive to set up a professional Internet based survey form. Each questionnaire would need to be developed separately.

Self-selection bias.

Questionnaires posted on Web sites ask visitors to answer while there. These surveys have no control over who answers and when and have therefore a large self-selection bias. It is very likely that the sample will consist largely of the extremely satisfied or dissatisfied.

It is possible to insert attention-grabbing mailing material to an extent into e-mails, as it is possible to do so in direct mail pieces. Online surveys have the distinction to introduce multimedia elements, but further complicate self-selection biases, as the interviewees must then go to the Web site where the survey resides

Appendix 3: Coded Questionnaire

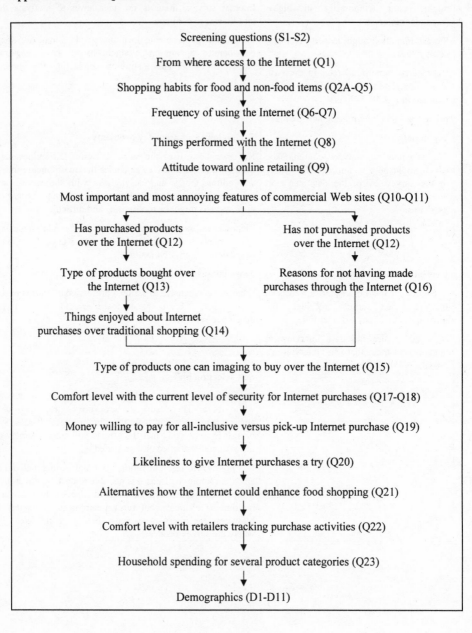

Screening questions (S1-S2)

From where access to the Internet (Q1)

Shopping habits for food and non-food items (Q2A-Q5)

Frequency of using the Internet (Q6-Q7)

Things performed with the Internet (Q8)

Attitude toward online retailing (Q9)

Most important and most annoying features of commercial Web sites (Q10-Q11)

Has purchased products over the Internet (Q12) | Has not purchased products over the Internet (Q12)

Type of products bought over the Internet (Q13) | Reasons for not having made purchases through the Internet (Q16)

Things enjoyed about Internet purchases over traditional shopping (Q14)

Type of products one can imaging to buy over the Internet (Q15)

Comfort level with the current level of security for Internet purchases (Q17-Q18)

Money willing to pay for all-inclusive versus pick-up Internet purchase (Q19)

Likeliness to give Internet purchases a try (Q20)

Alternatives how the Internet could enhance food shopping (Q21)

Comfort level with retailers tracking purchase activities (Q22)

Household spending for several product categories (Q23)

Demographics (D1-D11)

Appendix 4: Questionnaire

Introduction

Hello, my name is _____ calling from Market Decisions Corporation, an independent research and consulting firm. This is NOT a sales call. This evening we are conducting a brief research survey with Internet users. May I speak with the adult member of your household who most often accesses the World Wide Web?

Screening

S1	In order not to take up your time unnecessarily, let's first make sure that you qualify for the survey. Do you have Internet access?

1	Yes		
2	No	→	Terminate
7	Don't know	→	get referral or terminate

S2	Are you primarily responsible or share responsibility for the household's grocery shopping?

1	Yes		
2	No	→	get referral or terminate
8	Don't know	→	get referral or terminate

Question base

Q1	Where do you access the Internet? (Multiple Mention)

11	Work	15	Community Center
12	Home	16	Shopping Malls
13	School	17	At a Friend's place
14	Library	99	Other

Q2A	The following section will focus on your shopping habits. In an average month, how often do you normally shop for food?

1	Once
2	Twice
3	3 - 5 times
4	6 - 8
5	More than 8 times

Q2B	In general do you consider yourself (READ LIST, ROTATE 1&2)

1	A convenience, last minute food shopper
2	An organized, stock-up food shopper
3	Neither
4	Both

Q2C	Please tell me which category best describes the average monthly food expenditure of your household (excluding dining out).

1	less than $100	4	$501 - $750
2	$100 - $250	5	$751 - $1,000
3	$251 - $500	6	more than $1,000

Q3 Which of the following best describes your overall attitude. "I enjoy food shopping ...(READ LIST)"

1 All the time
2 Most of the time
3 Sometimes
4 Never, only do it because it needs to be done
7 (DO NOT READ) Don't know

Q4 In general, where do you do the majority of your food shopping? (unaided) (**NOTE** – Up to 5 mentions)

11	Albertson's	20	Red-Apple
12	Costco	21	Safeway
13	Cub Foods/Winco Foods	22	Selected Markets
14	Food-4-Less	23	Thriftway
15	AnyCo	24	Trader Joe's
16	Howard's	25	Waremart
17	IGA	26	Wizer's
18	Kienow's	27	Zupan's
19	Nature's	99	Other (specify)

Q5 Now, let's talk about products other than food. Where do you do the majority of your non-food shopping. (Please name the top 3) (unaided)

11	Bi-Mart	19	Kmart
12	Costco	20	Meier & Frank
13	Emporium	21	Mervyn's
14	AnyCo	22	Montgomery Ward
15	G.I. Joe's	23	Nordstrom
16	Home Base	24	Office Depot
17	Home Depot	25	Officemax
18	JCPenney	26	Pacific Linen

Q6 Now let's talk about the Internet. How long have you had access to the Internet?

1	Less than 3 months	5	2- 3 years
2	3-6 months	6	Over 3 years
3	7-12 months	7	Don't know
4	1 - 2 years		

Q7 How often do you use the Internet? (PROMPT WITH LIST IF NECESSARY)

1	Daily	5	Twice or three times a month
2	4 to 6 times a week	6	Once a month or less often
3	2 to 3 times a week	7	Don't know
4	Once a week		

Q8	Please name the 3 things you do most often with the Internet. (unaided)

11	Communicating with others (chat, e-mail)
12	News/daily information/newsgroups
13	Entertainment
14	Make purchase of a product/service
15	Access financial information
16	Use for work/business
17	Search for product/service information
18	Education related research
19	Games
20	Pass the time
99	Other (specify)
97	Don't know

Q9	If you use the Internet, you are probably aware that today more and more retailers offer their products over this new medium. Following are a few statements about Internet purchasing. Please rank your agreement to each of the statements from 1 to 5, with 1 meaning strongly disagree and 5 meaning strongly agree. How much do you agree or disagree that…(READ LIST, ROTATE)

5	Strongly agree
4	Agree
3	Neither agree nor disagree
2	Disagree
1	Strongly disagree

A.	Shopping over the Internet delivers the quality shopping experience I expect.
B.	Shopping over the Internet gives me better item selection.
C.	Shopping over the Internet saves me time.
D.	Shopping over the Internet fits into my life style.

Q10	Please answer the following question based on your Web experience and/or expectations. Name the 3 most important features of a commercial Web site from which you might make a purchase. (unaided)

11	Colorful and interesting site
12	Reflects the personality of the store
13	Site is simple to get around
14	Quick delivery of product purchased
15	Merchandise is simple to locate
16	Cheaper prices than in physical store
17	Detailed product information (e.g. picture, description)
18	Customer service
19	Number of payment alternatives
20	Suggestions, ideas, recommendations, new products, and trend information
21	Return policy and guarantees
22	1-800 telephone number
23	History of the company, store locations
24	Gift / bridal registry and gift ideas
25	Security issue
99	Other or Customer service (specify)
97	Don't know / no answer

Q11	Now let's talk about the opposite. What are the 3 things that you consider most annoying about the Web or about a Web site? (unaided)

11	Can't effectively organize the information I gather
12	Can't find a page I know is out there or that I once visited
13	Can't visualize where I have been and where I can go ("lost in cyberspace")
14	Don't find the information I am looking for
15	It takes too long (too slow)
16	Encounter links that do not work (broken links)
17	Web site too complex/chaotic
18	Pictures are too small
19	Fonts are too small
99	Other (specify)
97	Don't know / no answer
98	None, no complaints

Q12	Have you ever purchased products over the Internet?

1	Yes	→	(Do not ask Q16)
2	No	→	(skip to Q15)

Q13	Which of the following products you have purchased over the Internet. (READ LIST, ROTATE)

1	Yes, bought on-line (skip corresponding Q15 product)
2	No, never purchased these products on-line
7	Don't know/no response

A.	Jewelry or Accessories
B.	Clothing or Shoes
C.	Cosmetics, Health and Beauty, Vitamins, or Prescriptions
D.	Books, Music, or Computer Software or Peripherals
E.	Gardening or Floral Supplies
F.	Home Goods
G.	Toys or Sporting Goods
H.	Consumables, like Groceries, Wine or Perishables

Q13I.	What other products have you purchased on-line? (Probe & Clarify)

Q14	Compared to traditional shopping what are the 3 things you like most about shopping on the Internet? (Probe & Clarify)

Q15	Which of the following products might you consider buying over the Internet? (READ LIST, ROTATE) (IP NOTE: add again after buying for those products already purchased in Q13 series - Which of the following products might you consider buying *again* over the Internet?)

1	Yes, would buy on-line
2	No, would never purchase on-line
7	Don't know/no response

A.	Jewelry or Accessories
B.	Clothing or Shoes
C.	Cosmetics, Health and Beauty, Vitamins, or Prescriptions
D.	Books, Music, or Computer Software or Peripherals
E.	Gardening or Floral Supplies
F.	Home Goods

G.   Toys or Sporting Goods
H.   Consumables, like Groceries, Wine or Perishables

Q15I.	What other products would you consider buying over the Internet? (Probe & Clarify)

If Q12 = 2, ask Q16, else skip to Q17

Q16	Please name the top 3 reasons why you have never made a purchase through the Internet. (unaided)

11   Don't trust the security issue
12   Never thought of Internet shopping
13   Couldn't find the web site
14   Too hard to get around within the site
15   Didn't find what I was looking for
16   Want to touch, try or pick out the product
17   Prefer going to a physical store
18   Not enough to choose from
19   Merchandise too expensive
20   Shipping and handling fee too high
21   Don't know / trust the merchant
99   Other (specify)
97   Don't know

Q17	How comfortable are you with the current level of security associated with Internet purchases? Please rank your comfort level from 1 to 5, with 1 being not at all comfortable to 5 being very comfortable.

1   not at all comfortable
2   somewhat uncomfortable
3   neither uncomfortable nor uncomfortable
4   somewhat comfortable
5   very comfortable
7   Don't know

Q18	If security was not an issue how likely is it you would… (if Q12=2, ask) A. Change your mind and make Internet purchases? (If Q12 not equal 2, ask) B. Make Internet purchases more frequently? Please rank your answer from 1 to 5, with 1 being not at all likely and 5 being very likely

1   not at all likely   4   somewhat likely
2   somewhat unlikely   5   very likely
3   neither unlikely nor likely   7   Don't know

Q19	Let's return for a moment to the process of food shopping. Imagine your food store offers online shopping. All you have to do is fill out an online shopping list. Please tell me, what percentage of the total purchase amount would be a fair fee for this service if your food store did your food shopping for you and…(READ LIST, ROTATE)

A.   Delivered your groceries to your house at a time that is most convenient to you.
B.   Had your order available for you to pick-up in front of the store at a time that is most
      convenient to you.

1   up to 2% of the total purchase amount
2   2% - 5%
3   6% - 10%
4   11% - 20%
5   More than 20%
8   Would not pay anything for this service
7   Don't know

Q20	How likely are you to try online food shopping with a delivery procedure that is most convenient for you on a scale from 1 to 5, with 1 being not at all likely to 5 being very likely.

1	not at all likely	4	somewhat likely
2	somewhat unlikely	5	very likely
3	neither unlikely nor likely	7	Don't know

Q21	What other ways can you imagine the Internet helping you with food shopping? (Probe & Clarify)

Q22	How comfortable are you with both traditional and online retailers tracking your purchase activities to tailor their offers to your personal needs? Please rank your comfort level from 1 to 5, with 1 being not at all comfortable to 5 being very comfortable.

1   not at all comfortable
2   somewhat uncomfortable
3   neither uncomfortable nor comfortable
4   somewhat comfortable
5   very comfortable
7   Don't know

Q23	How much would you estimate your household spent in the last 12 months on...(READ LIST, Q13 or Q15 "yes" categories).

RECORD $_____
                    99997   Don't know
                    99998   Refused/no answer

A.   Jewelry or Accessories
B.   Clothing or Shoes
C.   Cosmetics, Health and Beauty, Vitamins, or Prescriptions
D.   Books, Music, or Computer Software or Peripherals
E.   Gardening or Floral Supplies
F.   Home Goods
G.   Toys or Sporting Goods
H.   Consumables, like Groceries, Wine or Perishables

Demographics

This last set of questions is simply to help classify your answers. All of your answers will remain completely confidential.

D1	Which of the following best describes your age?

11	Under 18	16	55 - 64
12	18 - 24	17	65 - 74
13	25 - 34	18	75 and older
14	35 - 44	97	No answer
15	45 – 54		

D2	What is the highest level of education you have had the opportunity to complete? (unaided)

11	Some High School	16	Some Post Grad. Work
12	Completed High School	17	Master's Degree
13	Vocational/Techn. School	18	Doctorate Degree
14	Some College	99	Other
15	Bachelor's Degree		

D3	Please name your current occupation. (unaided)

11   Business Owner
12   In-Home Business
13   Skilled Tradesman
14   Middle Management
15   Upper Management
16   Professional / Technical
17   Homemaker
18   Teacher
19   Secretary /Administration
20   Sales/Marketing
21   Government / Public
22   Nurse
23   Veteran
24   Retired
25   Unemployed (looking for work) (do not ask D7)
99   Other
97   No answer

D4	Altogether, how many people including yourself live in your household? (unaided)

1   1   →   skip to D7 (unless D3=25, then skip to D8)
2   2
3   3
4   4
5   5 or more
7   No answer

D5	How many children do you have living at home? (unaided)

1   one   4   four or more
2   two   8   None
3   three   .   7   Refused/No answer

D6	How many members of your household, including yourself are currently working?

1   1   3   3 and more
2   2   7   No answer

D7	Are you or any other member of your household working in the high-tech industry?

1   Yes
2   No
7   No answer

D5	How many children do you have living at home? (unaided)

1   one   4   four or more
2   two   8   None
3   three   7   Refused/No answer

D6	How many members of your household, including yourself are currently working?

1   1   3   3 and more
2   2   7   No answer

D7 Are you or any other member of your household working in the high-tech industry?

    1   Yes   7   No answer
    2   No

D8 What is your marital status? (unaided)

    1   Single   4   Widowed
    2   Married   7   No answer
    3   Divorced / separated

D9 Do you own or rent the home in which you live?

    1   Own   7   No answer
    2   Rent

D10 What hobbies or interests are actively pursued in your household? (Multiple Mention)
(**NOTE** – up to 7 mentions)

    11   Reading
    12   Outdoor recreation (such as Camping, Hiking, Hunting, or Fishing)
    13   Gourmet Cooking
    14   Do it yourself projects
    15   Going to the Movies
    16   Travel (domestic and foreign)
    17   Needlecraft, Sewing or Quilting
    18   Outdoor Sport Activities (Golf, Biking, Running, Walking,...)
    19   Indoor Team Sports
    20   Exercise
    21   Gardening
    22   Photography
    23   Stamps/Coins
    24   Music
    25   Theatre or Performing Arts
    26   Health/Light Food or Diet Conscious
    27   Volunteer Work
    99   Other (specify)
    97   No answer

D11 Which category best describes your annual household income (gross)?

    1   less than $25,000   5 $75,000 - $99,999
    2    $25,000 - $34,999   6 $100,000 - 149,999
    3    $35,000 - $49,999   7 $150,000 +
    4    $50,000 - $74,999   8   Refused/No answer

O1 As you have probably realized - this survey is meant to learn more about Internet shopping. Do you have any other on-line shopping experiences or opinions – good or bad - you would like to share?

V1 And, just in case my supervisor needs to verify that we completed this survey, could I have your first name?

RECORD GENDER

    1   Male   2   Female

Thank you for your time and your opinions. Have a nice evening.

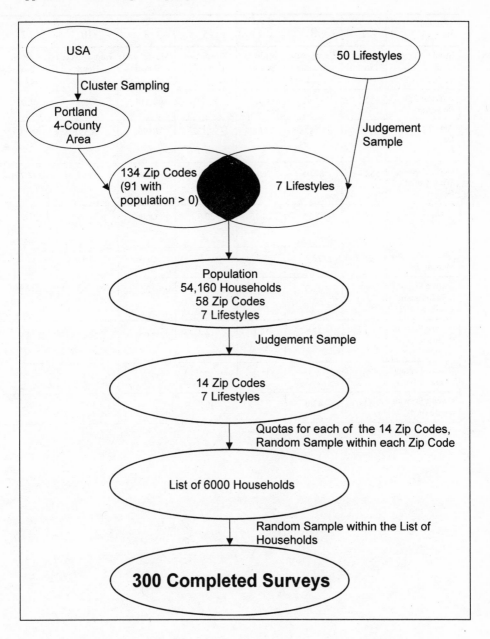

Appendix 6: The Seven Lifestyles "most likely" Internet Users[3]

Segment Number	2	3	4	5	8	10	12
Segment Title	Lap of Luxury	Established Wealth	Mid-life Success	Prosperous Metro Mix	Movers and Shakers	Home Sweet Home	A Good Step Forward
Average Age (in years)	32.27	35.92	37.03	32.09	39.14	37.29	40.23
Average Income (in U.S. $)	88,336	77,828	78,968	59,122	70,968	58,591	56,409
Occupation: White Collar (mean)	82.47	81.05	76.84	72.1	81.94	68.93	78.77
Occupation: Blue Collar (mean)	17.53	18.95	23.16	27.9	18.06	31.07	21.23
Owns a PC with Modem (in %)	28.3	22.4			21.4	7.4	
Owns a PC used for online services (in %)		13.9	15.7	12.6	12.2		10.8
Owns a PC with fax modem (in %)		12.6	14.1	12.5	11.4		11.6
Owns a Laptop/ notebook (in %)	9.1	7.5	11.2		7.9	5.3	
Owns a PC with mouse (in %)	51.0	42.0		40.0		30.9	

---

[3] Extracted from the Micro Vision database.

Appendix 7: Relative Demographic Profiles

Age distribution (in percent) among survey respondents

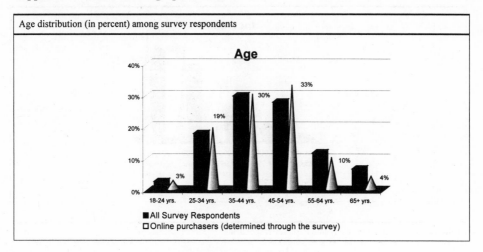

Level of education (in percent) among survey respondents

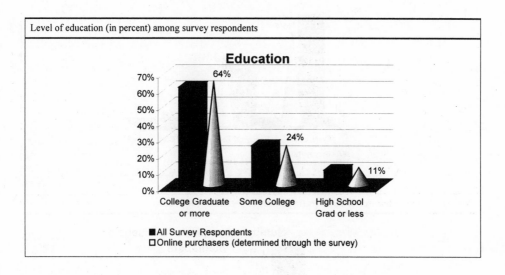

Income distribution (in percent) among survey respondents

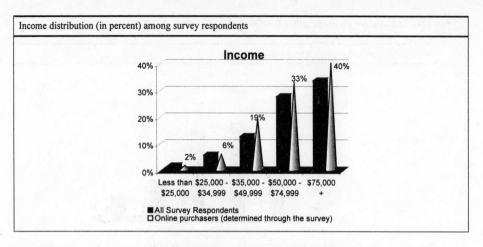

Different professions (in percent) among survey respondents

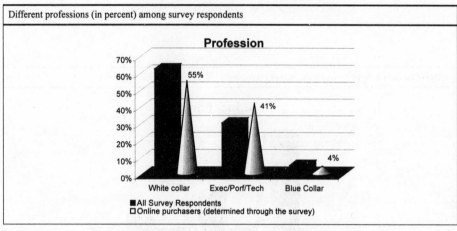

Number of employed household members (in percent) among survey respondents

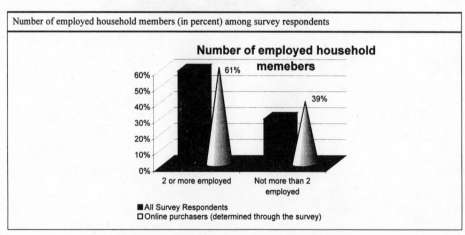

Marital status (in percent) among survey respondents

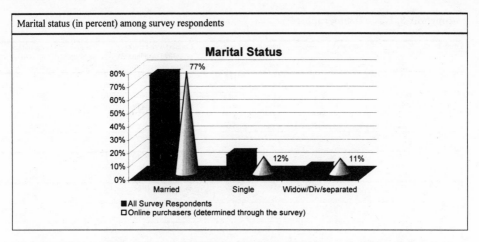

Children under 18 at home (in percent) among survey respondents

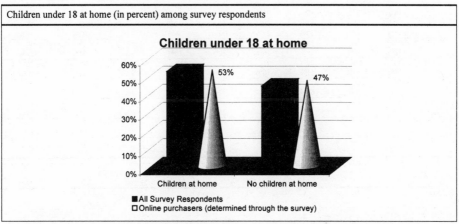

Home ownership (in percent) among survey respondents

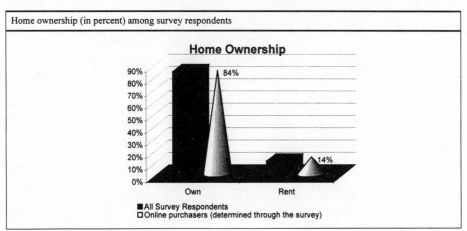

Appendix 8: Basic Demographics

Gender	Total	Internet access		Internet purchaser		Comfort with security associated with Internet ---		Comfort with being tracked by retailers ---	
		Home	Work	Yes	No	High	Low	High	Low
Total	300	127	270	140	117	95	117	78	164
Male	144	80	132	74	50	57	50	34	79
	48%	63%	49%	53%	43%	60%	43%	44%	48%
Female	156	47	138	38	67	38	67	44	85
	52%	37%	51%	40%	57%	40%	57%	56%	52%

D1	Total	Internet access		AnyCo customer ---		Comfort with being tracked by retailers ---		Gender ---	
		Home	Work	Yes	No	High	Low	Male	Female
Total	300	127	270	111	189	78	164	144	156
Under 18	3	2	3	2	1	1	1	3	-
	1%	2%	1%	2%	1%	1%	1%	2%	
18 - 24	8	2	8	2	6	1	6	2	6
	3%	2%	3%	2%	3%	1%	4%	1%	4%
25 - 34	55	23	48	24	31	20	24	29	26
	18%	26%	18%	22%	16%	26%	15%	20%	17%
35 - 44	91	39	81	30	61	28	46	33	58
	30%	31%	30%	27%	32%	36%	28%	23%	37%
45 - 54	85	34	78	29	56	14	56	45	40
	28%	27%	29%	26%	30%	18%	34%	31%	26%
55 - 64	35	13	29	11	24	8	19	19	16
	12%	10%	11%	10%	13%	10%	12%	13%	10%
65 - 74	17	3	17	10	7	5	8	9	8
	6%	2%	6%	9%	4%	6%	5%	6%	5%
75 and older	4	-	4	1	3	1	2	3	1
	1%		1%	1%	2%	1%	1%	2%	1%
No answer	2	1	2	2	-	-	2	1	1
	1%	1%	1%	2%			1%	1%	1%

D2	Total	Age				Gender ---	
		18 - 34	35 - 44	45 - 54	55 +	Male	Female
Total	300	63	91	85	56	144	156
Some high school	7	2	-	2	1	4	3
	2%	3% *		2%	2%	3%	2%
Completed high school	17	3	6	5	3	8	9
	6%	5%	7%	6%	5%	6%	6%
Technical school	9	3	2	1	3	4	5
	3%	5%	2%	1%	5%	3%	3%
Some college	77	20	24	20	13	35	42
	26%	32%	26%	24%	23%	24%	27%
Bachelor's degree	110	31	33	28	16	56	54
	37%	49%	36%	33%	29%	39%	35%
Some post grad.	22	-	8	6	8	10	12
	7%		9%	7%	14%	7%	8%
Master's degree	46	4	17	20	5	18	28
	15%	6%	19%	24%	9%	13%	18%
Doctorate degree	10	-	1	3	6	7	3
	3%		1%	4%	11%	5%	2%
Other	1	1	-	-	1	1	-
		1%			2%	1%	

* Reading example:
From 300 individuals having participated in the survey, 63 indicated to be between 18- 34 years old. Of those 63, 2 individuals (or 3%) indicated have "some high school" as their highest level of education.

Appendix 9: Household Information

D4	Total	Type of shopper			AnyCo customer	
		Convenience	Organized	Both	Yes	No
Total	300	67	123	93	111	189
1	25	8	6	9	11	14
	8%	12%	5%	10%	10%	7%
2	101	26	39	28	37	64
	34%	39%	32%	30%	33%	34%
3	61	14	27	18	24	37
	20%	21%	22%	19%	22%	20%
4	68	11	32	21	21	47
	23%	16%	26%	23%	19%	25%
5 or more	42	8	18	15	16	26
	14%	12%	15%	16%	14%	14%
No answer	3	-	1	2	2	1
	1%		1%	2%	2%	1%

D5	Total	Monthly food bill			AnyCo customer	
		< $250	$251 - $500	> $500	Yes	No
Total	275	102	138	35	100	175
1	50	19	26	5	16	34
	18%	19%	19%	14%	16%	19%
2	61	14	37	10	22	39
	22%	14%	27%	29%	22%	22%
3	25	44	12	9	8	17
	9%	4%	9%	26%	8%	10%
4 or more	10	-	4	6	5	5
	4%		3%	17%	5%	3%
None	126	64	57	5	47	79
	46%	63%	41%	14%	47%	45%
No answer	3	1	2	-	2	1
	1%	1%	1%		2%	1%

D8	Total	Type of shopper			Online purchaser	
		Convenience	Organized	Both	Yes	No
Total	300	67	123	93%	140	160
Single	48	16	15	15	17	31
	16%	24%	12%	16%	12%	19%
Married	227	45	103	68	108	122
	76%	67%	83%	73%	75%	76%
Divorced/ separated	19	6	3	6	14	5
	6%	9%	2%	6%	10%	3%
Widowed	1	-	1	-	1	-
			1%		1%	
No answer	5	-	1	4	3	2
	2%		1%	4%	2%	1%

	Total	Age				Annual household income			
		18 - 34	35 - 44	45 - 55	55+	$25 - 49K	$50 - 74K	$75 - $99K	$100K +
Total	300	63	91	85	56	58	83	61	43
Own	257	38	83	80	53	39	69	59	42
	86%	60%	91%	94%	95%	67%	83%	97%	98%
Rent	39	24	7	5	3	18	13	2	1
	13%	38%	8%	6%	5%	31%	16%	3%	2%
No answer	4	1	1	-	-	1	1	-	-
	1%	2%	1%			2%	1%		

Appendix 10: Occupational Life Information

D3	Internet purchasers		Annual household income			
			$25 - 49K	$50 - 74K	$75 - $99K	$100K +
Total	140	160	58	83	61	43
Professional/ technical	47 34%	33 21%	16 28%	20 24%	22 36%	9 19%
Homemaker	11 8%	18 11%	3 5%	10 12%	7 11%	3 7%
Teacher	13 9%	15 9%	8 14%	9 11%	4 7%	3 7%
Retired	9 6%	17 11%	5 9%	5 6%	4 7%	1 2%
Middle management	9 6%	15 9%	1 2%	10 12%	6 10%	4 9%
Sales/ marketing	12 9%	8 5%	3 5%	4 5%	3 5%	8 19%
Skilled tradesman	5 4%	13 8%	4 7%	4 5%	3 5%	2 5%
Secretary/ clerical/ administration	7 5%	7 4%	4 7%	4 5%	2 3%	3 7%
Business owner	5 4%	7 4%	1 2%	3 4%	-	6 14%
Upper management	3 2%	6 9%	2 3%	7 8%	2 3%	1 2%
Nurse	4 3%	4 3%	3 5%	2 2%	2 3%	1 2%
Unemployed	3 2%	3 2%	3 5%	1 1%	-	1 2%
In-home business	4 5%	-	2 3%	-	1 2%	-
Other	4 4%	3 2%	1 1%	1 1%	4 7%	2 3%
No answer	-	2 1%	-	-	2 2%	-

D7	Total	Internet access		Internet purchasers		Comfort with security associated with Internet		Comfort with being tracked by retailers	
		Work	Home	Yes	No	High	Low	High	Low
Total	288	123	259	134	154	91	112	75	156
Yes, working in high-tech industry	86 30%	54 44%	73 28%	51 38%	35 23%	33 36%	25 22%	21 28%	48 31%
No	200 69%	68 55%	184 71%	83 62%	117 76%	57 63%	86 77%	54 72%	106 68%
No answer	2 1%	1 1%	2 1%	-	2 1%	1 1%	1 1%	-	2 1%

D6	Total	Type of shopper			AnyCo customer		Internet purchasers	
		Convenience	Organized	Both	High	Low	High	Low
Total	275	59	117	84	100	175	132	143
1	82 30%	14 24%	38 32%	24 29%	27 27%	55 31%	42 32%	40 28%
2	141 51%	31 53%	58 50%	47 56%	56 56%	85 49%	66 50%	75 52%
3 and more	37 13%	10 17%	15 13%	9 11%	9 9%	28 16%	19 14%	18 13%
No answer	15 5%	4 7%	6 5%	4 5%	8 8%	7 4%	5 4%	10 7%

D11	Total	Type of shopper			AnyCo customer		Internet purchasers	
		Convenience	Organized	Both	High	Low	High	Low
Total	300	67	123	93	111	189	140	160
Less than $25,000	5 2%	-	3 2%	1 1%	2 2%	3 2%	2 1%	3 2%
$25,000 - $34,999	19 6%	5 7%	6 5%	5 5%	4 4%	15 8%	7 5%	12 8%
$35,000 - $49,999	39 13%	9 13%	13 16%	8 9%	16 14%	23 12%	23 16%	16 10%
$50,000 - $74,999	83 28%	20 30%	31 25%	28 30%	34 31%	49 26%	39 28%	44 28%
$75,000 - $99,999	61 28%	12 18%	30 24%	17 18%	23 21%	38 20%	24 17%	37 23%
$100,-149,000	25 8%	10 15%	7 6%	8 9%	7 6%	18 10%	15 11%	10 6%
$150,000 and more	18 6%	3 4%	6 5%	9 10%	3 3%	15 8%	9 6%	9 6%
No answer	50 17%	8 12%	24 20%	17 18%	22 20%	28 15%	21 15%	29 18%

D11	Total	Age			
		18 - 34	35 - 44	45 - 54	55+
Total	300	63	91	85	56
Less than $25,000	5 2%	1 2%	-	2 2%	2 4%
$25,000 - $34,999	19 6%	6 10%	9 10%	1 1%	3 5%
$35,000 - $49,999	39 13%	13 21%	5 5%	11 13%	10 18%
$50,000 - $74,999	83 28%	18 29%	27 30%	27 32%	11 20%
$75,000 - $99,999	61 28%	11 17%	26 20%	6 11%	-
$100,-149,000	25 8%	8 13%	7 8%	9 11%	1 2%
$150,000 and more	18 6%	2 3%	6 7%	5 6%	5 9%
No answer	50 17%	4 6%	11 12%	13 15%	18 32%

Appendix 11: Hobbies

D10	Total	AnyCo customer		Online purchaser	
		Yes	No	Yes	No
Total	300	111	189	140	160
Outdoor sports	153 51%	55 50%	98 52%	73 52%	80 50%
Reading	117 39%	37 33%	80 42%	50 36%	67 42%
Outdoor recreation	113 38%	39 35%	74 39%	47 34%	66 41%
Playing with animals	89 30%	39 35%	50 26%	56 40%	33 21%
Music	559 20%	19 17%	40 21%	29 21%	30 19%
Do it yourself projects	56 19%	21 19%	35 19%	27 19%	29 18%
Gardening	52 17%	24 22%	28 15%	24 17%	28 18%
Indoor team sports	43 14%	21 19%	22 12%	24 17%	19 12%
Travel	36 12%	9 8%	27 14%	17 12%	19 12%
Needlecraft, sewing	33 11%	15 14%	18 10%	12 9%	21 13%
Gourmet cooking	25 8%	9 8%	16 8%	15 11%	10 6%
Exercise	21 7%	4 4%	17 9%	11 8%	10 6%
Going to the movies	21 7%	5 5%	16 8%	6 4%	15 9%
Theatre, Arts	14 5%	9 8%	5 3%	8 6%	6 4%
Volunteer work	6 2%	- 	3 2%	2 1%	1 1%
Other	15 5%	8 8%	8 5%	9 6%	7 5%
No answer	24 8%	7 6%	17 9%	9 6%	15 9%

Appendix 12: Frequency of Shopping

Q2A	Total	Type of shopper			Monthly food bill		
		Convenience	Organized	Both	< $250	$251-$500	> $500
Total	300	67	123	93	120	145	35
Once	15	2	7	6	6	7	2
	5%	3%	6%	6%	5%	5%	6%
Twice	26	3	14	5	13	12	1
	9%	4%	11%	5%	11%	8%	3%
3 - 5 times	116	21	57	27	48	58	10
	39%	31%	46%	29%	40%	40%	29%
6 - 8 times	70	17	26	26	30	32	8
	23%	25%	21%	28%	25%	22%	23%
8 times +	73	24	19	29	23	36	14
	24%	36%	15%	31%	19%	25%	40%

Q2A	Total	Age				Annual household income			
		18-34	35-44	45-54	55+	$25 - 49K	$50 - 74K	$75 - $99K	$100K +
Total	300	63	91	85	56	58	83	61	43
Once	15	4	5	3	3	4	-	6	3
	5%	6%	5%	4%	5%	7%		10%	7%
Twice	26	11	8	2	4	6	9	3	4
	9%	17%	9%	2%	7%	10%	11%	5%	9%
3 - 5 times	116	26	38	35	16	28	25	24	15
	39%	41%	42%	41%	29%	48%	30%	39%	35%
6 - 8 times	70	14	18	22	14	13	23	13	7
	23%	22%	20%	26%	25%	22%	28%	21%	16%
8 times +	73	8	22	23	19	7	26	15	14
	24%	13%	24%	27%	34%	12%	31%	25%	33%

Appendix 13: Type of Shopper

Q2B	Total	Monthly Food bill			AnyCo customer -		Annual household income			
		< $250	$251 - $500	> $500	Yes	No	$25 - 49K	$50 - 74K	$75 - $99K	$100K +
Total	300	120	145	35	111	189	58	83	61	43
Convenience	67	30	33	4	31	36	14	20	12	13
	22%	25%	23%	11%	28%	19%	24%	24%	20%	30%
Organized	123	43	66	14	36	87	22	31	30	13
	41%	36%	46%	40%	32%	46%	38%	37%	49%	30%
Neither	17	7	8	2	6	11	9	4	2	-
	6%	6%	6%	6%	5%	6%	16%	5%	3%	
Both	93	40	38	15	38	55	13	28	17	17
	31%	33%	26%	43%	34%	29%	22%	34%	28%	40%

Appendix 14: Food Expenditure

Q2C	Total	Annual household income				AnyCo customer		Average number of per household	
		$25 - 49K	$50 - 74K	$75 - $99K	$100K +	Yes	No	Individuals	Children
Total	300	58	83	61	43	111	189		
Less than $100	16	2	4	3	1	7	9	2.2	1.5
	5%	3%	5%	5%	2%	6%	5%		
$100 - $250	104	24	28	20	14	44	60	2.5	1.5
	35%	41%	34%	33%	33%	40%	32%		
$251 - $500	145	27	43	27	23	53	92	3.3	1.9
	48%	47%	52%	44%	53%	48%	49%		
$501 - $750	30	5	8	8	4	7	23	4.0	2.6
	10%	9%	10%	13%	9%	6%	12%		
$751 - $1,001	4	-	-	3	1	-	4	4.4	2.4
	1%			5%	2%		2%		
More than $1,000	1	-	-	-	-	-	1		
	1%						1%		

Appendix 15: Food Shopping Locations

Q4	Total	Type of Shopper			Monthly Food Bill			Online Purchaser	
		Convenience	Organized	Both	< $250	$251 - $500	> $501	Yes	No
Total	300	67	123	93	120	145	35	140	160
Safeway	127 42%	23 34%	61 50%	34 37%	51 43%	64 44%	12 34%	58 41%	69 43%
AnyCo	122 41%	29 43%	49 40%	38 41%	53 44%	61 42%	8 23%	49 35%	73 46%
Albertons's	105 35%	25 37%	41 33%	34 37%	35 29%	57 39%	13 37%	49 35%	56 35%
Thriftway	82 27%	22 33%	33 27%	23 25%	34 28%	39 27%	9 26%	40 29%	42 26%
Cub Foods/ Winco Foods	68 23%	9 13%	38 31%	17 18%	24 20%	31 21%	13 37%	30 21%	38 24%
Costco	44 15%	7 10%	25 20%	12 13%	8 7%	23 16%	13 37%	23 16%	21 13%
Zupan's	28 9%	8 12%	6 5%	11 12%	8 7%	15 10%	5 14%	15 11%	13 8%
Nature's	20 7%	2 3%	8 7%	9 10%	4 3%	14 10%	2 6%	8 6%	12 8%
Trader Joe's	12 4%	2 3%	4 3%	6 6%	2 2%	8 6%	2 6%	3 2%	9 6%
Howard's	11 4%	2 3%	3 2%	6 6%	4 3%	5 3%	2 6%	6 4%	5 3%
Others[4]	55 19%	12 17%	18 15%	24 26%	23 19%	28 19%	4 11%	28 25%	27 14%

Q4	Total	Comfort level with being tracked by retailers		Annual household income			
		High	Low	$25 - 49K	$50 - 74K	$75 - $99K	$100K +
Total	300	78	164	58	83	61	43
Safeway	127 42%	28 36%	73 45%	25 43%	34 41%	25 41%	20 47%
AnyCo	122 41%	35 45%	65 40%	19 33%	37 45%	24 39%	13 30%
Albertons's	105 35%	29 37%	50 30%	17 29%	31 37%	20 33%	17 40%
Thriftway	82 27%	24 31%	43 26%	11 19%	23 28%	20 33%	17 40%
Cub Foods/ Winco Foods	68 23%	18 23%	35 21%	16 28%	24 29%	12 20%	7 16%
Costco	44 15%	10 13%	23 14%	5 9%	10 12%	8 13%	10 23%
Zupan's	28 9%	8 10%	15 9%	7 12%	6 7%	4 7%	6 14%
Nature's	20 7%	2 3%	15 9%	3 5%	6 7%	4 7%	5 12%
Trader Joe's	12 4%	2 3%	7 4%	1 2%	4 5%	2 3%	2 5%
Howard's	11 4%	1 1%	9 5%	1 2%	2 2%	1 2%	2 5%
Others	55 19%	23 29%	26 18%	10 17%	16 19%	9 15%	9 21%

---

[4] Others in % from Total are: Waremart (3%), Kienow's (3%), Wizer's (2%), Hagens (2%), Food Front (2%), Food-4-Less (1%), Selected Markets (1%), IGA (1%), Other (5%).

166

Appendix 16: Non-Food Shopping Locations

Q5	Total	Type of Shopper			Monthly Food Bill			Online Purchaser	
		Convenience	Organized	Both	< $250	$251 - $500	> $501	Yes	No
Total	300	67	123	93	120	145	35	140	160
AnyCo	107 36%	30 45%	37 30%	34 37%	44 37%	53 37%	10 29%	56 40%	51 32%
Meier & Frank	76 25%	15 22%	36 29%	19 20%	35 29%	33 23%	8 23%	35 25%	41 26%
Target	64 21%	10 15%	31 25%	21 23%	21 18%	35 24%	8 23%	36 26%	28 18%
Costo	58 19%	16 24%	24 20%	17 18%	15 13%	31 21%	12 34%	29 21%	29 18%
Nordstrom	48 16%	10 15%	15 12%	21 23%	21 18%	23 16%	4 11%	16 11%	32 20%
JCPenny	17 6%	3 4%	7 6%	4 4%	5 4%	9 6%	3 9%	11 8%	6 4%
Rite Aid/ Payless	16 6%	3 4%	9 7%	3 3%	10 8%	6 4%	1 3%	13 9%	4 3%
G/I.Joe's	13 4%	2 3%	3 4%	6 6%	6 5%	3 2%	4 11%	7 5%	6 4%
Home Depot	11 4%	2 3%	3 2%	5 5%	5 4%	5 3%	1 3%	2 1%	9 6%
Bi-Mart	10 3%	1 1%	5 4%	4 4%	3 3%	6 4%	1 3%	4 3%	6 4%
Kmart	10 3%	2 3%	4 3%	2 2%	4 3%	6 4%	-	5 4%	5 3%
Sears	10 3%	2 3%	3 2%	5 5%	7 6%	3 2%	-	3 2%	7 4%
Other[5]	64 21%	15 22%	27 22%	20 22%	24 20%	35 24%	7 20%	34 24%	31 19%
Don't know	61 20%	10 15%	30 24%	18 19%	27 23%	24 17%	10 29%	28 18%	36 23%

Appendix 17: Enjoyment of Food Shopping

Q3	Total	Type of Shopper			AnyCo Shopper		Online Purchaser	
		Convenience	Organized	Both	Yes	No	Yes	No
Total	300	67	123	93	111	189	140	160
All the time	15 5%	3 4%	5 4%	6 6%	5 5%	10 5%	8 6%	7 4%
Most of the time	72 24%	13 19%	37 30%	22 24%	26 23%	46 24%	35 25%	37 23%
Sometimes	116 39%	29 43%	42 34%	37 40%	47 42%	69 37%	54 39%	62 39%
Never	96 32%	22 33%	39 32%	28 30%	32 29%	64 34%	43 31%	53 33%
Don't know	1 %	-	-	-	-	-	-	1 1%

---

[5]   Others in % from Total are: Order by catalog (3%), Wal-Mart (2%), Mervyn's (1%), Home Base (1%), Winco/Cub Foods (1%), Washington Square Mall (1%), Gap (1%), Montgomery Ward (1%), Office Depot (1%), Eddie Bauer (1%), REI (1%), Ann Taylor (1%), Staples (1%), Officemax (1%), Eporium (1%), Order by Internet (1%), Other (7%).

Appendix 18: Comfort Level with Retailers Tracking Activities

Q22	Total	Age				Annual household income			
		18 - 34	35 - 44	45 - 54	55 +	$25 - $49K	$50 - $74K	$75 - $99K	$100K +
Total	300	63	91	85	56	58	83	61	43
Very comfortable	35 12%	10 16%	17 19%	4 5%	4 7%	9 16%	14 17%	5 8%	6 14%
Somewhat comfortable	43 14%	11 17%	11 12%	10 12%	10 18%	8 14%	11 13%	9 15%	8 19%
Neither Nor	53 18%	11 17%	15 16%	13 15%	13 23%	11 19%	12 14%	10 16%	9 21%
Somewhat uncomfortable	57 19%	13 21%	19 21%	19 22%	5 9%	7 12%	20 24%	13 21%	11 26%
Not at all comfortable	107 36%	17 27%	27 30%	37 44%	24 43%	21 36%	25 30%	22 36%	9 21%
Average	2.5	2.7	2.7	2.1	2.4	2.6	2.6	2.4	2.8
STD DEV	1.4	1.4	1.5	1.2	1.4	1.5	1.5	1.3	1.4
Don't know	5 2%	1 2%	2 2%	2 2%	-	2 3%	1 1%	2 3%	%%	-

Appendix 19: Internet Usage

Q1	Total	Internet access		Age				Annual household income			
		Work	Home	18 - 34	35 - 44	45 - 54	55 +	$25 - $49K	50 - $74K	$75 - $99K	$100K +
Total	300	127	270	63	91	85	56	58	83	61	43
Home	270	100	270	56	81	78	50	55	76	56	35
	90%	79	100%	89%	89%	92%	89%	95%	92%	92%	81%
Work	127	127	100	35	39	34	16	18	39	23	25
	42%	100	37%	56%	43%	40%	29%	31%	47%	38%	58%
School	4	1	4	1	-	2	-	1	1	-	1
	1%	1	1%	2%		2%		2%	1%		2%
Other	7	3	2	4	2	-	1	2	2	1	-
	2%	2	2%	7%	2%		2%	3%	2%	1%	

Q6	Total	Internet access		Online purchaser		Age				Gender	
		Work	Home	Yes	No	18 - 34	35 - 44	45 - 54	55 +	Male	Female
Total	300	127	270	140	160	63	91	85	56	144	156
Less than 3 months	14	4	14	-	14	2	5	2	4	5	9
	5%	3%	5%		9%	3%	5%	2%	7%	3%	6%
3 - 6 months	10	2	9	2	8	3	2	1	4	3	7
	3%	2%	3%	1%	5%	5%	2%	1%	7%	2%	4%
7 - 12 months	17	2	15	4	13	2	5	3	7	7	10
	6%	2%	6%	3%	8%	3%	5%	4%	13%	5%	6%
1 - 2 years	72	27	67	26	46	15	19	23	15	38	34
	24%	21%	25%	19%	29%	24%	21%	27%	27%	26%	22%
2 - 3 years	69	29	58	32	37	12	25	22	8	32	37
	23%	23%	21%	23%	23%	19%	27%	26%	14%	22%	24%
Over 3 years	117	63	107	76	41	29	35	34	17	59	58
	39%	50%	40%	54%	26%	46%	38%	40%	30%	41%	37%

Q7	Total	Internet access		Online purchaser		Comfort with security associated with Internet -		Gender	
		Work	Home	Yes	No	Yes	No	Male	Female
Total	300	127	270	140	160	95	117	144	156
Daily	183	92	170	103	80	81	53	101	82
	61%	72%	63%	74%	50%	85%	45%	70%	53%
4 - 6 times a week	33	14	32	13	20	5	17	20	13
	11%	11%	12%	9%	13%	5%	15%	14%	8%
2 - 3 times a week	39	9	34	10	29	5	21	13	26
	13%	7%	13%	7%	18%	5%	18%	9%	17%
Once a week	17	6	12	5	12	4	8	4	13
	6%	5%	4%	4%	8%	4%	7%	3%	8%
Twice or three times a month	19	2	16	7	12	-	11	4	15
	6%	2%	6%	5%	8%		9%	3%	10%
Once a month or less often	6	3	3	2	4	-	4	1	5
	2%	2%	1%	1%	3%		3%	1%	3%
Don't know	3	1	3	-	3	-	3	1	2
	1%	1%	1%		2%		3%	1%	1%

Appendix 20: Frequent Online Activities

Q8	Total	Internet access		Online purchaser		Age				Gender	
		Work	Home	Yes	No	18 - 34	35 - 44	45 - 54	55 +	Male	Female
Total	300	127	270	140	160	63	91	85	56	144	156
Communicating with others	198 66%	78 61%	188 70%	91 65%	107 67%	36 57%	60 66%	57 67%	41 73%	94 65%	107 67%
Search for product/ service information	121 40%	53 42%	108 40%	47 34%	74 46%	24 38%	42 46%	33 39%	20 36%	61 42%	60 38%
Education related research	81 27%	28 22%	75 28%	43 31%	38 24%	14 22%	28 31%	25 29%	12 21%	37 26%	44 28%
News/ daily information/ newsgroup	74 25%	35 28%	65 24%	38 27%	36 23%	20 32%	19 21%	15 18%	19 34%	39 27%	35 22%
Use for work/ business	69 23%	52 41%	55 20%	39 28%	30 19%	19 30%	19 21%	21 25%	8 14%	36 25%	3% 21%
Make purchase of a product/ service	41 14%	17 13%	35 13%	29 21%	12 8%	7 11%	11 12%	12 14%	10 18%	22 15%	19 12%
Access financial information	39 13%	16 13%	35 13%	22 16%	17 11%	4 6%	10 11%	14 16%	11 20%	28 19%	11 7%
Entertainment	35 12%	14 11%	33 12%	13 9%	22 14%	14 22%	10 11%	7 8%	2 4%	13 9%	22 14%
Pass the time	26 9%	8 6%	25 9%	13 9%	13 8%	6 10%	5 5%	8 9%	6 11%	17 7%	16 10%
Games	15 5%	5 4%	15 6%	7 5%	8 5%	1 2%	6 7%	7 8%	1 2%	9 6%	6 4%
Information on travel	10 3%	5 4%	8 3%	6 4%	4 3%	1 2%	5 5%	3 4%	1 2%	3 2%	7 4%
Other	10 3%	5 5%	8 3%	7 6%	3 3%	-	4 4%	5 6%	1 2%	6 4%	4 2%

Appendix 21: Positive Features of a Web Site

Q10	Total	Internet access ----		Online purchaser		Age --				Gender -------------	
		Work	Home	Yes	No	18 - 34	35 - 44	45 - 54	55 +	Male	Female
Total	300	127	270	140	160	63	91	85	56	144	156
Site is simple to get around	111 37%	57 45%	98 36%	66 47%	45 28%	28 44%	42 46%	28 33%	12 21%	50 35%	61 39%
Detailed product information	93 31%	44 35%	83 31%	55 39%	38 24%	21 33%	34 37%	23 27%	11 20%	38 26%	55 35%
Security issue	65 22%	29 23%	61 23%	35 25%	30 19%	13 21%	21 23%	23 27%	7 13%	38 26%	27 17%
Cheaper prices than in physical stores	62% 21%	27 21%	53 20%	31 22%	31 19%	12 19%	22 24%	19 22%	9 16%	33 23%	29 19%
Colorful and interesting site	45 15%	18 14%	43 16%	19 14%	26 16%	14 22%	16 18%	9 11%	5 9%	19 13%	26 17%
Merchandise is simple to locate	34 11%	16 13%	29 11%	17 12%	17 11%	8 13%	10 11%	7 8%	9 16%	14 105	20 13%
Variety/ selection of products	25 8%	17 13%	19 7%	19 14%	6 4%	2 3%	6 7%	11 13%	5 9%	15 10%	10 6%
Quick delivery of products purchased	20 7%	11 9%	16 6%	11 8%	9 6%	5 8%	5 5%	5 6%	5 9%	11 8%	9 6%
Customer service	13 4%	6 5%	12 4%	6 4%	7 4%	4 6%	3 3%	4 5%	2 4%	8 6%	5 3%
History of the company, store locations	13 4%	6 5%	13 5%	7 5%	6 4%	4 6%	5 5%	1 1%	3 5%	7 5%	6 4%
Return policy and guarantees	11 4%	6 5%	7 3%	3 2%	8 5%	2 3%	3 3%	4 5%	2 4%	5 3%	6 4%
Quickness	8 3%	6 5%	8 3%	6 4%	2 1%	3 5%	3 3%	2 2%	-	8 6%	-
Number of payment alternatives	5 2%	3 2%	5 2%	3 2%	2 1%	3 5%	1 1%	-	1 2%	3 2%	2 1%
Suggestions, ideas, recommend., trends	5 2%	4 3%	4 3%	3 2%	2 1%	1 2%	2 2%	-	1 2%	3 2%	2 1%
Reflects the personality of the store	3 1%	3 1%	2 2%	3 2%	-	1 2%	1 1%	1 1%	1 2%	1 1%	2 1%
1-800 telephone number	2 1%	2 1%	-	 21%	-	-	-	2 2%	-	2 1%	-
Other	12 3%	5 3%	12 3%	4 3%	8 5%	2 4%	6 6%	4 4%	3 3%	3 3%	4 6%
Don't know/ no answer	68 23%	18 14%	63 23%	16 11%	37 32%	12 19%	14 15%	21 25%	20 36%	29 20%	39 25%

Appendix 22: Negative Features of a Web Site

Q11	Total	Internet access		Online purchaser		Age				Gender	
		Work	Home	Yes	No	18 - 34	35 - 44	45 - 54	55 +	Male	Female
Total	300	127	270	140	160	63	91	85	56	144	156
It takes too long	136	65	126	72	64	36	48	27	21	70	66
	45%	51%	47%	51%	40%	57%	53%	32%	38%	49%	42%
Web site too complex/chaotic	70	39	60	40	30	13	24	18	13	37	33
	23%	31%	22%	29%	19%	21%	26%	21%	23%	26%	21%
Don't find information I am looking for	67	32	59	44	23	15	22	22	8	35	32
	22%	25%	22%	31%	14%	24%	24%	26%	14%	24%	21%
Ads/ junk mail	57	27	50	33	24	15	14	20	7	29	28
	19%	21%	19%	24%	15%	24%	15%	24%	13%	20%	18%
Can't organize the information I gather	33	18	33	16	17	7	13	8	3	17	16
	11%	14%	12%	11%	11%	11%	14%	9%	5%	12%	10%
Encounter links that do not work	30	12	27	15	15	6	7	11	6	13	17
	10%	9%	10%	11%	9%	10%	8%	13%	11%	9%	11%
Can't find a page I know is out there	26	14	25	11	15	6	8	6	5	10	16
	9%	11%	9%	8%	9%	10%	9%	7%	9%	7%	10%
Lost in cyberspace	19	7	17	5	14	3	8	4	3	13	6
	6%	6%	6%	4%	9%	5%	9%	5%	5%	9%	4%
Security w/ credit card	18	6	17	7	11	3	5	6	4	7	11
	6%	5%	6%	5%	7%	5%	5%	7%	7%	5%	7%
Pictures/ fonts are too small	20	9	18	10	10	6	10	1	6	5	15
	6%	8%	9%	7%	7%	9%	11%	1%	11%	3%	9%
Impersonal / don't like computers	8	3	5	4	4	-	4	1	3	5	3
	3%	2%	2%	3%	3%		3%	1%	5%	3%	2%
Other	11	9	10	4	5	4	5	1	1	5	6
	4%	7%	4%	6%	3%	6%	5%	1%	2%	3%	4%
Don't know	18	2	16	3	15	2	4	7	5	5	13
	6%	2%	6%	2%	9%	3%	4%	8%	9%	3%	8%
None, no other complaints	26	9	25	11	15	5	6	8	7	10	16
	9%	7%	9%	8%	9%	8%	7%	9%	13%	7%	10%

Appendix 23: Characterization of Current Online Purchasers

Q12	Total	Internet Access		Type of shopper			Monthly food bill			AnyCo customer	
		Work	Home	Con-venience	Orga-nized	Both	< $250	$251 - 500	> $500	Yes	No
Total	300	127	270	67	123	93	120	145	35	111	189
Yes	140	69	127	34	56	38	56	69	15	52	88
	47%	54%	47%	51%	46%	41%	47%	48%	43%	47%	47%
No	160	58	143	33	67	55	64	76	20	59	101
	53%	46%	53%	49%	54%	59%	53%	52%	57%	53%	53%

Q12	Total	Annual household income				Age				Gender	
		$25 - $49K	$50 - $74K	$75 - $99K	$100K +	18 - 34	35 - 44	45 - 54	55 +	Male	Female
Total	300	58	83	61	43	63	91	85	56	144	156
Yes	140	30	39	24	24	30	42	46	20	74	66
	47%	52%	47%	39%	56%	48%%	46%	54%	36%	51%	42%
No	160	28	44	37	19	33	49	39	36	70	90
	53%	48%	53%	61%	44%	52%	54%	46%	64%	49%	59%

Q12	Total	Comfort with security associated with Internet		Likeliness to try online food shopping		Comfort with being tracked by retailers	
		High	Low	High	Low	High	Low
Total	300	95	117	108	145	78	164
Yes	140	70	34	52	70	36	73
	47%	74%	29%	48%	48%	46%	45%
No	160	25	83	56	75	42	91
	53%	26%	71%	52%	52%	54%	55%

Appendix 24: Reasons for Online Purchases

Q14	Total	Internet Access		Type of shopper			Monthly food bill			AnyCo customer	
		Work	Home	Convenience	Organized	Both	< $250	$251-500	> $500	Yes	No
Total	140	69	127	34	56	38	56	69	15	52	88
Convenience / shop at home	83 59%	44 64%	75 59%	16 47%	35 63%	25 66%	32 57%	40 58%	11 73%	31 60%	52 59%
Easy access to products	55 39%	34 49%	50 39%	10 29%	25 45%	16 41%	18 32%	28 41%	9 60%	20 38%	35 40%
24 hour access	27 19%	13 19%	25 20%	5 15%	12 21%	6 16%	10 18%	13 19%	4 27%	4 8%	23 26%
Saves time	22 16%	10 14%	22 17%	9 26%	4 7%	8 21%	11 20%	7 10%	4 27%	9 17%	13 15%
Don't like crowds	19 14%	9 13%	18 14%	3 9%	8 14%	5 13%	10 18%	9 13%	-	4 8%	15 17%
Better prices	9 6%	6 9%	7 6%	3 9%	3 3%	3 8%	7 4%	5 7%	-	5 10%	4 5%
Other	12 9%	8 12%	11 9%	2 6%	4 7%	5 13%	5 9%	6 9%	1 7%	5 10%	7 8%
Don't know	12 9%	2 3%	12 9%	5 15%	3 5%	2 5%	4 7%	8 12%	-	5 10%	7 8%

Q14	Total	Annual household income				Age				Gender	
		$25-$49K	$50-$74K	$75-$99K	$100K+	18-34	35-44	45-54	55+	Male	Female
Total	140	30	39	24	24	30	42	46	20	74	66
Convenience / shop at home	83 59%	14 47%	27 69%	18 75%	12 50%	19 63%	26 62%	25 54%	11 55%	42 57%	41 62%
Easy access to products	55 39%	7 23%	18 46%	10 42%	10 42%	11 37%	12 29%	24 52%	8 40%	33 45%	22 33%
24 hour access	27 19%	10 33%	5 13%	4 17%	4 17%	6 20%	7 17%	9 20%	5 25%	16 22%	11 17%
Saves time	22 16%	3 10%	7 18%	4% 17%	7 29%	4 13%	8 19%	8 17%	1 5%	14 19%	8 12%
Don't like crowds	19 14%	6 20%	4 10%	4 17%	2 8%	5 17%	6 14%	6 13%	2 10%	10 14%	9 14%
Better prices	9 6%	1 3%	2 5%	2 8%	3 13%	1 3%	3 7%	3 7%	1 5%	7 9%	2 3%
Other	12 9%	3 10%	5 13%	-	3 13%	2 7%	5 12%	5 11%	-	8 11%	4 6%
Don't know	12 9%	4 13%	1 3%	2 8%	3 13%	4 13%	4 10%	2 4%	2 10%	5 7%	7 11%

Q14	Total	Comfort with security associated with Internet		Likeliness to try online food shopping		Comfort with being tracked by retailers	
		High	Low	High	Low	High	Low
Total	140	70	34	52	70	36	73
Convenience / shop at home	83 59%	45 64%	15 44%	32 62%	36 51%	23 72%	43 59%
Easy access to products	55 39%	31 44%	13 38%	20 38%	27 39%	11 31%	27 37%
24 hour access	27 19%	17 24%	2 6%	12 23%	12 17%	6 17%	16 22%
Saves time	22 16%	15 21%	3 9%	11 21%	8 11%	7 19%	10 14%
Don't like crowds	19 14%	6 9%	3 9%	6 12%	10 14%	6 17%	10 14%
Better prices	9 6%	5 7%	1 3%	7 13%	1 1%	4 11%	2 3%
Other	12 9%	5 7%	3 9%	4 8%	6 9%	3 8%	7 10%
Don't know	12 9%	3 4%	8 24%	2 4%	9 13%	2 6%	6 8%

174

Appendix 25: Reasons for Hesitating

Q16	Total	Internet Access		Type of shopper			Monthly food bill			AnyCo customer	
		Work	Home	Con-venience	Orga-nized	Both	< $250	$251 - 500	> $500	Yes	No
Total	160	58	143	33	67	55	64	76	20	59	101
Don't trust the security issue	92 58%	32 55%	88 62%	21 64%	44 66%	26 47%	39 61%	43 57%	10 50%	30 51%	62 61%
Want to touch, try or pick out the product	39 24%	12 21%	35 24%	8 24%	11 16%	19 35%	14 22%	18 24%	7 35%	14 24%	25 25%
Haven't been on the Internet for very long	35 22%	11 19%	30 21%	5 15%	14 21%	13 24%	17 27%	13 17%	5 25%	10 17%	25 25%
Prefer going to a physical store	17 11%	8 14%	16 11%	-	11 16%	5 9%	5 8%	10 13%	2 10%	6 10%	11 11%
Never thought of Internet shopping	17 11%	8 14%	13 9%	3 9%	4 6%	9 16%	7 11%	5 7%	5 25%	7 12%	10 10%
Didn't find what I was looking for	11 7%	4 7%	11 8%	-	7 10%	4 7%	5 8%	5 7%	1 5%	7 4%	7 7%
No time	10 6%	5 9%	7 5%	2 6%	4 6%	4 7%	6 9%	1 1%	3 15%	5 8%	5 5%
Don't know/ trust the merchant	9 6%	2 3%	8 6%	-	4 6%	5 9%	1 2%	5 7%	3 15%	3 5%	6 6%
Too hard to return/ waiting for products	8 5%	3 5%	8 6%	2 6%	2 3%	3 5%	1 2%	6 8%	1 5%	4 7%	4 4%
Shipping and handling fee too high	7 4%	3 5%	7 5%	1 3%	6 9%	-	-	6 8%	1 5%	4 7%	3 3%
No need/ lack of interest	7 4%	3 5%	6 4%	-	6 9%	-	5 8%	2 3%	-	2 3%	5 5%
Too hard to get around within the site	6 4%	2 3%	6 4%	-	2 3%	4 7%	1 2%	5 7%	-	2 3%	4 4%
Merchandise too expensive	5 3%	4 7%	5 3%	1 3%	1 1%	3 5%	-	4 5%	1 5%	2 3%	3 3%
Other	12 8%	6 10%	12 8%	2 6%	3 4%	6 11%	6 9%	3 3%	2 10%	4 7%	7 7%
Don't know	9 6%	4 7%	4 3%	2 6%	3 4%	2 4%	2 3%	5 7%	-	3 5%	4 4%

Q16	Total	Annual household income				Age				Gender	
		$25 - $49K	$50 - $74K	$75 - $99K	$100K +	18 - 34	35 - 44	45 - 54	55 +	Male	Female
Total	160	28	44	37	19	33	49	39	36	70	90
Don't trust the security issue	92 58%	16 57%	29 66%	18 49%	15 79%	20 61%	27 55%	26 67%	18 50%	46 66%	46 51%
Want to touch, try or pick out the product	39 24%	9 32%	8 18%	15 41%	3 16%	7 21%	16 33%	6 15%	10 28%	13 19%	26 29%
Haven't been on the Internet for very long	35 22%	10 36%	8 18%	6 16%	5 26%	8 24%	5 10%	9 23%	12 33%	14 20%	21 23%
Prefer going to a physical store	17 11%	4 14%	4 9%	4 11%	2 11%	4 12%	3 6%	6 15%	2 6%	9 13%	8 9%
Never thought of Internet shopping	17 11%	2 7%	4 9%	5 14%	2 11%	4 12%	3 6%	5 13%	4 11%	10 14%	7 8%
Didn't find what I was looking for	11 7%	1 4%	3 7%	4 11%	-	2 6%	6 12%	-	3 8%	6 9%	5 6%
No time	10 6%	1 4%	2 5%	5 14%	1 5%	3 9%	6 12%	-	1 3%	1 1%	9 10%
Don't know/ trust the merchant	9 6%	2 7%	3 7%	2 5%	1 5%	1 3%	4 8%	2 5%	2 6%	3 4%	6 7%
Too hard to return/ waiting for products	8 5%	-	2 5%	3 8%	-	2 6%	3 6%	2 5%	1 3%	3 4%	5 6%
Shipping and handling fee too high	7 4%	4 14%	1 2%	2 5%	-	-	3 6%	3 8%	1 3%	4 6%	3 3%

No need/ lack of interest	7 4%	-	-	3 8%	-	1 3%	3 6%	1 3%	2 6%	4 6%	3 3%
Too hard to get around within the site	6 4%	2 7%	1 2%	-	-	2 6%	2 4%	2 5%	-	2 35	4 4%
Merchandise too expensive	5 3%	-	2 5%	2 5%	-	1 3%	3 6%	1 3%	-	2 3%	3 3%
Other	12 8%	2 7%	2 5%	3 8%	1 5%	4 12%	5 10%	1 3%	1 3%	8 12%	4 4%
Don't know	9 6%	1 4%	2 5%	2 5%	1 5%	2 6%	1 2%	2 5%	2 6%	3 4%	4 4%

Q16	Total	Comfort with security associated with Internet --------		Likeliness to try online food shopping -----------		Comfort with being tracked by retailers-	
		High	Low	High	Low	High	Low
Total	160	25	83	56	75	42	91
Don't trust the security issue	92 58%	7 28%	64 77%	30 54%	44 59%	24 57%	53 58%
Want to touch, try or pick out the product	39 24%	2 8%	22 27%	11 20%	23 31%	10 24%	20 22%
Haven't been on the Internet for very long	35 22%	6 24%	15 18%	17 30%	9 17%	8 19%	23 25%
Prefer going to a physical store	17 11%	4 16%	6 7%	4 7%	9 12%	4 10%	11 12%
Never thought of Internet shopping	17 11%	5 20%	3 4%	10 18%	5 7%	2 5%	12 13%
Didn't find what I was looking for	11 7%	2 8%	1 1%	5 9%	2 3%	3 7%	5 5%
No time	10 6%	-	4 5%	3 5%	6 8%	4 10%	2 2%
Don't know/ trust the merchant	9 6%	1 45	6 7%	4 7%	3 4%	4 10%	4 4%
Too hard to return/ waiting for products	8 5%	1 4%	4 5%	3 5%	3 4%	2 5%	4 4%
Shipping and handling fee too high	7 4%	2 8%	2 2%	2 4%	4 5%	-	6 7%
No need/ lack of interest	7 4%	3 12%	1 1%	1 2%	4 5%	2 5%	4 4%
Too hard to get around within the site	6 4%	1 4%	4 5%	1 2%	4 5%	-	6 7%
Merchandise too expensive	5 3%	1 4%	1 1%	4 7%	1 1%	2 5%	2 2%
Other	12 8%	3 12%	4 5%	7 13%	3 4%	3 7%	7 7%
Don't know	9 6%	2 8%	3 4%	2 4%	5 7%	2 5%	3 3%

176

Appendix 26: Potentials for Different Product Categories

Q13	Yes	AnyCo customer		Comfort level with security associated with Internet		Comfort level with retailers tracking		Gender	
		Yes	No	High	Low	High	Low	Male	Female
Total	140	52	88	70	34	36	73	74	66
Jewelry or accessories	6 4%	1 2%	5 6%	5 7%	1 3%	3 8%	2 3%	3 4%	3 5%
Clothing or shoes	30 21%	8 15%	22 25%	19 27%	2 6%	12 33%	10 14%	17 23%	13 20%
Cosmetics, HAB, vitamins, prescriptions	11 8%	6 12%	5 6%	6 9%	2 6%	5 14%	3 4%	6 8%	5 8%
Books, music, computer items	124 89%	46 88%	78 89%	63 90%	27 79%	32 89%	66 90%	68 92%	56 85%
Gardening or floral supplies	11 8%	5 10%	6 7%	8 11%	- 	4 11%	4 5%	7 9%	4 6%
Home goods	30 21%	12 23%	18 20%	22 31%	2 6%	13 36%	8 11%	15 20%	15 23%
Toys or sporting goods	35 25%	17 33%	18 20%	21 30%	4 12%	11 31%	15 21%	21 28%	14 21%
Consumables	13 9%	5 10%	8 9%	12 17%	- 	7 19%	3 4%	7 9%	6 9%

Q13	Yes	Age				Annual household income			
		18 - 34	35 - 44	45 - 54	55 +	$25 -$49K	$50 -$74K	$75 -$99K	$100K+
Total	140	30	42	46	20	30	39	24	24
Jewelry or accessories	6 4%	2 7%	4 10%	- 	- 	2 7%	4 10%	- 	-
Clothing or shoes	30 21%	7 23%	14 33%	8 17%	1 5%	5 17%	12 31%	6 25%	5 21%
Cosmetics, HAB, vitamins, prescriptions	11 8%	2 7%	3 7%	3 7%	3 15%	2 7%	3 8%	1 4%	2 8%
Books, music, computer items	124 89%	28 93%	37 88%	37 80%	20 100%	29 97%	34 87%	19 79%	23 96%
Gardening or floral supplies	11 8%	2 7%	4 10%	4 9%	1 5%	1 3%	4 10%	- 	4 17%
Home goods	30 21%	4 13%	13 31%	9 20%	3 15%	5 17%	8 21%	6 25%	7 29%
Toys or sporting goods	35 25%	11 37%	10 24%	8 17%	4 20%	5 17%	11 28%	6 25%	8 33%
Consumables	13 9%	- 	5 12%	8 17%	- 	2 7%	2 5%	3 13%	5 21%

Question 23: How much would you estimate your household spent in the last 12 months on …   Multiple mention

Q23	Total "Yes" on Q13 A-H or Q13 A-H	Average household spending per category (in U.S. $)	STD DEV
Jewelry or accessories	55	1,214	3,167
Clothing or shoes	125	1,789	2,109
Cosmetics, HAB, vitamins, prescriptions	119	982	1,1811
Books, music, computer items	260	1,272	3,203
Gardening or floral supplies	130	364	411
Home goods	157	1,828	3,111
Toys or sporting goods	176	750	1,039
Consumables	84	4,553	6,285

Appendix 27: Distribution of Future Growth

	# of current online purchaser - will buy this category online again in the future	# of current online purchaser who have previously not bought this category - will buy this category online in the future	# of going-to-be online purchaser - will buy this category online in the future	# of total future purchasers
Jewelry or Accessories	6	33	16	55
Clothing or Shoes	30	45	50	125
Cosmetics, Health & beauty, Vitamins	11	63	45	119
Books, Music, Computer	124	13	123	260
Gardening or Floral Supplies	11	65	54	130
Home Goods	30	65	62	157
Toys or Sporting Goods	35	65	76	176
Consumables	13	44	27	84

Appendix 28: Willingness to Pay for Service

Q19A	Total	Type of shopper			Monthly food bill			Comfort level with online security	
		Convenience	Organized	Both	< $250	$251 - $500	> $500	High	Low
Total	300	67	123	93	120	145	35	95	117
Up to 2%	36	7	13	14	7	20	9	10	14
	12%	10%	11%	15%	6%	14%	26%	11%	12%
2% - 5%	63	12	29	20	28	24	11	17	25
	21%	18%	24%	22%	23%	17%	31%	18%	21%
6% - 10%	47	15	17	11	18	27	2	17	16
	16%	22%	14%	12%	15%	19%	6%	18%	14%
11% - 20%	20	6	9	5	9	9	2	9	6
	7%	9%	7%	5%	8%	6%	6%	9%	5%
More than 20%	17	6	4	7	5	7	5	4	7
	6%	9%	3%	8%	4%	5%	14%	4%	6%
Would not pay anything	102	19	47	28	46	50	6	33	43
	34%	28%	38%	30%	38%	34%	17%	35%	37%
Don't know	15	2	4	8	7	8	-	5	6
	5%	3%	3%	9%	6%	6%		5%	5%

Q19A	Total	Comfort with being tracked by retailers		Age				Annual household income			
		High	Low	18 - 34	35 - 44	45 - 54	55 +	$25 - $49K	$50 - $74K	$75 - $99K	$100K +
Total	300	78	164	63	91	85	56	58	83	61	43
Up to 2%	36	3	24	4	14	12	5	5	8	10	7
	12%	4%	15%	6%	15%	14%	9%	9%	10%	16%	16%
2% - 5%	63	16	31	12	19	20	11	10	22	8	10
	21%	21%	19%	19%	21%	24%	20%	17%	27%	13%	23%
6% - 10%	47	22	20	20	16	8	2	5	15	17	8
	16%	28%	12%	32%	18%	9%	4%	9%	18%	28%	19%
11% - 20%	20	7	9	6	11	1	2	4	4	6	5
	7%	9%	5%	10%	12%	1	4%	7%	5%	10%	12%
More than 20%	17	7	6	5	6	3	2	4	4	1	2
	6%	9%	4%	8%	7%	4%	4%	7%	5%	2%	5%
Would not pay anything	102	18	64	12	22	36	31	26	25	18	10
	34%	23%	39%	19%	24%	42%	55%	45%	30%	30%	23%
Don't know	15	5	10	4	3	5	3	4	5	1	1
	5%	6%	6%	6%	3%	6%	5%	7%	6%	2%	2%

Q19B	Total	Type of shopper			Monthly food bill			Comfort level with online security	
		Convenience	Organized	Both	< $250	$251 - $500	> $500	High	Low
Total	300	67	123	93	120	145	35	95	117
Up to 2%	62 21%	14 21%	24 20%	20 22%	21 18%	29 20%	12 34%	18 19%	25 21%
2% - 5%	65 22%	18 27%	27 22%	17 18%	32 27%	25 17%	8 23%	23 24%	22 19%
6% - 10%	14 5%	2 3%	5 4%	6 6%	4 3%	8 6%	2 6%	5 5%	4 3%
11% - 20%	17 6%	3 4%	9 7%	5 5%	4 3%	11 8%	2 6%	3 3%	7 6%
More than 20%	11 4%	6 9%	1 1%	4 4%	4 3%	5 3%	2 6%	3 3%	4 3%
Would not pay anything	113 38%	21 31%	50 41%	34 37%	50 42%	57 39%	6 17%	37 39%	48 41%
Don't know	18 6%	3 4%	7 6%	7 8%	5 4%	10 7%	3 9%	6 6%	7 6%

Q19B	Total	Comfort with being tracked by retailers		Age				Annual household income			
		High	Low	18 - 34	35 - 44	45 - 54	55 +	$25 - $49K	$50 - $74K	$75 - $99K	$100K +
Total	300	78	164	63	91	85	56	58	83	61	43
Up to 2%	62 21%	11 14%	36 22%	13 21%	19 21%	21 25%	9 16%	11 19%	22 27%	11 18%	11 26%
2% - 5%	65 22%	28 36%	26 16%	22 35%	20 22%	14 16%	7 13%	11 19%	19 23%	16 26%	9 21%
6% - 10%	14 5%	5 6%	6 4%	5 8%	6 7%	2 2%	1 2%	-	4 5%	4 7%	4 9%
11% - 20%	17 6%	4 5%	11 7%	2 3%	10 11%	3 4%	1 2%	3 5%	3 4%	6 10%	4 9%
More than 20%	11 4%	5 6%	4 2%	4 6%	3 3%	2 2%	1 2%	3 5%	2 2%	-	-
Would not pay anything	113 38%	19 24%	71 43%	14 22%	29 32%	36 42%	33 59%	25 43%	26 31%	23 38%	12 28%
Don't know	18 6%	6 8%	10 6%	3 5%	4 4%	7 8%	4 7%	5 9%	7 8%	1 2%	3 7%

Appendix 29: Willingness to Try Service

Q20		Type of shopper			Monthly food bill			AnyCo customer		Comfort with Internet security	
		Con-venience	Orga-nized	Both	< $250	$251 - $500	> $500	Yes	No		
Total	300	67	123	93	120	145	35	111	189	95	117
Very likely	42	12	15	13	17	15	10	13	29	22	7
	14%	18%	12%	14%	14%	10%	29%	12%	15%	23%	6%
Somewhat likely	66	15	27	22	20	38	8	25	41	21	24
	22%	22%	22%	24%	17%	26%	23%	23%	22%	22%	21%
Neither likely nor unlikely	45	7	20	17	24	17	4	19	26	16	16
	15%	10%	16%	18%	20%	12%	11%	17%	14%	17%	14%
Somewhat unlikely	44	12	15	13	16	23	5	11	33	9	22
	15%	18%	12%	14%	13%	16%	14%	10%	17%	9%	19%
Not at all likely	101	21	45	27	42	51	8	42	59	27	47
	34%	31%	37%	29%	35%	35%	23%	38%	31%	28%	40%
Average	2.7	2.8	2.6	2.8	2.6	2.6	3.2	2.6	2.7	3.0	2.3
STD DEV	1.5	1.5	1.5	1.4	1.5	1.5	1.6	1.5	1.5	1.6	1.3

Q20	Total	Comfort with being tracked by retailers		Age				Annual household income			
		High	Low	18 - 34	35 - 44	45 - 54	55 +	$25 - $49K	$50 - $74K	$75 - $99K	$100K +
Total	300	78	164	63	91	85	56	58	83	61	43
Very likely	42	19	16	11	16	12	2	4	10	5	14
	14%	24%	10%	17%	18%	14%	4%	7%	12%	8%	33%
Somewhat likely	66	28	23	16	21	15	11	13	22	14	10
	22%	36%	14%	25%	23%	18%	20%	22%	27%	23%	23%
Neither likely nor unlikely	45	11	24	13	14	8	9	9	13	9	5
	15%	14%	15%	21%	15%	9%	16%	16%	16%	15%	12%
Somewhat unlikely	44	6	31	11	12	14	7	9	12	7	6
	15%	8%	19%	17%	13%	16%	13%	16%	14%	11%	14%
Not at all likely	101	14	68	12	27	35	27	23	25	25	8
	34%	18%	41%	19%	30%	41%	48%	40%	30%	41%	19%
Average	2.7	3.4	2.3	3.0	2.9	2.5	2.2	2.4	2.8	2.5	3.4
STD DEV	1.5	1.4	1.4	1.4	1.5	1.5	1.3	1.4	1.4	1.4	1.5

Appendix 30: Comfort Level with Security

Question 17: How comfortable are you with the current level of security associated with Internet purchases? Please rank your comfort level from 1 to 5, with 1 being not at all comfortable to 5 being very comfortable.   Total of 300

Q17		AnyCo customer ----------		Internet purchaser --------		Comfort level with being tracked by retailer ----------		Gender ---------------------	
		Yes	No	Yes	No	High	Low	Male	Female
Total	300	111	189	140	160	78	164	144	156
Very comfortable	35 / 12%	13 / 12%	22 / 12%	29 / 21%	6 / 4%	13 / 17%	12 / 7%	23 / 16%	12 / 8%
Somewhat comfortable	60 / 20%	26 / 23%	34 / 18%	41 / 29%	19 / 12%	20 / 26%	28 / 17%	34 / 24%	26 / 17%
Neither nor	78 / 26%	26 / 23%	52 / 28%	35 / 25%	43 / 27%	22 / 28%	45 / 27%	35 / 24%	43 / 28%
Somewhat uncomfortable	46 / 15%	21 / 19%	25 / 13%	19 / 14%	27 / 17%	11 / 14%	23 / 14%	17 / 12%	29 / 19%
Not at all comfortable	71 / 24%	21 / 19%	50 / 26%	15 / 11%	56 / 35%	11 / 14%	49 / 30%	33 / 23%	38 / 24%
Average	2.7	2.9	2.7	3.4	2.3	3.2	2.6	3.0	2.6
STD DEV	1.3	1.3	1.4	1.3	1.2	1.3	1.3	1.4	1.3
Don't know	10 / 3%	4 / 4%	6 / 3%	1 / 1%	9 / 6%	1 / 1%	7 / 4%	2 / 1%	8 / 5%

Q17	Total	Age ---				Annual household income -------------------------------------			
		18 - 34	35 - 44	45 - 54	55+	$25 - $49K	$50 - $74K	$75 - $99K	$100K
Total	300	63	91	85	56	58	83	61	43
Very comfortable	35 / 12%	6 / 10%	9 / 10%	14 / 16%	5 / 9%	7 / 12%	7 / 8%	5 / 8%	9 / 21%
Somewhat comfortable	60 / 20%	13 / 21%	17 / 19%	20 / 24%	8 / 14%	15 / 26%	19 / 23%	9 / 15%	6 / 14%
Neither nor	78 / 26%	25 / 40%	26 / 29%	10 / 12%	16 / 29%	15 / 26%	23 / 28%	13 / 21%	12 / 28%
Somewhat uncomfortable	46 / 15%	8 / 13%	14 / 15%	16 / 19%	7 / 13%	9 / 16%	10 / 12%	14 / 23%	5 / 12%
Not at all comfortable	71 / 24%	9 / 14%	23 / 25%	23 / 27%	16 / 29%	11 / 19%	19 / 23%	19 / 31%	10 / 23%
Average	2.7	3.0	2.7	2.8	2.6	3.0	2.8	2.5	3.0
STD DEV	1.3	1.2	1.3	1.5	1.3	1.3	1.3	1.3	1.5
Don't know	10 / 3%	2 / 3%	2 / 2%	2 / 2%	4 / 7%	1 / 2%	5 / 6%	1 / 2%	1 / 2%

182

Appendix 31: If Security was not an Issue

Q18A	Total	Comfort level with being tracked by retailers		Age				Annual household income			
		High	Low	18 - 34	35 - 44	45 - 54	55+	$25 - $49K	$50 - $74k	$75 - $99k	$100k
Total	160	42	91	33	49	39	36	28		37	19
Very likely	38	12	22	9	13	8	8	8	6	11	5
	24%	29%	24%	27%	27%	21%	22%	29%	14%	30%	26%
Somewhat likely	44	13	23	12	11	15	5	9	16	9	6
	28%	31%	25%	36%	22%	38%	14%	32%	36%	24%	32%
Neither nor	40	11	19	7	13	8	11	7	14	5	3
	25%	26%	21%	21%	27%	21%	31%	25%	32%	14%	16%
Somewhat unlikely	13	3	9	1	5	3	4	2	3	3	2
	8%	7%	10%	3%	10%	8%	11%	7%	7%	8%	11%
Not at all likely	19	2	13	4	7	2	6	2	4	7	3
	12%	5%	14%	12%	14%	5%	17%	7%	9%	19%	16%
Average	3.4	3.7	3.4	3.6	3.4	3.7	3.1	3.7	3.4	3.4	3.4
STD DEV	1.3	1.1	1.6	1.3	1.4	1.1	1.4	1.2	1.1	1.5	1.4
Don't know	6	1	5	-	-	3	2	1	1	2	-
	4%	2%	5%			8%	6%	2%	2%	5%	

Q18B	Total	Comfort level with being tracked by retailers		Age				Annual household income			
		High	Low	18 - 34	35 - 44	45 - 54	55+	$25 - $49K	$50 - $74k	$75 - $99k	$100k
Total	140	36	73	30	42	46	20	30	39	24	24
Very likely	35	13	14	8	16	8	2	2	9	11	10
	25%	36%	19%	27%	38%	17%	10%	7%	23%	46%	42%
Somewhat likely	34	7	22	5	11	13	5	7	11	9	3
	24%	19%	30%	17%	26%	28%	25%	23%	28%	38%	13%
Neither nor	38	11	15	12	9	10	7	10	15	2	6
	27%	31%	21%	40%	21%	22%	35%	33%	38%	8%	25%
Somewhat unlikely	8	1	6	2	2	4	-	3	2	-	1
	6%	3%	8%	7%	5%	9%		10%	5%		4%
Not at all likely	12	1	10	1	2	6	3	3	2	-	2
	9%	3%	14%	3%	5%	13%	15%	10%	5%		8%
Average	3.6	3.9	3.4	3.6	3.9	3.3	3.2	3.1	3.6	4.4	3.8
STD DEV	1.2	1.1	1.3	1.1	1.1	1.3	1.2	1.1	1.1	0.7	1.3
Don't know	13	3	6	2	2	5	3	5	-	2	2
	9%	8%	8%	7%	5%	11%	15%	17%		8%	8%

Appendix 32: Attitude toward Online Purchasing

Q9A	Total	Internet access		Internet purchaser		Comfort level with Internet security		Likeliness to try online food shopping		Comfort level with being tracked by retailers	
		Work	Home	Yes	No	High	Low	High	Low	High	Low
Total	300	127	270	140	160	95	117	108	145	78	164
Strongly agree	9	4	9	9	-	8	-	6	3	3	2
	3%	3%	3%	6%		8%		6%	2%	4%	1%
Agree	49	23	43	39	10	26	9	20	21	13	27
	16%	18%	16%	28%	6%	27%	8%	19%	14%	17%	16%
Neither nor	154	70	140	56	98	41	66	54	75	46	78
	51%	55%	52%	40%	61%	43%	56%	50%	52%	59%	48%
Disagree	55	21	51	26	29	16	26	21	25	8	37
	18%	17%	19%	19%	18%	17%	22%	19%	17%	10%	23%
Strongly disagree	33	9	27	10	23	4	16	7	21	8	20
	11%	7%	10%	7%	14%	4%	14%	6%	14%	10%	12%
Average	2.8	2.9	2.8	3	2.6	3.2	2.6	3.0	2.7	2.9	2.7
STD DEV	0.9	0.9	0.9	1.0	0.8	1.0	0.8	0.9	1.0	0.9	0.9

Q9B	Total	Internet access		Internet purchaser		Comfort level with Internet security		Likeliness to try online food shopping		Comfort level with being tracked by retailers	
		Work	Home	Yes	No	High	Low	High	Low	High	Low
Total	300	127	270	140	160	95	117	108	145	78	164
Strongly agree	21	10	20	15	6	12	5	10	8	7	5
	7%	8%	7%	11%	4%	13%	4%	9%	6%	9%	3%
Agree	40	15	37	24	16	17	12	16	20	9	20
	13%	12%	14%	17%	10%	18%	10%	15%	14%	12%	12%
Neither nor	142	69	125	56	86	36	60	49	68	43	74
	47%	54%	46%	40%	54%	38%	51%	45%	47%	55%	45%
Disagree	60	25	55	33	27	20	22	23	27	11	40
	20%	20%	20%	24%	17%	21%	19%	21%	19%	14%	24%
Strongly disagree	37	8	33	12	25	10	18	10	22	8	25
	12%	6%	12%	9%	16%	11%	15%	9%	15%	10%	15%
Average	2.8	3.0	2.8	3.0	2.7	3.0	2.7	2.9	2.8	2.9	2.6
STD DEV	1.0	0.9	1.1	1.1	1.0	1.2	1.0	1.1	1.0	1.0	1.0

Q9C	Total	Internet access		Internet purchaser		Comfort level with Internet security		Likeliness to try online food shopping		Comfort level with being tracked by retailers	
		Work	Home	Yes	No	High	Low	High	Low	High	Low
Total	300	127	270	140	160	95	117	108	145	78	164
Strongly agree	82	37	71	56	26	40	17	36	33	23	38
	27%	29%	26%	40%	16%	42%	15%	33%	23%	29%	23%
Agree	67	31	62	37	30	21	28	29	29	18	61
	22%	24%	23%	26%	19%	22%	24%	27%	20%	23%	23%
Neither nor	98	37	91	27	71	19	48	26	50	25	61
	33%	29%	34%	19%	44%	20%	41%	24%	34%	32%	37%
Disagree	26	13	23	13	13	6	12	8	17	3	15
	9%	10%	9%	9%	8%	6%	10%	7%	12%	4%	9%
Strongly disagree	27	9	23	7	20	9	12	9	16	9	13
	9%	7%	9%	5%	13%	9%	10%	8%	11%	12%	8%
Average	3.5	3.6	3.5	3.9	3.2	3.8	3.2	3.7	3.3	3.6	3.4
STD DEV	1.2	1.2	1.2	1.2	1.2	1.3	1.1	1.2	1.3	1.3	1.2

Q9D	Total	Internet access		Internet purchaser		Comfort level with Internet security		Likeliness to try online food shopping		Comfort level with being tracked by retailers	
		Work	Home	Yes	No	High	Low	High	Low	High	Low
Total	300	127	270	140	160	95	117	108	145	78	164
Strongly agree	41	20	38	32	9	28	6	25	11	17	13
	14%	16%	14%	23%	6%	29%	5%	23%	8%	22%	8%
Agree	67	32	62	37	30	25	21	27	29	14	38
	22%	25%	23%	26%	19%	26%	18%	25%	20%	18%	23%
Neither nor	83	43	72	31	52	18	33	28	42	17	49
	28%	34%	27%	22%	33%	19%	28%	26%	29%	22%	30%
Disagree	45	14	43	18	27	9	20	13	24	16	25
	15%	11%	16%	13%	17%	9%	17%	12%	17%	21%	15%
Strongly disagree	64	18	55	22	42	15	37	15	39	14	39
	21%	14%	20%	16%	26%	16%	32%	14%	27%	18%	24%
Average	2.9	3.2	2.9	3.3	2.6	3.4	2.5	3.3	2.6	3.1	2.8
STD DEV	1.3	1.2	1.3	1.4	1.2	1.4	1.2	1.3	1.3	1.4	1.3

Appendix to Section IV: Entrance to the Electronic Commerce World

Appendix 33: Wal-Mart.com as External Benchmark

Wal Mart Inc. (WM), a $104 billion revenue creating retailer, was the first discount store chain to jump into the rapidly evolving online market, announcing an agreement with Microsoft to begin a business-to-consumer electronic commerce Web site, which was launched in July 1996.[6] Numbers of the venture are rare to find. The company's president and CEO David Glass, stated that the Internet venture eventually would represent "a significant portion" of the company's revenues, while an industry expert recently estimated online sales to be less than 5% of total revenues.[7]

Challenges

Different Rules. WM discovered that the rules of the game of online retailing and the environment in which it is played are far different online than in the physical world. The average household income of online customers is about $15,000 above the average income range of Wal-Mart store customers. This distinctive difference in demographics of present online purchasers and the WM clientele has turned out to be one of the largest challenges the company has been facing in the past. Such seems to raise the following questions: Should the company's merchandising staff seek out new vendors to better service the needs of online customers, and if so, what would be the risk to traditional vendor relationships in case new brands were added online? Conversely, it can be argued if the online traffic and sales could or would continue to grow without the addition of such brands? Also new for WM is a serious competition from niche operators finding themselves able to compete much more effectively against traditional retail Goliath's online than offline.[8]

Advertising. Additionally, the retail giant had to discover that as strong as its store network and off-line advertising campaigns are, building site traffic requires extensive online marketing and promotions, actions that WM has obviously been reluctant to take in the past. Until now, it has done almost nothing to promote its Web site, neither within stores or in its advertising efforts, only on the site itself.[9]

Strategic Goals

Objectives. Phil Martz, the director of Wal-Mart online, defined the venture's objective to offer the concept of one-stop shopping and offer everything, in order to accommodate, help and service more customers than they have in the past, by simultaneously providing low prices, great merchandise and superior convenience. In other words, becoming a dominant player in key Web merchandising categories, using the Internet in a complimentary way by offering Internet-only specials to the Web audience as well as "traditional" products to be reflective of its brick-and-mortar store assortments and to serve a wider customer base.[10]

Strategy to Get There. The company's goal is to reach a class of customers, who may not shop at a brick-and-mortar Wal-Mart store. Also, the hope that Wal-Mart's successful brand can be leveraged to new categories on the Web, such as custom-made computers, fresh meat and

---

[6] Scally 1998, p. 8 and Smith 1996, p. 24.
[7] Kuchinskas 1998, p. IQ 12 and Rubinstein 1997, p. 66.
[8] Bivens 1998, p. 122 and Rubinstein 1997, p. 68.
[9] Bivens 1998, p. 122 and Scally 1998, p. 8.
[10] Machlis 1998b, p. C1.

seafood can be acknowledged. Nevertheless, the decision-makers expressed no intention to replace the experience of going to the real store, but rather to enhance this. One very important goal for the company seems to move the customer even more in to the center of attention by seeking closer contacts with them and obtaining more feedback from them. Here, WM understands Internet retailing as an opportunity to "let the customer tell [the company] what they are after."[11] Additionally, WM seeks to also use the Web site as a marketing test pad for the chain's brick-and mortar stores. [12] This is an interesting approach, since it aims to work backwards applying the knowledge and experience gained on the Web to the brick-and-mortar stores. It becomes apparent that the decision-makers at WM do not view Web site and physical stores as separate entities, instead they search for synergies and opportunities to complement one another.

Tentative Future Undertakings. Currently, also under observation, it seems there is an alternative to the conventional way of online purchasing, namely offering customers over the Wal-mart.com site a service informing them whether the particular item of interest is in stock at a given store. If so, this item could then be ordered online and be picked up at this particular store.[13] Such undertaking appears innovative, however, since WM has a similar technique already in place for the business side, it should not be very difficult to also implement it for the customer side of their operations.

Mix of Online Merchandise

Traditional Merchandise. Wal-Mart went online quietly making sure everything worked, when it initially started the venture in 1996 with 1,550 stock-keeping units (SKUs) in six categories. By the end of 1996, the company sold about 2,500 SKUs and six months later, it expanded its online merchandise to 40,000 SKUs, representing 21 categories. By the end of 1998, it offered more than 500,000 SKUs on its site (including 20,000 items of computer-related products, 30,000 videos, and 7,000 music titles) and intended to eventually offer up to 3 million SKUs in the future. This reflects the company's decision to roll out a growing variety of items expanding the depth and breadth of merchandise offered, while more and more customers discover the Web as a purchasing tool. Compared to other online retailers, WM's current Web site is among those with the most complete merchandise in the "mainstream retail" categories, including home improvement and toys.[14] Particularly interesting is taking a look at company's efforts to sell books online, since this episode illustrates that even Wal-Mart needed to learn how to perform on the new sales medium. In summer 1997, the retailer increased its book selection from 350 titles to more than 300,000 titles, however, in late 1998, it cut back its online offering to 50,000 titles. WM's category manager justified this step with the following, "We found out that quantity was not as important as quality, being in stock and getting it out the door quickly are more important." Also, the company generated most of the revenue with only the 50,000 titles.[15] For books, WM's new online focus is on service and price[16] and shipping price is $3.00 regardless of the quantity of books ordered. Also available for purchase over the Web site are gift certificates

---

[11] Supermarket News 1997, p. 30.
[12] Scally 1998, p. 8, Shein 1996, p. E3, Supermarket News 1997, p. 30 and Zimmerman 1998, p. 27.
[13] Rubenstein 1997, p. 68.
[14] Bivens 1998, p. 122, Forbes 1998, p. 44, Jeffrey & Atwood 1997, p. 1, Leccese 1998, p. 46, Rubenstein 1997, p. 66, Scally 1998, p. 8, Smith 1996, p. 24, Shein 1996, pp. E1-E2 and Zimmerman 1998, pp. 27-28.
[15] Patrick 1998, p. 11.
[16] Bestsellers are discounted 45%, hardcover 30%, and paperback 25%.

(from \$5 to \$50), that can be redeemed for merchandise in all Wal-Mart and Sam's club locations, but not for online merchandise.[17]

New Merchandise. By the beginning of 1999, Wal-Mart's Web merchandise covers, besides its traditional brick-and-mortar store categories, also additional and more upscale product categories, not available in stores.

In May 1997, the company began offering fresh meat and seafood.[18] [19] In June 1998, WM experimented with selling china, crystal and sterling flatware strictly online. However, vendors of this exclusive merchandise were not aware of the fact that their products were sold online over the WM site, since the company was not an authorized dealer and therefore bought from a trans-shipper. One vendor put it this way, "we have no relationship with WM whatsoever. It's not our class of trade."[20] It seems more than questionable, whether this kind of approach is suitable to build long term relationships with a higher customer clientele. Two months later, Wal-Mart launched a campaign of selling custom-configured computers on the Web (an area in which Dell Computer Corporation pulls in approximately \$6 million per day). For this undertaking, WM is partnering with a company from Colorado Springs, which produces and ships computers and supports the customers. The target customers for these computers seem to be occasional home users and those, who are more focused on price than on brand names and service. Concluding it can be said that electronics, office equipment, books, music and videos, appliances and home accessories appear to be top sellers. Wal-Mart's online customers evidently do not want clothing, shoes, cosmetics, tools, auto accessories or linens, the mainstays of its brick-and-mortar stores.[21]

Pricing and Logistics

Pricing. Wal-Mart, with intention of being the lowest priced merchandiser, has extended its marketing strategy on the Web and, therefore, has taken the price war to cyberspace. For example, industry experts assumed that the company purposefully calculated the prices for hit CDs too low knowing they would not generate any profit. Overall, the company started out pricing Web merchandise about 30% cheaper than in stores (plus shipping costs). By the beginning of 1999, it implemented a fixed shipping fee of \$3 anywhere in the U.S., additionally it offers special features where shipping fees are already included.[22]

Logistics. The site has constantly evolved over the last 2 years. The Web site applies a so-called shopping cart system allowing customers to place items in their carts as they shop and review them before placing the actual order.[23] Analysts contend that WM's vast capabilities regarding distribution and information technology proves to best position it for online sales compared to many other online retail stores (the company has 1,500 employees in the Information Systems department). It seems especially helpful that Wal-Mart's approach allows suppliers to electronically access its warehouses, which makes it possible to match the

---

[17] Patrick 1998, p. 11 and www.wal-mart.com.
[18] As pointed out earlier, motivator for such a step seemed to be the wish to obtain a different and more upscale customer segment than the ones usually attracted by physical stores.
[19] Supermarket News 1997, p. 30 and Zimmerman 1998, p. 27.
[20] Kehoe 1998, p. 39.
[21] Diederich 1998a, www.computerworld.com, Kuchinskas 1998, p. IQ12 and Machelis 1998, p. C1.
[22] Jeffrey & Atwood 1997, p. 1 and Shein 1996, E2.
[23] Rubinstein 1997, p. 68, Scally 1998, p.8 and Shein 1996, p. E2.

190

quantities of goods supplied more closely with demand.[24] In some instances, the company engages in strong alliances with suppliers (currently applicable for meat and seafood, custom-made computers, and most of the music items) making them responsible for directly shipping to the customers. Such saves time (for seafood the slogan is "shore to door" in 24 hours) and disburdens Wal-Mart's distribution centers. For any other online merchandise, Wal-Mart uses more than 100 locations to handle fulfillment, which as the company claims, enables it to ship faster than most of its competitors, and to ship a wider variety of goods from a single location. However it is interesting to note that - ignoring these assumed advantages over other online retailers - industry experts remark that Wal-Mart "needs to be careful not to somehow get lost in the crowd."[25]

---

[24] Black 1998, p. FTS8 and Rubinstein 1997, p. 66.
[25] Jeffrey & Atwood 1997, p. 1, Machlis 1998b, p. C1, Supermarket News 1997, p. 30 and Zimmerman 1998, p. 28.

References

Aaker, David A. (1995): *Developing Business Strategies.* Fourth Edition. New York, NJ: John Wiley & Sons, Inc.

Aggarwal, Praveen, Taihoon Cha, and David Wilemon (1998): Barriers to the Adoption of Really-New Products and the Role of Surrogate Buyers. *Journal of Consumer Marketing, 15 (4), 1998:* 358-371.

Allen, Cliff, Deborah Kania, and Beth Yaeckel (1998): *Guide to One-To-One Web Marketing. Build a Relationship Marketing Strategy One Customer at a Time.* New York, NY: John Wiley & Sons, Inc.

Amazon (1999): *Amazon.com, February 1999,* [http://www.amazon.com].

Anderer, Bernd (1998): *Marketing Strategies for Business-to-Consumer Electronic Commerce and the Strategic Implications of Software Agents and XML.* December 1998. German Master Thesis (Diplomarbeit) handed in at the University of Karlsruhe, Germany.

Ansoff, H. I. (1959): Strategies for Diversification. *Harvard Business Review, 35 (5), September-October, 1957*: 113-124.

Arlen, Gary (1998): The Agora Beyond the Web: Tele-Shopping in the Interactive Age. *Digitrends Online, Digitrends Quarterly Review, Summer 1998,* [http://www.4interactivemarketing.com].

A.T. Kearney (1998): *Strategies 2005. Vision for the Wholesale – Supplied System.* Falls Church, VA: Food Distributors International, Inc.

Audette, John (1998): Adapting to the Internet: Reports From Inside the Net. *Adventive.com, December 8, 1998,* [http://www.adventive.com].

Barabba, Vincent P. (1990): The Market Research Encyclopedia. *Harvard Business Review, 68 (1), January-February, 1990:* 105-117.

Barnack, Renee (1998): Redefining Food: Home Meal Replacement Trend Takes Hold. *National Petroleum News, 90 (1), January 1998:* 30-33.

Bass, M., Vijay Mahajan, and Eitan Muller (1990): New Product Diffusion Models in Marketing: A Review and Directions for Research. *Journal of Marketing, 54 (1), January 1990:* 1-27.

Berekhoven, Ludwig, Werner Eckert, and Peter Ellenrieder (1996): *Marktforschung. Methodische Grundlagen und praktische Anwendung.* Seventh Edition. Wiesbaden, Germany: Gabler Verlag.

Berger, Paul D. and Bada I. Nasr (1998): Customer Lifetime Value: Marketing Models and Applications. *Journal of Interactive Marketing, 12 (1), Winter 1998:* 17-29.

Berkman, Robert I. (1996): *How to Find Market Research Online.* New York, NY: Find/SVP Publishing, Inc.

Bivens, Jackie (1998): On Line Not Yet on Target. *Discount Store News, 37 (11), June, 1998:* 122.

Blankenship, Albert, George E. Breen, and Alan Dutka (1998): *State of the Art Marketing Research.* Second Edition. Chicago, IL: NTC Business Books.

Boston Consulting Group, The (1998): *The State of Online Retailing.* November 1998. Shop.org.

Brody, Herbert (1991): Great Expectations: Why Technology Predictions Go Awry. *Technology Review, 94 (5), July 1991:* 39-44.

Brown, Francis E. (1980): *Marketing Research: A Structure for Decision Making.* Reading, MA: Addison-Wesley Publishing Company.

Bureau of the Census (1998a): *U.S. Bureau of the Census, Population Projections of the United States by Age, Sex, Race, and Hispanic Origin: 1995 to 2050, Current Population Reports, P25-1130.* Washington, WA: U.S. Government Printing Office.

Bureau of the Census (1998b): *U.S. Bureau of the Census, Current Population Reports, P60-200, Money Income in the United States: 1997.* Washington, WA: U.S. Government Printing Office.

Campbell, A. J. (1997): Relationship Marketing in Consumer Markets: A Comparison of Managerial and Consumer Attitudes about Information Privacy. *Journal of Direct Marketing, 11 (3), Summer 1997:* 44-56.

Carmichael, Matt (1998): Building a Web Site? Cost Keeps Climbing. *Business Marketing, 83 (6), June 1998:* 1-2.

Carr, Robert E. (1998): The Internet & other Vaporous Issues. *Sporting Goods Business, 31 (3), February 4, 1998:* 146.

Carter, Dennis (1996): You've Got to Maintain a Beginner's Mind about Interactive Marketing. In: Deighton, John (introduction): The Future of Interactive Marketing. *Harvard Business Review, 74 (6), November-December 1996:* 156-157.

CDNow (1999): *CDNow, February 1999,* [http://www.cdnow.com].

Ching Leong, Kathy (1998): Toys "R" Us Restructures for E-Comm. *Internet Week,* June 8, 1998, [http://www.internetwk.com].

Chposky, J. and T. Leonsis (1988): *Blue Magic: The People, Power, and Politics Behind the IBM Personal Computer.* New York, NY: Facts on File Publications.

Churchill, Jr., Gilbert A. (1995): *Marketing Research, Methodological Foundations.* Sixth Edition. Orlando, FL: The Dryden Press.

CommerceNet (1998): Internet Statistics. *Research Center: Internet Population, December 1998,* [http://www.commerce.net/research/stats/].

Cox, Beth (1998): Online, Men Do More of the Shopping. *Electronic Commerce News. Internet.com, November 6, 1998,* [http://www.internetnews.com/ec-news/].

Crimp, Margaret and Len Tiu Wright (1995): *The Marketing Research Process.* Fourth Edition. Herfordshire, Great Britain: Prentice Hall.

Cybermeals (1998): *Cybermeals, December 1998,* [http://www.cybermeals.com].

Davy, Jo Ann (1998): Electronic Commerce: Is Going Online the Right Road for Your Company? *Managing Office Technology, June 1998:* 20-24.

Diederich, Tom (1998a): Wal-Mart Launches Build-to-Order PC Effort. *Computerworld, August 5, 1998,* [http://www.computerworld.com].

Diederich, Tom (1998b): Online Shopping Frustrates Consumers. *Online News, October, 1 1998,* [http://www.computerworld.com].

DMA (1997): *Marketing Online: Privacy Principles and Guidance.* The Direct Marketing Association, Inc., July 1997. New York, NY: The Direct Marketing Association.

DMA (1999): *The Direct Marketing Association, March 1999,* [http://www.the-dma.org].

Dodd, Honathan (1998): Market Research on the Internet - Threat or Opportunity? *Marketing and Research Today, 26 (1), February 1998:* 60-66.

Dowling, Geoff R. and Richard Staelin (1994): A Model of Perceived Risk and Intended Risk-Handling Activity. *Journal of Consumer Research, 21 (1), June 1994:* 119-134.

Dutka, Alan (1991): How to Maximize the Benefits of Computer Assisted Telephone Interviewing. *Quirk's Marketing Research Review, May 1991,* [http://www.quirks.org].

Dwyer, Steve (1997): A Recipe for the Next Century. *Prepared Foods, 165 (11), November 1996:* 13-19.

Edmondson, Brad (1997): The Wired Bunch: Online Surveys and Focus Groups Might Solve the Toughest Problems in Market Research. But Can Internet Users Really Speak for Everyone? *American Demographics, 19 (6), June 1997:* 10-15.

Ernst & Young (1998): *Internet Shopping. An Ernst & Young Special Report.* Ernst & Young, January 1998.

Ernst & Young (1999): *The Second Annual Ernst & Young Internet Shopping Study. The Digital Channel Continues to Gather Steam. An Ernst & Young Special Report.* Ernst & Young, January 1999.

EToys (1999): *EToys, February 1999,* [http://www.etoys.com].

Evans, Philip B. and Thomas S. Wurster (1997): Strategy and the New Economics of Information. *Harvard Business Review, 75 (5), September-October 1997:* 71-82.

Flycast (1999): *Flycast, March 1999,* [http://www.flycast.com].

Forbes (1998): Future Shop. *Forbes, 161 (7), April 6, 1998:* S37-S49.

Fournier, Susan, Susan Dobscha, and David Glen Mick (1998): Preventing the Premature Death of Relationship Marketing. *Harvard Business Review 76 (1), January-February 1998*: 42-51.

FTC (1998): Federal Trade Commission: Privacy Online: A Report to Congress. *Federal Trade Commission, June 1998,* [http://www.ftc.gov].

Fukuyama, Francis (1998): *The Virtual Handshake: E-Commerce and the Challenge of Trust.* The Merrill Lynch Forum, March 1998.

Goldman Sachs (1997): *U.S. Research: Cyber Commerce – Internet Tsunami.* New York, NY: Goldman Sachs.

Ghosh, Shikhar (1998): Making Business Sense of the Internet. *Harvard Business Review, 76 (2), March-April 1998:* 126-135.

Green, Heather and Seanna Browder (1998): Online Merchants – Cyberspace Winners: How They Did It. *Business Week, 3583, June 22, 1998:* 154-162.

Green, Paul E., Donald S. Tull, and Gerald Albaum (1988): *Research for Marketing Decisions.* Fifth Edition. Englewood Cliffs, NJ: Prentice-Hall, Inc.

Grewal, Gotlieb D. and H. Marmostein (1994): The Moderating Effects of Message Framing and Source Credibility on the Price-Perceived Risk Relationship. *Journal of Consumer Research, 21 (1), June 1994:* 145-153.

Gross, Neil and Sager Ira (1998): Caution Sign Along the Road. *Business Week, 3583, June 22, 1998:* 166-168.

Gupta, Sunil and Rabikar Chatterjee (1997): Consumer and Corporate Adoption of the World Wide Web as a Commercial Medium. In: Peterson, Robert A. (editor): *Electronic Marketing and the Consumers.* Thousand Oaks, CA: SAGE Publications, Inc.: 123-138.

Guttman, Robert H., Alexandros G. Moukas and Pattie Maes (1997): *Agent-Mediated Electronic Commerce: A Survey. Software Agents Group.* MIT Media Laboratory, [http://ecommerce.media.mit.edu].

GVU (1997): Graphic, Visualization & Usability Center's (GVU) 8th WWW User Survey, *GVU, October 1997,* [http://www.gvu.gatech.edu/user_surveys/survey-1997-10/].

GVU (1998): Graphic, Visualization & Usability Center's (GVU) 9th WWW User Survey, *GVU, April 1998,* [http://www.gvu.gatech.edu/user_surveys/survey-1998-04/].

Hagel III, John and, A.G. Armstrong (1997): *Net Gain. Expanding Markets Through Virtual Communities.* Boston, MA: Harvard Business Press.

Hagel III, John and Jeffrey F. Rayport (1998): The Coming Battle for Customer Information. *Harvard Business Review, 75 (1), January-February 1997:* 53-65.

Hagel III, John and Marc Singer (1999): *Net Worth. Shaping Markets When Customers Make the Rules.* Boston, MA: Harvard Business Press.

Hamel, Gary and Jeff Sampler (1998): The E-Corporation. More Than Just Web-Based, it's Building a New Industrial Order. *Fortune, December 7, 1998,* [http://www.pathfinder.com/fortune/1998/981207/eco.html].

Hanson, Ward (1998): The Original WWW: Web Lessons from the Early Days of Radio. *Journal of Interactive Marketing, 12 (3), Summer 1998*: 46-55.

Harris, Cheryl (1997): Developing Online Market Research Methods and Tools - Considering Theorizing Interactivity: Models and Cases. *Marketing and Research Today, 25 (4), November 1997:* 267-273.

Hartnett, Michael (1999): Home Improvement Retailers Urged to Step Up e-Commerce Efforts. *Stores, 81 (3), March 1999:* 76-77.

Hawkins, Del I. and Donald S. Tull (1994): *Essentials of Marketing Research.* First Edition. New York, NY: Maxwell Macmillan Publishing Company.

Hawkins, Del I., Roger J. Best and Kenneth A. Coney (1998): *Consumer Behavior: Building Marketing Strategy.* Seventh Edition. Boston, MA: The McGraw-Hill Companies, Inc.

Heller, Laura (1998): Real Store Environment Key to Web Sales Growth. *Discount Store News, 37 (13), July 13, 1998:* 23.

Hennessy, Terry (1998): Sense of Sell. *Progressive Grocer, 77 (8), August 1998:* 107-110.

Herzberg, Frederick (1972): *Work and the Nature of Man.* New York, NY: The World Publishing Company.

Herzberg, Frederick (1987): One More Time: How Do You Motivate Employees? *Harvard Business Review, 65 (5), September-October 1987:* 109-120.

Hill, Jim (1998): Leaping Into Big Leagues. *The Oregonian, 75, June 21, 1998:* R04.

Hof, Robert D., Gary McWilliams and Gabrielle Saveri (1998): The "Click Here" Economy. *Business Week, 3583, June 22, 1998:* 122-128.

Hoffman, Donna L. (1996): Cyberspace to Congress: The Net is Mainstream –And it Votes! *MicroTimes, 148, March 4, 1996,* [http://www.microtimes.com].

Hunt, Shelby D., Richard D. Sparkam, Jr. and James B. Wilcox (1982): The Pretest in Survey Research: Issues and Preliminary Findings. *Journal of Marketing Research, 19, May 1982:* 269-273.

Jarvenpaa, Sirkka L. and Peter A. Todd (1997): In: Peterson, Robert A. (editor): *Electronic Marketing and the Consumers.* Thousand Oaks, CA: SAGE Publications, Inc.: 138-154.

Jeffrey, Don and Brett Atwood (1997): Price War on the Web? *Billboard, 109 (24), June 14, 1997:* 1-2.

Jones, Thomas O. and Earl W. Sasser, Jr. (1995): Why Satisfied Customers Defect. *Harvard Business Review, 73 (6), November – December 1995:* 88–99.

Jupiter Communications (1998): Press Release: Jupiter/NFO Study Shows New Online Buyers Will be Tough to Convert. *Jupiter Communications, October 20, 1998,* [http://www.jup.com].

Kalakota, Ravi and Andrew B. Whinston (1997): *Electronic Commerce. A Manager's Guide.* Menlo Park, CA: Addison Wesley Longman, Inc.

Kehoe, Ann-Margaret (1998): Wal-Mart Online: Moving Upstairs. *HFN: The Weekly Newspaper for the Home Furnishing Network, 72 (25), June 22, 1998:* 39.

Knnear, Thomas C. and James R. Taylor (1996): M*arketing Research: An Applied Approach.* Fifth Edition. New York, NY: McGraw-Hill, Inc.

KPMG (1997): *Electronic Commerce. Research Report 1997.* KPMG, 1997.

Kraft (1999): *Kraft Interactive Kitchen, February 1999,* [http://www.kraft.com].

Kuchinskas, Susan (1998): The E-Commerce Cometh. *Brandweek, 39 (35), September 21, 1998:* I8-I12.

Land's End (1999): *Land's End Direct Merchant, February 1999,* [http://www.landsend.com].

Leccese, Donna (1998): Retail Alternatives Gain Ground. *Playthings, 96 (11), November 1998:* 46-49.

Lehmann, Donald R. (1989): *Market Research and Analysis. Third Edition.* Boston, MA: Irwin.

Levin, Martin (1996): A Corporate Web Site is Different From a Marketing Web Site. In: Deighton, John (introduction): The Future of Interactive Marketing. *Harvard Business Review. 74 (6), November-December 1996:* 154-156.

Levitt, Theodore (1960): Marketing Myopia. *Harvard Business Review, 38 (4), July-August 1960:* 45-56.

Machlis, Sharon (1998a): Internet Commerce Expo; Wires aren't only Things Tripping up E-Commerce. *Computerworld, 32 (13), March 30, 1998:* 43.

Machlis, Sharon (1998b): Two of the Best-Known Names in Retailing, One Real-World, the Other Virtual, Moved to Expand Their Electronic-Commerce Operations Last Week, In Hopes That Their Successful Brands Can be Leveraged to New Categories on the Web. *Computerworld, 32 (32), August 10, 1998:* C1.

Macht, Joshua (1998): Toy Seller Plays Internet Hardball. *Inc, 20 (14), October, 1998:* 17-18.

Maguire, Tom (1998): Web Nets the Masses. *American Demographics, 20 (12), December 1998:*18-20.

Martinez, Eva, Yolanda Polo, and Carlos Flavián (1998): The Acceptance and Diffusion of New Consumer Durables: Differences Between First and Last.

Mathews, Ryan (1997): The Power of the Internet. *Progressive Grocer, 76 (3), March 1997:* 39-44.

Mathews, Ryan (1998a): Consumer-Direct: You Say You Want a Revolution? *Progressive Grocer, 77 (3), March 1998:* 22-29.

Mathews, Ryan (1998b): The Power of the Internet: As the World Becomes Increasingly Wired, Traditional Food Retailers Risk Losing Upscale, High-Margin Customers to Electronic-Commerce Marketers. *Progressive Grocer, 77 (3), March 1998:* 39-43.

McKenzie, J. R. (1977): An Investigation into Interviewing Effect in Market Research. *Journal of Marketing Research, Volume 14, August 1977:* 330-336.

MicroVison (1995): *MicroVision Marketing Guide.* Atlanta, GA: Equifax Marketing Decision Systems Inc.

Moore, Geoffrey A. (1991): *Crossing the Chasm: Marketing and Selling Technology Products to Mainstream Customers.* New York, NY: Harper Collins Publishers, Inc.

Morgan Stanley (1997): *U.S. Investment Research – Internet Retail.* Morgan Stanley, May 1997.

Moschella, David (1998): Web Competition May Look Frighteningly Familiar. *Computerworld, 32 (45), November 9, 1998:* 34.

Nadilo, Rudy (1998): On-Line Research Taps Consumers Who Spend. *Marketing News, 32 (12), June 8, 1998:* 12.

Nielsen Media Research (1998): Number of Internet Users and Shoppers Surges in United States and Canada, *Nielsen Media Research, November 1998,* [http://www.nielsenmedia.com/news/commnet2.html].

Nieschlag, Robert, Erwin Dichtl and Hans Hörschgen (1994): *Marketing. Seventeenth Edition.* Berlin, Germany: Duncker & Humbolt.

Nunnally, Jum C. (1978): *Psychometric Theory. Second Edition.* New York, NY: McGraw-Hill.

Online Privacy Alliance (1998): *Privacy Alliance, December 1998,* [http:///www.privacyalliance.org].

Oregonian (1998): Internet Use Climbs Above 33% in U.S. *The Oregonian, 75, August 26, 1998:* C02.

Orler, Victor J. and David H. Friedman (199 a): Consumer-Direct: Here to Stay. *Progressive Grocer, 77 (1), January 1998:* 51-54.

Orler, Victor J. and David H. Friedman (1998b): The Consumer Behind Consumer-Direct. *Progressive Grocer, 77 (2), February 1998:* 39-42.

Orler, Victor J. and David H. Friedman (1998c): What Consumer-Direct Means to You. *Progressive Grocer, 77 (4), April 1998:* 51-54.

Patrick, Diane (1998): Wal-Mart Trims Online Title Inventory. *Publishers Weekly, November 2, 1998:* 11.

Peppers, Don and Martha Rogers (1997): *Enterprise One To One. Tools for Competing in the Interactive Age.* New York, NY: Currency and Doubleday, Inc.

Peppers, Don and Martha Rogers (1998a): Europe and the Future of One To One. *Inside 1 to 1, November 5, 1998,* [http://www.1to1.com].

Peppers, Don and Martha Rogers (1998b): Fingerhut Forever: The Advantages of Modeling Lifetime Value. *Inside 1 to 1, November 19, 1998,* [http://www.1to1.com].

Perlitz, Manfred (1997): *Internationales Management.* Third Edition. Stuttgart, Germany: Lucius & Lucius Verlag.

Peterson, Robert A. (1982): *Marketing Research.* Plano, TX: Business Publications, Inc.

Peterson, Robert A. (1997): Electronic Marketing: Vision, Definitions, and Implications. In: Peterson, Robert A. (editor): M*arketing and the Consumers.* Thousand Oaks, CA: SAGE Publications, Inc.: 1-15.

Predow-James, Karen (1996): *Ten Top Insights About Tracking the Effect of Advertising That Came Out of the ARF's November 1996 workshop,* [http://www2.worldopinion.com].

Pricewaterhouse Coopers (1998a): *Technology Forecast: 1998.* Menlo Park, CA: Price Waterhouse Global Technology Center.

Pricewaterhouse Coopers (1998b): *Electronic Business Outlook. A Survey of E-Business Goals, Practices, and Results. Sponsored by The Conference Board and Pricewatehouse Coopers.* Menlo Park, CA: Pricewaterhouse Global Technology Center.

Progressive Grocer (1998): Building a Virtual Community. *Progressive Grocer, 77 (9), September 1998*: 93-96.

Puryear, Rudy C. (1998): A Call to eAction. *Andersen Consulting Outlook Magazine, October 6, 1998,* [http://www.ac.com/overview/outlook/].

Radoce, Carol (1998): The Virtual Future. Today's Web Sites are Redefining Tomorrow's Retailer. *Progressive Grocer, 77 (7), July 1998*: 49-52.

Reda, Susan (1998): On-line Marketers Struggle to Avoid Privacy "Land Mine". *Stores, 80 (7), July 1998*: 41-44.

Reda, Susan (1999): Websites and Stores: Integrate or Separate? *Stores, 81 (3), March 1999*: 26-30.

Reinhardt, Andy (1998): Log On, Link Up, Save Big. *Business Week, 3583, June 22, 1998:* 132-138.

Reynoldsen, David (1999): *How to Analyze the Effectiveness of Your Web Site?* American Marketing Association, Oregon Chapter, Portland, Oregon, February 2, 1999.

Roberton, Stephens & Company (1997): *The Webolution. E-Tailing - The Electronic Advantage.* San Francisco, CA: Robertson, Stephens & Company.

Rogers, E. M. (1983): *Diffusion of Innovations.* New York, NY: The Free Press.

Rubinstein, Ed (1997): Wal-Mart On-Line Looking for $$.com; Next on the Agenda: 80,000 SKUs. *Discount Store News, 36 (5), March 3, 1997:* 66-69.

Safeway (1999): *Safeway, February 1999,* [http://www.safeway.com].

Savage, Lou and Scott Warner (1998): *Marketing on the Internet.* American Marketing Association, Oregon Chapter, Portland, Oregon, November 3, 1998.

Scally, Robert (1998): Wal-Mart Online celebrates 2nd Birthday. *Discount Store News, 37 (15), August 10, 1998:* 8.

Schrage, Michael (1997): *The Relationship Revolution: Understanding the Essence of the Digital Age.* The Merrill Lynch Forum, March 1997.

Schulz, David P. (1999): Growth of Direct-to-Consumer Channels Reshapes Retail Distribution. *Stores, 81 (3), March 1999*: 48-51.

Schwartz, Evan I. (1997): *Webonomics.* New York, NY: Broadway Books.

Seattle Times, The (1998): The Market Reporter. Puget Sound Economy, Retail Sales Forecast by Category, and Consumer Retail Trend. *The Seattle Times and Seattle Post-Intelligencer,* Seattle, WA.

Shein, Esther (1996): The Virtual Storefronts. *PC Week, Volume 13, 38 (23), June 8, 1996:* E1-E3.

Shein, Esther (1998): Back-End Transactions Are No Bargain. Outsourcers Handle Order Processing for New Online Companies. *PC Week, 15 (34), August 24, 1998:* 55.

Sheth, Jagdish N. and Rajendra S. Sisodia (1996): Consumer Behavior in the Future In: Peterson, Robert A. (editor): *Electronic Marketing and the Consumers.* Thousand Oaks, CA: SAGE Publications, Inc.: 17-37.

Smith, David (1996): Stagnant Growth Common for Arkansas' Retailers. *Arkansas Business, 13 (53), December 30, 1996:* 24.

Smith, Michelle L. (1999): One To One: Put the Customer in the Driver Seat and Build Better Relationships. *Direct Marketing, 60 (9), January 1999: 37-39.*

Spiegel Online (19999): USA – Internet-Wirtschaft boomt. *Spiegel Online, 43, Oktober 1999,* [http://www.spiegel.de/wirtschaft/konjunktur/].

Stark, Myra (1998): A Fly on the Virtual Wall; Cybercommunities Observed. *Digitrends Online, Research, 1998,* [http://www.4interactivemarketing.com].

Sterne, Jim (1995): World Wide Web Marketing: Integrating the Internet into Your Marketing Strategy. New York, NY: John Wiley & Sons, Inc.

Stevens, Robert E. (1997): *The Marketing Research Guide.* Binghamton, NY: The Haworth Press, Inc.

Stewart, Trevor R. (1998): Doing Business in Cyberspace. *In the E-Business Tidal Wave, Perspectives on Business in Cyberspace. Deloitte Touch Tohmats,* [http://www.deloitte.com/tidalwave/].

Stone, Bob (1996): *Successful Direct Marketing Methods.* Sixth Edition. Chicago, IL: NTC / Contemporary Publishing Group, Inc.

Supermarket Business (1998a): E-Commerce and the Food Industry's. *Supermarket Business, 53 (6), June 1998:* 30-31.

Supermarket News (1997): Wal-Mart Web Site to add Exotics to Menu. *Supermarket News, 47 (33), August 18, 1997:* 30.

TAP 98 (1998): *Trade Area Profiles 1998. /Electronics.* Portland, OR: The Oregonian.

Thompson, Stephanie (1997): Food 'Packaging' a Hot Topic as HMR Turns to Pies and Meal Kits. *Brandweek, 38 (35), September 22, 1997:* 16.

Tripod (1999): *Tripod, February 1999,* [http://www.tripod.com].

TRUSTe (1998): *TRUSTe, December 1998,* [http://www.truste.org].

Tushman, Michael L. and Philip Anderson (1988): In: Pettigrew, Andrew, M. (editor): *The Management of Strategic Change.* Oxford, United Kingdom: Basil Blackwell Ltd.: 89-122.

Urban, G. L., B. D. Weinberg and J.R. Hauser (1996): *Premarket Forecasting of Really-New-Products.* Journal of Marketing, *60 (1),* January 1996: 47-60.

U.S. Department of Commerce, Secretariat on Electronic Commerce (1998): *The Emerging Digital Economy,* [http://www.ecommerce.gov].

Venkatraman N. and John C. Henderson (1998): Real Strategies for Virtual Organizing. *Sloan Management Review, 40 (1), Fall 1998:* 33-49.

Wal-Mart.com (1999): *Wal-Mart, February 1999,* [http://www.wal-mart.com].

Wang, Huaiqing, K.O. Lee and Chen Wang (1998): Consumer Privacy Concerns About Internet Marketing. *Communications of the ACM, 41 (3), March 1998:* 63-70.

WebTrust (1998): *VeriSign WebTrust, December 1998,* [http://www.verisign.com/webtrust/].

Weiers, Ronald M. (1984): *arketing Research.* Englewood Cliffs, NJ: Prentice-Hall, Inc.

Wilson, Bob (1998): *PlanetU. The Internet: Strategic Platform or Over-Hyped Distraction?* Presentation on the 1998 Fourth Annual Fall Conference of the Food Industry Leadership Center on "The Changing Face of the Food Industry", Portland, Oregon, October 27, 1998.

Wilson, Ralph F. (1999): Multiple Streams of Revenue for Your Website. *Web Marketing Today, 52, January 1, 1999,* [http://www.wilsonweb.com].

Wingfield, Nick (1998): A Marketer's Dream. *The Wall Street Journal, 126, December 7, 1998:* R20.

Wolfe, David B. (1996): *A Behavior Model for Imparting Empathy to Relationship Marketing in Cyberspace.* In: Proceedings of the Third Research Conference on Relationship Marketing: Contemporary Knowledge of Relationship Marketing, Center for Relationship Marketing, Emory University, Atlanta, GA, 1996.

Wolfe, David B. (1998): Developmental Relationship Marketing (Connecting Messages with Mind: An Empathetic Marketing System). *Journal of Consumer Marketing, 15 (5), 1998:* 449-467.

Ziff-Davis (1998a): InternetTrak: The Web explored. *Ziff-Davis, First Quarter 1998*, [http://www.ziffdavis.com/marketresearch/internettrak.htm].

Ziff-Davis (1998b): InternetTrak: The Web explored. *Ziff-Davis, Second Quarter 1998*, [http://www.ziffdavis.com/marketresearch/internettrak.htm].

Zimmerman, Liza B. (1997*):* Home Delivery of Seafood is On-Line Lure for Wal-Mart. *Supermarket News, 47 (33), August 18, 1997:* 27-29.

Markt, Kommunikation, Innovation (MKI)

herausgegeben von Michael Schenk
(Forschungsstelle für Empirische
Kommunikationsforschung (FEK), Universität
Hohenheim)
und Bruno Neibecker (Institut für
Entscheidungstheorie und
Unternehmungsforschung, Universität Karlsruhe)

Michael Schenk; Hermann Dahm;
Deziderio Šonje
Innovationen im Kommunikationssystem
Eine empirische Studie zur Diffusion von
Datenfernübertragung und Mobilfunk
Im Beruf wie im Privatleben setzen sich informa-
tionstechnische Innovationen zunehmend durch.
Allen voran sind hier der Mobilfunk und die
Online-Kommunikation (Datenfernübertragung)
zu nennen. Trotz des derzeitigen Booms ist noch
wenig über den konkreten Nutzen und die Folgen
der Techniken bekannt. Gleiches gilt für die Me-
chanismen, die bei der Marktdurchdringung von
Bedeutung sind. In der vorliegenden empirischen
Studie werden u. a. folgende Fragen untersucht:
Wie wirken sich Nutzenkalküle auf Kaufent-
scheidungen und den Gebrauch der Techniken
aus? Welche Rolle spielt dabei das soziale Um-
feld? Durch welche Merkmale zeichnen sich die
Innovatoren des Mobilfunks und der Datenfernübertragung aus?
Bd. 1, 1996, 480 S., 68,80 DM, br., ISBN 3-8258-3023-3

Hans Georg Gemünden; Achim Walter;
Gabi Helfert
**Grenzüberschreitende
Geschäftsbeziehungen**
Erfolgsfaktoren und Gestaltungsempfehlun-
gen für kleine und mittlere Unternehmen
Grenzüberschreitende Geschäftsbeziehungen tragen
entscheidend zum wirtschaftlichen und technischen
Erfolg kleiner und mittlerer Unternehmen bei.
Dies ist jedoch nicht selbstverständlich. Beacht-
liche Barrieren behindern die Zusammenarbeit
mit Kunden im Ausland. Auf der Grundlage von
Interviews mit deutschen Herstellern und de-
ren ausländischen Kunden werden wesentliche
Erfolgsfaktoren grenzüberschreitender Kundenbe-
ziehungen diskutiert und insbesondere konkrete
Empfehlungen für die Gestaltung dieser Bezie-
hungen abgeleitet. Die Inhalte werden praxisnah
präsentiert und anhand zahlreicher konkreter Fall-
beispiele illustriert. Der Band wendet sich in erster

Linie an Personen aus der Praxis, denen das Ma-
nagement von Geschäftsbeziehungen obliegt, ist
aber auch für Dozenten und Studenten aus den
Bereichen Marketing, Unternehmensführung und
Innovationsmanagement von Interesse.
Bd. 2, 1996, 216 S., 38,80 DM, br., ISBN 3-8258-3111-6

Hermann Dahm; Patrick Rössler;
Michael Schenk
Vom Zuschauer zum Anwender
Akzeptanz und Folgen digitaler Fernseh-
dienste
Trotz euphorischer Prognosen ist die Vermark-
tung des digitalen bzw. interaktiven Fernsehens in
Deutschland bisher eher von Fehlstarts geprägt.
Welche Marktchancen hat das digitale bzw. inter-
aktive Fernsehen in Deutschland? Welches sind die
Erfolgsfaktoren für eine Akzeptanz im breiten Pu-
blikum? Die vorliegende Untersuchung gibt einen
Überblick über die Marktsituation und die techni-
schen Voraussetzungen des digitalen Fernsehens.
In einer Befragung unter Multimedia-Pionieren
wurden zudem verschiedene Angebotsoptionen des
digitalen Fernsehens auf ihre Akzeptanz getestet.
Mit Hilfe einer Conjoint-Analyse können erste
Anhaltspunkte für die spezifischen Präferenzen
der innovativen Anwender gewonnen werden. Die
Befunde werden auch mit Ergebnissen anderer
Forschungsarbeiten verknüpft. Aus kommunika-
tionswissenschaftlicher Sicht werden schließlich
mögliche Chancen und Risiken, welche sich aus
der neuen Technologie für Individuum und Gesellschaft ergeben, diskutiert.
Bd. 3, 1998, 146 S., 39,80 DM, br., ISBN 3-8258-3677-0

Telekommunikation und Multimedia

herausgegeben von
Prof. Dr. Klaus Backhaus,
Prof. Dr. Heinz Lothar Grob,
Prof. Dr. Bernd Holznagel,
Prof. Dr. Wolfram-Manfred Lippe
und Prof. Dr. Gerhard W. Wittkämper

Klaus Backhaus; Markus Voeth
Stadtinformationssysteme
Ergebnisse einer Akzeptanzuntersuchung bei
Privathaushalten
Kommunalen Informations- und Kommunikations-
systemen, sogenannten Stadtinformationssystemen,
kommt zukünftig eine besondere Bedeutung für
den kommunalen Wirtschaftsstandort zu. Daher
befinden sich solche Systeme augenblicklich in
praktisch jeder größeren Stadt Deutschlands im
Aufbau.

LIT Verlag Münster – Hamburg – London
Bestellungen über:
Grevener Str. 179 48159 Münster
Tel.: 0251 – 23 50 91 – Fax: 0251 – 23 19 72
e-Mail: lit@lit-verlag.de – http://www.lit-verlag.de
Preise: unverbindliche Preisempfehlung

Obwohl der Erfolg von Stadtinformationssystemen wesentlich von der Akzeptanz der Privathaushalte abhängt, liegen bislang keine Informationen über die Präferenzen, Einstellungen und Anforderungen aus Sicht von Privathaushalten vor. Backhaus und Voeth versuchen, dieses Informationsdefizit abzubauen, indem sie die Akzeptanz von Stadtinformationssystemen bei Privathaushalten auf Basis einer Befragung von 3.500 Haushalten analysieren.
Bd. 1, 1997, 136 S., 19,80 DM, br., ISBN 3-8258-3296-1

Guido Schröder
**Die Ökonomie des Fernsehens –
eine mikroökonomische Analyse**
Mit einem Vorwort von Hans-Jürgen Ewers
Die Frage „Wieviel Markt verträgt der Rundfunk?" ist – nicht nur in Deutschland – so alt wie das Medium selbst. Doch nicht allein aus historischer Perspektive ist die Diskussion um das Verhältnis von Publizistik und Ökonomie in den Medien interessant. Sie wird vielmehr vor dem Hintergrund der sich im Rundfunkbereich abzeichnenden Trends zu Digitalisierung und Konvergenz in Zukunft noch an Bedeutung gewinnen.
Das vorliegende Buch versucht, in knapper Form in die ökonomischen Eigenschaften des Fernsehens einzuführen. In allgemeinverständlicher Weise werden die Kernprobleme des Mediums aus mikroökonomischer Sicht betrachtet, und es wird untersucht, wie das Fernsehen der Zukunft aussehen soll.
Bd. 2, 1997, 128 S., 29,80 DM, br., ISBN 3-8258-3387-9

Klaus Backhaus; Ekkehard Stadie;
Markus Voeth
**Standortfaktor Telekommunikation und
Multimedia**
Ein Handlungskonzept für ländliche Regionen am Beispiel des Münsterlandes
Der Telekommunikations- und Multimedia-Markt wird in den kommenden Jahren zu einem immer wichtigeren Schlüsselsektor für die wirtschaftliche Entwicklung der gesamten Bundesrepublik Deutschland, aber auch einzelner Regionen in Deutschland. Da der zum 1.1.1998 in allen Bereichen der Telekommunikation entstehende Wettbewerb dazu führt, daß die Carrier ihr Angebot den jeweiligen regionalen Marktbedingungen anpassen, droht ländlichen Regionen die Gefahr, von den im Aufbau befindlichen "Datenautobahnen" abgeschnitten zu werden. Um ein solches zukünftiges Zurückfallen im regionalen Standortwettbewerb zu verhindern, ist bereits zum jetzigen Zeitpunkt ein gezieltes regionalpolitisches Handeln in ländlichen Regionen erforderlich. Aus einer detaillierten Bestandsaufnahme der allgemeinen Marktsituation und der speziellen Ausgangssituation der Beispielregion "Münsterland" leiten Backhaus, Stadie und Voeth ein operationales Handlungskonzept und einen konkreten Maßnahmenkatalog für ländliche Regionen ab.
Bd. 3, 1997, 368 S., 79,80 DM, br., ISBN 3-8258-3517-0

Klaus Backhaus; Ekkehard Stadie;
Markus Voeth
**Was bringt der Wettbewerb im
Telekommunikationsmarkt?**
Erste Erfahrungen aus dem liberalisierten Markt. Unter Mitarbeit von Corinna Bohle, Frank Kleinhesseling, Frank Schockemöhle, Christoph Steens, Steffi Wolf
Mit dem Wegfall des Telefondienstes zum 1. 1. 1998 ist der letzte und wichtigste Schritt der Liberalisierung des Telekommunikationsmarktes erfolgt. Da die Carrier über keine Wettbewerbserfahrungen im Telekommunikationsbereich verfügen, müssen sich erst noch Spielregeln im Markt herausbilden, so daß zum jetzigen Zeitpunkt noch viele Fragen z. B. in bezug auf die Folgen des Wettbewerbs oder die Erfolgsstrategien für Carrier offen sind.
Backhaus, Stadie und Voeth greifen einige dieser Fragen im vorliegenden Buch heraus und legen hierfür auf Basis aktueller empirischer Untersuchungen erste Ergebnisse vor. Im einzelnen werden folgende Fragestellungen untersucht:
Inwieweit führt die Liberalisierung zu regionalen Preisunterschieden?
Was ist in der Zwischenzeit aus den in vielen Kommunen geplanten City-Carrier-Aktivitäten geworden?
Wie werden Preise von Privatkunden im Telefongeschäft wahrgenommen?
Anhand welcher Kriterien treffen Geschäftskunden die Carrier-Entscheidung?
Welche generellen Empfehlungen lassen sich für die Einführung innovativer Leistungen im Telekommunikationsmarkt ableiten?
Bd. 4, 1998, 148 S., 39,80 DM, br., ISBN 3-8258-3835-8

Ekkehard Stadie
**Medial gestützte Limit Conjoint-Analyse
als Innovationstest für technologische
Basisinnovationen – Eine explorative
Analyse**
Innovationen gelten als Triebfeder des Wirtschaftswachstums. Den beträchtlichen Chancen stehen jedoch auch erhebliche Risiken gegenüber. So zeigen verschiedenste Studien, daß nur eine Minderheit an Neuproduktprojekten am Markt erfolgreich ist. Da diese Floprate in der Vergangenheit stetig zu-

LIT Verlag Münster – Hamburg – London
Bestellungen über:
Grevener Str. 179 48159 Münster
Tel.: 0251 – 23 50 91 – Fax: 0251 – 23 19 72
e-Mail: lit@lit-verlag.de – http://www.lit-verlag.de
Preise: unverbindliche Preisempfehlung

genommen hat und zudem mit dem Neuigkeitsgrad der Innovation positiv korreliert ist, kommt einer leistungsfähigen Innovationsmarktforschung eine wachsende Bedeutung zu. Dies gilt insbesondere für Produkte, bei denen der Hauptteil der Kosten des Innovationsprozesses in der Phase der Entwicklung anfällt. Dieses Charakteristikum gilt u. a. für technische Leistungen.

Der Autor zeigt anhand technologischer Basisinnovationen, daß ein Verzicht auf reale Produkte als Marktforschungsprojekte zwar Effizienzgewinne verspricht, gleichzeitig aber auch erhebliche Probleme bezüglich der validen Schätzung des Marktpotentials erzeugt. Am Beispiel des Digital Radio weist er empirisch nach, daß die als Ersatz für reale Prototypen überwiegend verwandten verbalen Beschreibungen zu signifikant anderen Ergebnissen führen. Als Lösungsvorschlag wird ein Marktlabor auf Basis der multimedialen Limit Conjoint-Analyse entwickelt. Das Beispiel des Desktop-Videoconferencing zeigt darauf aufbauend, daß multimediale und reale Stimuli zu vergleichbaren Ergebnissen führen.

Bd. 5, 1998, 218 S., 59,80 DM, br., ISBN 3-8258-4111-1

Medienzukunft heute
herausgegeben von
Dr. Gerd Peter
(Landesinstitut Sozialforschungsstelle Dortmund)
und Prof. Dr. Heinz-Reiner Treichel (Bergische
Universität Gesamthochschule Wuppertal)
Redaktion: Kurt-Georg Ciesinger
(IBI – Gesellschaft für Innovationsforschung
und Beratung, Düsseldorf)
und Rainer Ollmann (GAUS – Gesellschaft für
angewandte Unternehmensforschung und
Sozialstatistik, Dortmund)
Redaktionsassistenz: Ingrid Goertz (sfs)

Kurt-Georg Ciesinger;
Rainer Ollmann (Hrsg.)
**Vom Druckunternehmen zum
Mediendienstleister**
Unternehmensstrategien beim Übergang in
die Informationsgesellschaft
Die immer enger werdenden Stammärkte der Druckbranche und die Substitutionspotentiale der "Neuen Medien" zwingen die traditionellen Betriebe der Branche zur raschen Umorientierung und Neupositionierung. Der aktuelle Umbruch – der sich für viele unvorbereitete Unternehmen zu einer massiven Krise ausgeweitet hat – rückt dabei insbesondere zwei Handlungsfelder

ins Blickfeld. Einerseits geht es im Sinne einer Kerngeschäftsorientierung um die Optimierung der Produktionsprozesse mit dem Ziel der flexibleren und zugleich kostenwirtschaftlicheren Erstellung eines Printproduktes. "Best practice"-Modelle hierfür wurden in einem Projekt erarbeitet, das im Rahmen des Programms Arbeit und Technik des Bundesministers für Bildung, Wissenschaft, Forschung und Technologie durchgeführt wurde. Andererseits – und dies ist derzeit in der Praxis die sehr viel größere Herausforderung – geht es um die Entwicklung und betriebliche Umsetzung des notwendigen Strukturwandels "vom Druckunternehmen zum Mediendienstleister". Diese Leitidee ist auch Inhalt eines noch laufenden, vom Land NRW und der EU über das NRW-Landesprogramm QUATRO geförderten Innovationsprojektes, das sich mit der betrieblichen Kompetenzentwicklung und Innovationsgestaltung im sich ausdifferenzierenden neuen Medienmarkt befaßt.

Der vorliegende Sammelband verknüpft in systematischer Weise Erfahrungen und Ergebnisse aus beiden Projekten. Aufgrund der handlungsorientierten Darstellung kann das Werk als praxisnahes "Handbuch der Innovation" für zentrale unternehmerische Handlungsfelder in den noch weitestgehend traditionell orientierten Betrieben der Druckbranche genutzt werden. Die Autoren wollen damit einen Beitrag zur Integration der ältesten und vielleicht wichtigsten Medienbranche in eine künftige "dienstleistungsintensive Medienwirtschaft" leisten.

Bd. 1, 1998, 248 S., 39,80 DM, br., ISBN 3-8258-3646-0

Dagmar Siebecke
**Unternehmerische Entscheidungen im
Medienumbruch**
Eine Verhaltensstudie in kleinen und mittleren Unternehmen
In zwei Untersuchungen werden Investitionsentscheidungsprozesse von strategischem Charakter analysiert. Ziel ist, das Entscheidungsverhalten zu modellieren, um für die Entscheidungsträger in der derzeitigen Umbruchsituation von der klassischen Druckindustrie zum Mediendienstleister Unterstützungsinstrumente entwickeln zu können, die an den aktuellen Problemen orientiert sind.
In einer ersten Untersuchung wird daher anhand von Fallstudien geprüft, welche Einflußfaktoren betriebliche Entscheidungsprozesse in der Medienindustrie determinieren. Die Ergebnisse werden in Form eines Entscheidungsmodells zusammengefaßt. Besonders herausgestellt werden dabei Einflüsse von betrieblichen und investitionsobjektbezogenen Faktoren sowie von Auswirkungen,

LIT Verlag Münster – Hamburg – London
Bestellungen über:
Grevener Str. 179 48159 Münster
Tel.: 0251 – 23 50 91 – Fax: 0251 – 23 19 72
e-Mail: lit@lit-verlag.de – http://www.lit-verlag.de

Preise: unverbindliche Preisempfehlung

die von der Person des Entscheiders ausgehen. In der zweiten Studie wird durch eine schriftliche Befragung das Informationsverhalten im Entscheidungsprozeß näher untersucht.

Aus der endgültigen Modellierung des Entscheidungsverhaltens, die Ergebnis beider Studien ist, werden fünf Interventionsbereiche begründet, in denen eine Unterstützung der Entscheider der Druckbranche sinnvoll ist:

Unterstützung bei der markt-, kunden- und potentialorientierten Strategiefindung und der Herleitung operativer Ziele aus diesen Strategien.

Hilfen zur Strukturierung und Erhöhung der Effizienz des Entscheidungsprozesses.

Beeinflussung der Informationsqualität durch Vermittlung zwischen Anwendern und Informationsanbietern. Erstellung von Anforderungskatalogen an die Informationen über technologische Innovationen.

Training für Führungskräfte zur Förderung der Aufmerksamkeits-, Motivations- und Emotionskontrolle sowie zur Bewältigung von Rückschlägen mit dem Ziel der Erhöhung der Handlungsorientierung in Entscheidungsfällen.

Initiierung und Unterstützung des zwischenbetrieblichen Erfahrungsaustauschs bis hin zur Kooperation.

Bd. 2, 1998, 288 S., 49,80 DM, br., ISBN 3-8258-3684-3

Kurt-Georg Ciesinger; Rüdiger Klatt; Rainer Ollmann; Dagmar Siebecke
Print and Publishing 2001
Die Druckindustrie befindet sich derzeit in einem tiefgreifenden Strukturwandel, indem sie sich weg von der reinen Informationsaufbereitung und -verbreitung ausschließlich über das Medium Print hin zur Informations- und Medienwirtschaft mit einer Integration der verschiedensten Medien bewegt. Hieraus ergeben sich zum Teil vollständig gewandelte – in weiten Teilen noch unbekannte – Anforderungen.

Zur Schaffung von mehr Transparenz hinsichtlich dieser Anforderungen wurden vier empirische Erhebungen durchgeführt. Befragt wurden
Experten der Medienwirtschaft zum erforderlichen Kompetenzprofil in den neuen Medienmärkten,
Unternehmen der Druck- und Verlagsbranche zu den aktuellen betrieblichen Stärken und Schwächen,
Kunden dieser Unternehmen bezüglich ihrer Anforderungen an die Branche sowie
Multimedia-Unternehmen hinsichtlich ihres "Erfolgsgeheimnisses".
Die Ergebnisse dieser Untersuchungen zeigen: Die Betriebe der Druckbranche verfügen über zahlreiche Potentiale. Diese lassen sich jedoch nur dann

ausschöpfen und weiterentwickeln, wenn die konservativen Strukturen und Innovationsblockaden in der Branche überwunden werden. Gefordert sind ein aktives Management und eine neue Beweglichkeit auf allen Ebenen.
Bd. 3, 1998, 176 S., 39,80 DM, br., ISBN 3-8258-3849-8

Heinz-Reiner Treichel (Hrsg.)
Innovation durch Kooperation
Das Beispiel Medien Zentrum Duisburg
Das Thema Kooperation wird derzeit als eines der wichtigsten Managementkonzepte für kleine und mittlere Unternehmen diskutiert. Verschiedene Formen zwischenbetrieblicher Zusammenarbeit bis hin zu virtuellen Verbünden sollen dazu beitragen, die aus dem Ressourcenbeschränkungen von KMU resultierenden Folgeprobleme zu lösen. Insbesondere in der expandierenden Medienwirtschaft sind neue Märkte kaum mehr im Alleingang, sondern nur noch durch kooperative Synchronisierung verschieden spezialisierter Partner zu erobern.

Das hier berichtete "Duisburger Modell" stellte einen sehr weitreichenden Ansatz zur Etablierung kooperativer Strukturen in der Medienwirtschaft dar. Unter dem Dach eines Medien Zentrums haben sich annähernd zwei Dutzend kleine Unternehmen zusammengefunden, um gemeinsam neue Dienstleistungen zu entwicklen, neue Produktiosstrukturen zu legen und sich damit auf neuen Märkte zu etablieren.

Diese Initiative wurde über mehr als drei Jahre begleitet und im Rahmen zweier Projekte der Landesregierung NRW unterstützt und ausgewertet: »Initiative Medienkooperation Duisburg«, gefördert durch die Landesinitiative media NRW, sowie »Kompetenzentwicklung im Übergang zu virtuellen Unternehmensstrukturen«, gefördert durch das Land NRW und die EU im Rahmen des Programms QUATRO.

Das vorliegende Buch verdichtet die Erfahrungen des Medien Zentrums Duisburg. Aus verschiedenen disziplinären Perspektiven werden die Aspekte der technologischen, konzeptionellen und organisatorischen Entwicklung nachgezeichnet und die zentralen Fragen der Kooperation – Kompetenzentwicklung, Kommunikation und Marketing – behandelt.

In der Summe läßt sich festhalten: Kooperationen wie das Medien Zentrum Duisburg sind nicht strategisch planbare Strukturen, sondern gewachsene Prozesse, die unter dem Einfluß ihrer dynamischen internen und externen Umwelt ständig ihre Form verändern. Aber gerade dies macht solche Formen der Zusammenarbeit extrem flexibel und wettbewerbsfähig. So konnte sich das Medien Zentrum Duisburg als Modell weit über den regionalen

LIT Verlag Münster – Hamburg – London
Bestellungen über:
Grevener Str. 179 48159 Münster
Tel.: 0251 – 23 50 91 – Fax: 0251 – 23 19 72
e-Mail: lit@lit-verlag.de – http://www.lit-verlag.de
Preise: unverbindliche Preisempfehlung

Kontext hinaus etablieren und wird derzeit in vielen anderen Initiativen kopiert.
Bd. 4, 1999, 248 S., 39,90 DM, br., ISBN 3-8258-4091-3

Kurt-Georg Ciesinger; Dagmar Siebecke;
Frank Thielemann
Innovationsintegral Mittelstand
Kompetenzentwicklung in Medienkooperationen
Kleine und mittlere Unternehmen werden aktuell als "Innovationsmotor" und "Jobmaschine" diskutiert. In der Realität ist die Innovationskraft dieser Unternehmen jedoch oftmals aufgrund fehlender Ressourcen eingeschränkt, die notwendige zukunftsgerichtete Qualifizierung wird dem Tagesgeschäft untergeordnet.
Durch Kompetenzentwicklung in zwischenbetrieblichen Kooperationen kann dieses Dilemma aufgebrochen werden. Dargestellt am Beispiel der Umbruchsituation innerhalb der Medienindustrie wird aufgezeigt, wie Innovationen durch strategische Allianzen erfolgreich umgesetzt werden können und wie diese überbetrieblichen Strukturen die notwendige Kompetenzentwicklung unterstützen.
Als Umsetzungsbeispiel und als Richtungsweiser für kleine und mittlere Unternehmen im strukturellen Umbruch werden die Realisierungskonzepte des Medien Zentrums Duisburg dargestellt. In einem durch das Land NRW und die EU im Rahmen des Programms QUATRO geförderten Projekt wurden hier neue Formen der Kompetenzentwicklung in Kooperationen konzipiert und erprobt. Die Erfahrungen des Projektes – Erfolge und Niederlagen – werden im vorliegenden Buch dargestellt und Erfolgsfaktoren für Kooperationen im Mittelstand hergeleitet.
Das Medien Zentrum etablierte sich im Projektverlauf nicht nur als virtuelles Unternehmen, sondern wurde selbst zum Weiterbildungsanbieter – ein Indiz dafür, daß die eigene Kompetenzentwicklung hier sehr erfolgreich betrieben wurde.
Bd. 5, 1999, 192 S., 39,80 DM, br., ISBN 3-8258-4217-7

ikö-Publikationen
herausgegeben vom Institut für Informations- und Kommunikationsökologie e. V.

Christian Schicha; Rüdiger Ontrup (Hrsg.)
Medieninszenierungen im Wandel
Interdisziplinäre Zugänge
In der "Inszenierungsgesellschaft" wird die Betrachtung von Wirklichkeit in zunehmendem Maße zur Beobachtung inszenierter Wirklichkeit. Dort setzen strategische Kommunikation, Dramaturgie, Erlebnis-Marketing und Zeicheneffekte ein. Die Autoren sehen ihre Aufgabe nicht darin, die "Medienrealität" als Manipulation zu "entlarven". Sie analysieren vielmehr die differierenden historischen, technischen und gesellschaftlichen Bedingungen, unter denen Medienwelten konstruiert und inszeniert werden. Formen von Grenzüberschreitungen in den Massenmedien zeigen sich im Ausstrahlungsbereich des Kult-und Erlebnismarketing, der Werbung und des "Infotainments". Die Beiträge skizzieren aktuelle Inszenierungsstrategien sowohl in den klassischen, als auch den "neuen" Medien, um zentrale Korrespondenzen und Differenzen der unterschiedlichen Mediengattungen herauszuarbeiten und zu reflektieren.
Bd. 1, 1999, 272 S., 48,80 DM, br., ISBN 3-8258-4125-1

LIT Verlag Münster – Hamburg – London
Bestellungen über:
Grevener Str. 179 48159 Münster
Tel.: 0251 – 23 50 91 – Fax: 0251 – 23 19 72
e-Mail: lit@lit-verlag.de – http://www.lit-verlag.de
Preise: unverbindliche Preisempfehlung